Who Is Our Example?

Grade Three Teacher's Manual

Michelle Richardson
Camille Kohner

Educational and
Theological Advisors

Rev. Richard M. Hogan
Rev. John M. LeVoir
Mary Jo Smith

IMAGE OF GOD SERIES
Image of God, Inc., Brooklyn Center, MN 55430
Ignatius Press, San Francisco

Nihil obstat: Mark B. Dosh
                  Censor Librorum

Imprimatur: ✠ John R. Roach, D.D.
                  Archbishop of St. Paul and Minneapolis
                  July 25, 1989

Cover design and illustrations: Barbara Harasyn
Book composition: Shoreline Graphics, Rockland, Maine

For additional information about the Image of God program: 1-800-635-3827

Published 1991 by Ignatius Press, San Francisco
© 1989 by Image of God, Inc.
All rights reserved
ISBN 0-89870-331-X
Printed in Hong Kong
Third Edition

Contents

Introduction

Lesson Plans

Introduction

Scope and Sequence

The Seven Basic Topics
God, creation, Christ, Church, grace, sacraments, and commandments.

Topics Emphasized by Grade Level
Preschool and Kindergarten: . . . . *God and creation.*
Grade 1 . . . . *Grace and sacraments.*
Grade 2 . . . . *Sacraments and commandments.*
Grade 3 . . . . *Christ and Church.*

Grade 4 . . . . *God, grace, and commandments.*
Grade 5 . . . . *Christ, Church, and sacraments.*
Grade 6 . . . . *Old Testament—creation.*

Grade 7 . . . . *God, creation, Christ, and commandments.*
Grade 8 . . . . *Church, grace, and sacraments.*

Grade 9 . . . . *Review of all seven basic topics.*
Grade 10 . . . . *Sacred Scripture.*
Grade 11 . . . . *History of the Church.*
Grade 12 . . . . *Communion of persons.*

Each of the seven topics is included in all grades; however, at each grade level, certain topics have been given special emphasis.

The "Who Is Our Example?" Program

The "Who Is Our Example?" program is a Catholic religion curriculum for children in the third grade. This program is based on Sacred Scripture, the Second Vatican Council, and the writings and teachings of Pope John Paul II.

This approach emphasizes the dignity of each individual as a person made in the image of God. The "Who Is Our Example?" program emphasizes in particular two truths of the Faith: Christ and Church. These key truths serve as the unifying elements of the lessons. The material in each lesson draws upon fundamentals of our Faith and expresses them in terms the children can understand and remember. This program was designed to be used equally well in a five-day parochial school setting and in a CCD setting. Suggestions for using the program in either setting follow.

This third-grade program consists of the following materials: this teacher's manual and a children's textbook. The teacher's manual consists of 21 basic lessons, a review lesson for each unit, and 3 liturgical and holiday lessons.

The textbooks contain activities related either to the stories suggested in the lesson or to the focus of the lesson. A children's version of most of the Scripture stories is included. The pages of the textbook can be sent home to be completed or can be completed in the classroom and then sent home. In either case, these pages should be used as take-home material so as to provide occasions for parent–child faith discussions.

It is the hope of the authors that the materials of the program will assist catechists in presenting to the children the teachings of Christ and the Church.

Using "Who Is Our Example?" in a Parochial School Setting

This third-grade curriculum contains 21 lessons, a review lesson that recaps the teaching in each of the units, and three liturgical and holiday lessons. The typical lesson is made up of the following components: *Lesson Focus* (Emphasis), *Concepts of Faith* (Things to Remember), *Vocabulary* (Words to Know), *Lesson Presentation* (Application), *Living the Lesson*, and lists of materials needed and related activities.

The Lesson Focus section gives you an insight into the main emphasis of the lesson.

The Concepts of Faith section is in question-answer format and restates the main ideas of the lesson. This same material appears at the end of each lesson in the student textbook, so that it can be used to review the lesson and check the students' comprehension of the lesson.

The Vocabulary section lists words important to an understanding of the lesson. Each word is presented with a definition that can be understood and remembered by the children. In the teacher manual, the vocabulary list is given before the section of the lesson in which they appear. Thus you can present all the vocabulary words at the start of the lesson and review them before using them in presenting the lesson.

When preparing for the lesson each week, you should read the whole lesson first. You can then decide which activities will be completed in class, and you will be aware of the materials and supplies needed for those activities. You will also then be able to remind the children to bring to school any supplies that they will be asked to provide.

The Lesson Presentation section in each lesson is made up of several parts, usually labeled A, B, C, . . . Each part presents a way to teach the lesson's concepts to the class. You can present more than one part each day. Sometimes the presentation involves a visual demonstration or role-playing. Sometimes it will include reading a story or portion from the student textbook. In this section too, the children are often given an opportunity to apply what they have learned to situations they might face in their daily lives. Again, our recommendation is that the whole lesson be read before any part of it is presented, so that you can determine which parts to present and which activities to complete each day.

The Living the Lesson section offers the students a chance to show their understanding of the preceding section of the lesson. The students might be asked to recall portions of the information they have been given and to restate it in their own words. We provide typical or sample answers in parentheses as an indication of the type of response you will look for.

The activities included in the lessons are intended to be reinforcements of the learning of the lesson's concepts through "hands-on" experience. You can use some of these activities in the classroom, as time permits, or send some home with the children to do with their families.

The lessons on Advent and Lent should be read in their entirety before presenting them in the classroom. Both lessons provide sufficient material for several class periods during each season. The last unit includes also a lesson on All Saints' Day; this lesson contains a list of saints and their feast days, as well as a "saint report" form, and provides you with a variety of options. To help your students become more familiar with the saints, you might read to them about one or two saints each month. You could also have students select a name from the list of saints and, by doing some research, prepare a class report or presentation on the saints they have selected.

Because prayer should be an important part of the students' daily lives, we recommend that each day at school begin and end with a prayer. We strongly encourage using the formal prayers of the Church—the "Our Father", "Hail Mary", "Glory Be", and the "Apostles' Creed", in particular. Informal, spontaneous prayer can also be introduced.

We suggest the following schedule for the parochial-school classroom. Obviously, time cannot be rigidly structured when working with young children, so you will wish to make suitable adjustments in this schedule.

Day 1. Introduction of all vocabulary words; Lesson Presentation (specific part chosen for this day); corresponding work from children's textbook.
Day 2. Review of specific vocabulary words; Lesson Presentation (specific part chosen for this day); corresponding work from children's textbook.
Day 3. Review of specific vocabulary words; Lesson Presentation (specific part chosen for this day); corresponding work from children's textbook.
Day 4. Activities included in the lesson.
Day 5. Review of the lesson, using Concepts of Faith.

Using "Who Is Our Example?" in a CCD Setting

This third-grade curriculum contains 21 lessons, a review lesson that recaps each unit, and 3 liturgical and holiday lessons. Each lesson is made up of the following components: *Lesson Focus* (Emphasis), *Concepts of Faith* (Things to Remember), *Vocabulary* (Words to Know), *Lesson Presentation* (Application), *Living the Lesson*, and lists of materials needed and related activities.

The Lesson Focus section gives you an insight into the main emphasis of the lesson. This section also contains information specifically for CCD teachers, such as suggestions as to which parts of the lesson to complete as classwork, and suggestions as to which activities and stories to send home with the children if time does not allow the entire lesson to be completed during class time.

The Concepts of Faith section is in question-answer format and restates the main ideas of the lesson. This same material appears at the end of each lesson in the student textbook, so that it can be used to review the lesson and check the students' comprehension of the lesson.

The Vocabulary section lists words important to an understanding of the lesson. Each word is presented with a definition that can be understood and remembered by the children. In the teacher manual, the vocabulary list is given before the section of the lesson in which they appear. Thus you can present all the vocabulary words at the start of the lesson and review them before using them in presenting the lesson.

When preparing for the lesson each week, you should read the whole lesson first. You can then decide which activities will be completed in class, and you will be aware of the materials and supplies needed for those activities. You will also then be able to remind the children to bring to school any supplies that they will be asked to provide.

The Lesson Presentation section in each lesson is made up of several parts, usually labeled A, B, C, . . . Each part presents a way to teach the lesson's concepts to the class. You can present more than one part each day. Sometimes the presentation involves a visual demonstration or role-playing. Sometimes it will include reading a story or portion from the student textbook. In this section too, the children are often given an opportunity to apply what they have learned to situations they might face in their daily lives. Again, our recommendation is that the whole lesson be read before any part of it is presented, so that you can determine which parts to present and which activities to complete during the class period.

The Living the Lesson section offers the students a chance to show their understanding of the preceding section of the lesson. The students might be asked to recall portions of the information they have been given and to restate it in their own words. We provide typical or sample answers in parentheses as an indication of the type of response you will look for.

The activities included in the lessons are intended to be reinforcements of the learning of the lesson's concepts through "hands-on" experience. You can use some of these activities in the classroom, as time permits, or send some home with the children to do with their families.

The lessons on Advent and Lent should be read in their entirety before presenting them in the classroom. Both lessons provide sufficient material for several class periods during each season. The last unit includes also a lesson on All Saints' Day; this lesson contains a list of saints and their feast days, as well as a "saint report" form, and provides you with a variety of options. To help your students become more familiar with the saints, you might read to them about one or two saints each month. You could also have students select a name from the list of saints and, by doing some research, prepare a class presentation on the saints they have selected.

Because prayer should be an important part of the students' daily lives, we recommend that each class begin and end with a prayer. We strongly encourage using the formal prayers of the Church—the "Our Father", "Hail Mary", "Glory Be", and the "Apostles' Creed", in particular. Informal, spontaneous prayer can also be introduced.

We suggest the following schedule for the CCD classroom. Obviously, time cannot be rigidly structured when working with young children, so you will wish to make suitable adjustments in this schedule.

1. Welcome the children; sharing; and opening prayer—5 minutes.

2. Introduction of vocabulary words—5 minutes.

3. *Lesson Presentation*—using the specific parts suggested—25 minutes.

4. Activities included in the lesson—15 minutes.

5. Review of the lesson, using *Concepts of Faith*—5 minutes.

6. Cleaning of the classroom; closing prayer—5 minutes.

Unit 1

THE MYSTERY OF GOD

1

God Is a Mystery

1. Lesson Focus

God is a mystery. He is outside of space and time. Yet He is also a living, free, personal being, Who created everything, but Who Himself is not created. God is.

Love is the gift of oneself. When God created the world, He gave Himself to the world. He loved. God created man and woman in His own image and likeness to do what He does: love. When we do what God does, love, our actions reflect His actions.

Note to CCD teachers: Use Parts A, B, C, and D in class. Activities in Part E may be sent home as family projects or used in class as time permits.

2. Concepts of Faith

Student Book, page 10

Things to Remember

Who is God?
God is the all-powerful, all-wise, and all-loving Being Who created everything.

How do we come to know God?
We come to know God by studying the things He has made, by reading Bible stories about Him, and by listening to what the Church teaches.

3. Lesson Presentation
Part A

Student Book, page 2

VOCABULARY
mystery: A truth that our minds cannot completely understand.
being: Someone that is, that exists.
choose: To decide; to make a choice.
believe: To know and to accept by faith.
source: A person, place, or thing from which something comes.

Materials needed:
   Phenolphthalein—order through a hobby shop or chemical supply shop.
   An alkali—baking soda (¼ cup).
   An acid—vinegar (1 cup).
   3 clear glass containers.
   3 cups of warm water.
   1 large, clear, glass bowl.
   1 spoon.
   Drawing paper, pencils, and crayons.

Note to teachers: Practice the following experiment before doing it in front of the children! Be sure to keep the phenolphthalein away from the children!

Application

Before class begins, put ¼ cup of baking soda, one cup of vinegar, and the small bottle of phenolphthalein in three separate glass containers for the children to see. Place the three containers, plus the glass bowl containing three cups of warm water, on a table (or desk). Make sure there is room in front of the table or desk for the children to sit on the floor.

Ask the class to come and sit on the floor in front of the table (or desk). Tell the class: "I have something special to show you today. Please watch carefully from where you are sitting. Do not come up to the table.

"I have four things in front of me: [*Hold them up as you name them*] a clear liquid [*phenolphthalein*], vinegar, baking soda, and water. First, I am going to dissolve the baking soda in the water." (*Pour the baking soda into the water in the glass bowl and mix them together until the baking soda dissolves.*) "Now I am going to put some of the clear liquid and the vinegar into the bowl of baking soda and water." (*Pour in ½ cup of vinegar and add the phenolphthalein, drop by drop, until the mixture turns pink.*) "What happened?" (*The mixture turned pink.*) "Now I am going to add some more vinegar to the mixture." (*Add vinegar until the mixture becomes clear.*) "What happened?" (*The mixture became clear.*)

"Why did these changes take place?" (*Students may say that one of the ingredients caused the change or that it's a mystery.*) "Do you know why that happened?" (*The students will not know why, but accept any reasonable answers.*)

"You may not completely understand why this experiment works. We call something that we cannot completely understand a mystery. Right now this experiment is a mystery to you.

"God is a mystery, too. God is someone we cannot completely understand. We will never completely understand Him.

"We believe that God is. No one created God. He always was, He is now, and He always will be."

Living the Lesson

1. What does the word mystery mean? (*Something we cannot completely understand.*)
2. Whom do we consider a mystery? (*God.*)
3. Why is God a mystery to us? (*We cannot completely understand Him.*)
4. Will we ever completely understand Him? (*No.*) Can we still know something about God? (*Yes.*)
5. Did anyone create God? (*God always was, He is now, and He always will be.*)

Activity

Say to the class: "If you could see God, what would He look like? (A king, a dad, a super-hero.) Draw a picture of what you think God would look like. Color your picture. When you are all finished, we will share and discuss our drawings."

Part B

Student Book, page 2

VOCABULARY
robed: Clothed with a robe.
image: A copy or reflection of something.
perfection: Without mistake; excellence; completeness.

Materials needed:
    One picture per child of something God made. These may be drawn or cut from a magazine.
    Glue.
    Paper large enough to hold all the pictures.

Application

Say to the class: "Let's think of how God might look as we read the following pages. Please open your books to page 3. We will be reading a description from the Bible of what God might look like." (*Ask one child to read the psalm as the others follow along.*)

Student Book, page 3

Bless the LORD, O my soul!
    O LORD, my God, you are great indeed!
You are clothed with majesty and glory,
    robed in light as with a cloak.
You have spread out the heavens like a tent-cloth;
    you have constructed your palace upon the waters.
You make the clouds your chariot;
    you travel on the wings of the wind.

                Psalm 104

When we are asked, "What might God look like?", we may think of Him as our Creator robed in glory above the clouds—just like the one in the picture! We cannot see God.

Still, we can imagine what He might look like.

Then, who is God? God is the source of all life. He is the all-powerful, all-wise, and all-loving Being Who created everything. He is a mystery that we cannot completely understand.

Because God is a supreme mystery, how do we come to know Him? We can come to know God by studying the things He has made, by reading Bible stories about Him, and by listening to what the Church teaches.

Say: "One way we can learn about God is to study the things He has made." (*Stop and have the children go up in small groups and glue pictures on the paper that was prepared earlier. Make sure they overlap the pictures as in a collage. Look at all of the pictures and discuss how each one reveals something about God.*)

Ask the children questions about the pictures. For example:

1. What is this a picture of? (*Point to a picture.*)
2. Who brought this picture? Why did you choose this picture? Can you describe the picture?
3. Where is this object found? Does it have to be in a certain place?
4. What does it need to survive?
5. Could you create another one just like it? Why, or why not?

Note to teachers: As time allows, repeat the above questions for other pictures in the mural. It is not necessary to discuss all of the pictures.

Living the Lesson

1. How do you describe God? (*Wise, powerful, loving, hard to understand, a mystery.*)
2. Is there only one way to describe God? (*No, there are many ways.*)
3. How do we come to know about God? (*By studying the things He has made, by reading Bible stories about Him, by listening to what the Church teaches.*)

Part C

Student Book, page 2

VOCABULARY
beauty: A quality that is delightful to look at, to listen to, or to think about.
truth: Something true or right.
love: To choose freely to give oneself to God and others.

Materials needed: A globe (optional).

Application

Say to the class: "We have shared pictures of some of the things God has made. We come to know God by studying the things He has made. Please open your books to page 5."

Student Book, page 5

All of creation was wonderfully planned and was created by God from nothing. The earth on which we live spins on its own axis. Day turns into night, and night turns into day. The seasons return year after year at the same time, providing sunshine and showers for all of God's creatures. Plans such as these show us that God is all-wise. The handiwork of creation shows us that He is all-powerful.

Demonstrate the spinning of the earth with the globe.

Above all the fine things God has made, He created living persons. When God creates, He gives. He who gives something to others loves. This wise and powerful God must have loved us very much because He gave us so much. Creation shows us that God is all-loving.

From the tiny ant to the lion, all creatures have a purpose. Their habits, powers, beauty, and perfection remind us of how mysterious life is. Only a living God could create such living beings for us!

God is the all-powerful, all-wise, and all-loving Being Who created everything. He is the source of everything. In addition, there was nothing before God. He was not created. God always was, He is now, and He always will be.

Living the Lesson

1. Did God create the world the way we create things? (*No. God created the world from nothing.*)
2. What kind of Being created the world? (*Wise, powerful, loving, living.*)
3. Who made God? (*No one. God was not made. He was, is, and always will be.*)
4. How do we know God is living? (*It takes a living Being to create living things.*)
5. How can we come to know God? (*By studying the things He has made, by reading Bible stories about Him, and by listening to what the Church teaches.*)
6. How can we thank God? (*Take care of the things He has made; love and praise Him.*)

Part D

VOCABULARY
reveal: To make known; to show.
inspire: To give someone an idea to act.
Bible: The book that contains God's word.

Application

Say to the class: "We have learned that by studying God's creations we can come to know something about God. Now we will read about two other ways we can come to know something about God. Open your books to page 8."

How wonderful are your works, O Lord!
You have made all things from nothing.
We know that you are wise and powerful!
Thank you for your marvelous gifts!

We learned that we can come to know God by studying the wonders of His world. But God also reveals Himself to us by speaking to us. His word can be found in stories about Him in the Bible.

Student Book, page 9

Long ago, before there were any books, God spoke to a certain group of people. He revealed His great power in the things He did for them. They were so inspired by His words and deeds that they told stories about Him.

Years passed and other people began writing down those stories about the wonder of our Creator. The writings were saved and collected over many hundreds of years. A book was formed by the Church. One of the ways God speaks to us today is through this book. It tells us about God. This book of holy writings is called "the Bible".

The word *Bible* comes from the Greek word *biblion*, meaning "book". The Bible is not just one book; it is a library of books in one volume. The Bible is one of the ways that the Church teaches us about God. There are other things about God that are not in the Bible. The Church teaches us these things, too. In order for us to know all there is to know about God, we should listen to the teachings of the Church.

Living the Lesson

1. We know that one way to learn about God is through what He has made. What are two other ways? (*Bible stories about Him and the teachings of the Church.*)
2. How were the special events of long ago shared with others? (*They were passed on from person to person through stories.*)
3. A new group of people wanted to save those stories. How did they do this? (*They wrote them down.*)
4. The stories were collected, saved, and placed in a book. What is the name of this book? (*The Bible.*)
5. What language does the word *Bible* come from? (*The Greek language.*)
6. What does the word *Bible* mean? (*Book.*)
7. What is the purpose of the Bible? (*God speaks to us and tells us about Himself.*)
8. How can we come to know all there is to know about God? (*We should listen to the teachings of the Church.*)

Part E

Note to teachers: Two activities follow. Both require scissors; only the first requires paper and glue.

Materials needed:
Scissors.
Two 8½" x 11" sheets of white paper per student.
Glue.

Application

Say to the class: "Please open your books to pages 11 and 13. Notice the 'keys' and 'keyholes' found on the two pages.

"First, beginning at the top of each page, carefully tear the pages out of your books. The edges of the pages have a line of holes that will help you tear them. Then, carefully cut out the keys and keyholes. Throw away any paper scraps."

A. Say to the class: "Place the keys and keyholes in two separate piles and wait for others to finish. While you wait, see if you can match the words on the keys to the definitions on the keyholes."

When all of the students have cut out their keys and keyholes, say: "Please take out your glue while I pass out two sheets of paper for each of you. Be careful not to knock over your piles of keys and keyholes! When you receive your two sheets of paper, write your name in the top right-hand corner of each one.

"Now, look at the vocabulary word printed on one of your keys. Find the keyhole with the correct definition of that word. Glue the key next to the keyhole on one sheet of paper. Continue matching keys and keyholes and gluing them on that sheet of paper until it is full. Then match the remaining keys and keyholes and glue them onto the second sheet of paper."

B. Say to the class: "When you have finished cutting, place the keyholes in one stack and the keys in another stack on your desk. Now, notice the vocabulary words that are printed on each of your keys. Try to match the words on the keys with the definitions on the keyholes."

Matching can be done in small groups or teams.

While the students are working, pass out an envelope for each of them so that they can keep their keys and keyholes. When most of the students have finished, discuss the correct words and definitions. Ask the students to write their names on their envelopes, place keys and keyholes inside the envelopes, and take them home to study.

2

Three Persons in One God

1. Lesson Focus

Student Book, page 16

There is only one God. Yet there are three Persons in God. God the Father, God the Son, and God the Holy Spirit are three Persons in one God. We call the mystery of three Persons in one God the Blessed Trinity.

We can *think* of God the Father as our Creator; we can *think* of God the Son as our Teacher and Savior; and we can *think* of God the Holy Spirit as our Helper. We only *think* of them as acting separately, but God the Father, Son, and Holy Spirit create, teach, save, and help together.

Remember, the Blessed Trinity is a mystery. It is difficult for us to understand. To help us learn about each Person, we are going to look at each one in succession.

When God the Father created the world and all of us, He showed us His power. He brought the world into existence out of nothing. He also created us in His image and likeness.

Student Book, page 17

God the Father's perfect image, God the Son, became man. We call Him Jesus. Through His teaching, Jesus tells us that we are images of God. He also teaches us how we should act as images of God. As our Savior, Jesus returned God's love and helps us return God's love.

God the Holy Spirit comes to us to give us grace, God's life. He comes to us every time we receive the sacraments. He helps us act as images of God.

Again, we must remember that God (all three Persons) creates us, saves and teaches us, helps us, and loves us. All three Persons work together as one.

Note to CCD teachers: Use Parts A, B, C, and D in class. All activities can be sent home as family projects, or used in class as time permits.

2. Concepts of Faith

Things to Remember
What is the Blessed Trinity?
The mystery of the three Persons in one God.

Who are the members of the Blessed Trinity?
We call the first Person God the Father, the second Person God the Son, and the third Person God the Holy Spirit.

How can we think of each Person?
We can think of God the Father as our Creator, God the Son as our Teacher and Savior, and God the Holy Spirit as our Helper.

3. Lesson Presentation

Part A

Materials needed:
A crystal prism with three long sides.
An apple.
4 strips of red construction paper (½" x 18") per student.
4 strips of white construction paper (½" x 12") per student.
1 square piece of black construction paper (2" x 2") per student.
2 pieces of string (12" long) per student.
Scissors and glue.

Application

Note to Teachers: Adapt the following instructions and questions to the shape of the prism, so that the children will be able to give the suggested answers.

Hold up the crystal prism and say to the class, "This is a crystal prism." Ask the class, "How many long sides does it have?" (*Three.*) "That's right. The prism has three sides. Now, when we look at the end, tell me how many corners the prism has." (*Three.*) "Yes, the prism has three corners. How many prisms are there?" (*One.*) "So in this one prism there are three sides and three corners, but only one prism."

Point to the sides and corners of the prism, one at a time, and say: "When we look at this prism we can think of the mystery of the Blessed Trinity, three Persons in one God. God the Father, God the Son, and God the Holy Spirit are the three Persons in one God." (*Point to the whole prism.*) "This prism helps us learn about the mystery of the Blessed Trinity. I have one prism. There is one God. There are three sides to one prism. There are three Persons in one God.

"To help us to understand and appreciate the mystery of the Trinity better, let's take a look at one of God's creations."

Hold up the apple. Cut the apple so the class can see the seeds. Ask the class, "Even though this apple has three parts—the skin, fruit, and seeds—is it one apple or three apples?" (*One.*) "That's right. There are three parts to one apple. The Blessed Trinity is three Persons in one God."

Say to the class: "The Blessed Trinity is a mystery. It is hard for us to understand. We believe in the mystery of the Blessed Trinity because Jesus, God the Son, taught us about it when He was on earth."

Activity

Note to teachers: Pass out the strips of red, white, and black construction paper. Make sure that students have their scissors and glue.

A

Say to the class: "We are going to make our own apples to help us think about the Trinity. Take one strip of white construction paper. Place a small drop of glue on one end. Hold on to that end with one hand. Be careful not to touch the drop of glue! Now, hold on to the other end with the other hand. Bring the two ends together to form a circle. Press the two ends together to hold them in place." (*Demonstrate. See figure A.*) "Take a second strip of white construction paper. Place a small drop of glue on one end. Glue that end in the place where the ends of the circle meet." (*Demonstrate. See figure B.*) "Take the other end of the second strip and form a circle. Make sure the two circles cross each other. Glue that end in place." (*Demonstrate. See figure C.*) "Continue adding white strips and making circles until all four white strips have been used up. Make sure that the circles are an even distance apart." (*Demonstrate. See figure D.*) "Now, take a red strip of construction paper. Place a small drop of glue on one end. Glue that end in the place where the white circles meet. Take the other end of the red strip, form a circle, and glue it in place. Continue adding red strips and making circles until all of the four red strips have been used up. The red circles will be around the white circles." (*Demonstrate. See figure E.*)

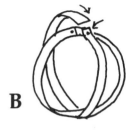

B

C

"While the circles are drying, tie one piece of string through the 'apples'. This will be used for hanging the apples. Now cut four seeds, each the size of a penny, out of the black construction paper. Punch a hole near the top of each one. Be careful not to tear the edges! Thread the other piece of string through the holes on the seeds. Tie the string with the seeds to your red and white circles." (*Demonstrate. Show your completed apple. See figure F.*) "Make sure that the seeds hang in the center of all of your circles!"

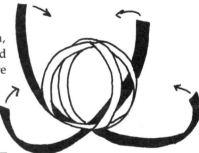

D

Say to the class: "Now, look at your finished apples. Each one has three parts—red skin, white fruit, and black seeds. Together, they are three parts in one apple. The Blessed Trinity has three Persons—God the Father, God the Son, and God the Holy Spirit. There are three Persons in one God."

Part B

E

Student Book, page 15
VOCABULARY
person: Someone who has a mind and a will.

Materials needed: 1 potted plant.

F

Application

Say to the class, "Because there are three Persons in one God, there must be differences among the three Persons. We call the first Person God the Father, we call the second Person God the Son, and we call the third Person God the Holy Spirit.

"We can think of God the Father as our Creator, we can think of God the Son as our Teacher and Savior, and we can think of God the Holy Spirit as our Helper. Yet God the Father, Son, and Holy Spirit create, teach, save, and help together. All three Persons work together as one.

"Remember, the Blessed Trinity is a mystery. It is difficult for us to understand. To help us learn more about the Blessed Trinity, we will learn about each Person."

Show the class a potted plant and ask: "Could I make a living plant like this out of nothing?" (*No.*) "Why not?" (*You don't know how. You have to have seeds.*)

Say to the class: "I couldn't make a plant. I couldn't even make the seeds that would grow into a plant. Only God can create things out of nothing. We can think of God the Father, the first Person of the Blessed Trinity, as our Creator.

"Please open your book to page 18, and we'll read a story about the creation of the world."

Student Book, pages 18–19

When God the Father created the world and all of us, He showed us His power. He brought the world into existence out of nothing. He also created us in His image and likeness.

In the beginning, before God created the heavens and the earth, there was darkness everywhere. Then God said, "Let there be light", and there was light. He called the light "day" and the darkness "night".

Next, God made the blue sky. He made the beautiful oceans, lakes, rivers, and streams. He filled the sky with everything that flies and the waters with everything that swims.

Between the waters He placed dry lands, grassy fields, hills, and mountains. To add to the landscape, God created flowers and trees. He then made every kind of animal: wild and tame, big and small.

God looked at everything that He had made. He was pleased.

Then God made Adam, the first man. Adam was special. He was an image of God. He could share God's life. He could think, love, and work. Adam was a person.

Even though Adam enjoyed taking care of God's world, he was lonesome. He was the only person with a body! There were angels. Angels are persons, but they do not have bodies. Adam could not see them and talk to them. He wanted to share his life with someone.

God did not want Adam to be lonely. So God created the first woman—Eve. Although Eve did not look exactly like Adam, she was created in the image and likeness of God, too. Adam and Eve loved each other as God's images. They formed the first family.

God told Adam and Eve that He had made the world and everything in it for them. He asked them to take care of everything in this world.
—Adapted from Genesis 1:1–31

We can think of God the Father as our Creator. However, we must remember that God (all three Persons) created us. All three Persons work together as one.

> **Student Book, page 20**
>
> 1. Who created the world and everything in it out of nothing? (*God.*)
> 2. Whom can we think of as our Creator? (*God the Father.*)
> 3. In the beginning, there was darkness everywhere. Then God said, "_____ _____." (*Let there be light.*)
> 4. Next, God created the sky and the water. What forms of life can be found in the sky and water? (*Every creature that flies or swims; water plants.*)
> 5. What forms of life can be found on land? (*Plants, animals, and people.*)
> 6. The first man, Adam, was special. Why? (*He was a person, an image of God. He could share God's life. He could think, love, and work.*)
> 7. The first woman, Eve, was special. Why? (*She was a person, an image of God. She could share God's life. She could think, love, and work.*)
> 8. Adam and Eve loved each other as God's images. They formed the first _____. (*family.*)

Activity

> **Student Book, page 21**
>
> Fill in the blanks with letters to form words that we can use to describe God the Father.
>
> ```
>                     C  R  E  A  T  O  R
>        F  A  T  H  E  R
>              P  O  W  E  R  F  U  L
>                     A  L  M  I  G  H  T  Y
>  P  E  R  F  E  C  T
>              L  O  V  I  N  G
>                     R  E  V  E  A  L  S
> ```
>
> *Powerful, Almighty, Creator, Perfect, Loving, Reveals, Father*

Part C

Materials needed:
1 piece of cardboard (8½" x 11") for each student.
Pattern of the cross from teacher's manual (make extra copies as needed). See Appendix.
Crayons or markers, scissors.
Transparent tape (optional).

Application

Say to the class: "When we look at pictures of ourselves we notice that the pictures are identical images of us. When we look in the mirror we see a perfect mirror image of ourselves. Let's read page 22 to find out about the perfect image of God the Father."

An identical image of God the Father does exist. He is the second Person of the Blessed Trinity, God the Son.

Say to the class: "God the Father's perfect image, God the Son, became man. We call Him Jesus. Jesus came to show us who we are and how we should act, to return God's love and to help us return God's love. We can think of Jesus as our Teacher and Savior."

When Jesus was a baby, some of the people of that time knew that He had come to teach them the truth and to save them from sin! Read the following story about two of those people.

THE PRESENTATION IN THE TEMPLE

After the birth of the baby Jesus, Mary and Joseph took Him to Jerusalem to present Him to the Lord. There was a man in Jerusalem by the name of Simeon. Simeon was a kind and loving man. He was old. Simeon was very holy. The Holy Spirit was with him.

When Mary and Joseph arrived at the temple, Simeon was already there. When he saw Mary and Joseph carrying baby Jesus, Simeon went up to them. He took the baby Jesus in his arms and prayed out loud saying, "Now, Master, I can die peacefully, for I have seen the glory of the Lord."

Mary and Joseph were amazed at what Simeon had to say about Jesus. Simeon told them that their child would speak the truth about who we are and how we should act. He told them that many people would not accept what Jesus would say. But he also said that many people would believe in what Jesus would say.

Anna, an eighty-four-year-old widow, was also in the temple. She saw baby Jesus too. She gave thanks to God the Father for allowing her to see Jesus. Then she went to tell all of the people who were waiting for news that the Savior had come!
—Adapted from Luke 2:22–38

God the Son is the perfect image of God the Father. He became man to be our Teacher and Savior. Through His teaching, Jesus tells us that we are images of God. He also teaches us how we should act as images of God.

When Jesus, God the Son, died on the cross, He freed us from sin and returned the Father's love. He also made it possible for us to return the Father's love.

We can think of God the Son as our Teacher and Savior. However, we must remember that God (all three Persons) creates us, saves us, helps us, and teaches us. All three Persons work together as one.

Living the Lesson

1. Who is the second Person of the Blessed Trinity? (*God the Son.*)
2. Why did God the Son become man? (*To show us who we are and how we should act, to return the Father's love, and to help us return the Father's love.*)
3. Why do you think God the Son came to us as a baby and grew like all of us? (*It is easier to understand someone who is like us. Accept other appropriate answers.*)
4. Who was in the temple when Mary, Joseph, and Jesus arrived? (*Simeon and Anna.*)
5. What did Simeon predict? (*That Jesus would speak the truth about who we are and how we should act. Not all people would believe Him, but many people would.*)
6. Who are we? (*Images of God.*)
7. How did Jesus tell us that we are images of God? (*Through His teaching.*)
8. Is God the Son an image of God the Father too? (*Yes, the perfect image.*)
9. How did Jesus free us from sin and return the Father's love? (*By dying on the cross.*)

Activity

> **Student Book, page 24**
>
> Fill in the blanks with letters that form words we can use to describe God the Son.
>
> ```
>              S   H   E   P   H   E   R   D
>      I   M   A   G   E
>      S   A   V   I   O   R
>          L   I   F   E
>          L   O   R   D
>          R   E   D   E   E   M   E   R
> ```
>
> *Savior, Lord, Redeemer, Image, Life, Shepherd*

Activity

Note to teachers: Print the word "Savior" on the blackboard. Pass out the patterns of the cross and the cardboard. Students should have scissors and crayons or markers ready.

Say to the class: "The cross reminds us of what Jesus has done for us. We are going to make crosses that we may keep to help us remember what Jesus did for us.

"First, trace the cross onto the cardboard. Then, using a brown or black crayon or marker, trace over the lines you've just drawn. Cut out the cardboard cross.

"Write 'Savior' on the front of your cross. Write your name on the back of your cross."

Note to parochial-school teachers: Say to students: "Roll a piece of transparent tape onto the back of your cross and tape it to your desk to remind you of what Jesus did for us."

Note to CCD teachers: Say to students: "Take your cross home and keep it in your room to remind you of what Jesus did for us."

Part D

Application

Say to the class: "God the Father, God the Son, and God the Holy Spirit all love each other. God the Father, God the Son, and God the Holy Spirit love us, too.

"God the Holy Spirit comes to us to give us grace, God's life. He comes to us every time we receive the sacraments. We can think of the Holy Spirit as our Helper.

"Whenever we need Him, He is there with His grace to help us act as images of God.

"Please open your books to page 24, and we'll read about the first time the Holy Spirit came to the Apostles."

Student Book, pages 24–25

The Apostles were gathered together, all in one place. Suddenly, a noise like a strong wind filled the entire house that they were in. Tongues of fire appeared above each one of them. They were all filled with the Holy Spirit.

The noise caused a large crowd to gather. Everyone in the crowd was from a different country. When the Apostles were speaking, they all spoke a different language. Yet every one of the people could understand what the Apostles were saying.

All of the people in the crowd were amazed! They asked one another, "Aren't these people Galilean? Then how does each of us hear them in his own language?"

Peter stood up, raised his voice, and said, "Listen to my words. God promised King David that He would send us a Savior. God also promised that He would never leave us.

"The Savior Jesus did come. And, as you have just seen, Jesus sent us the Holy Spirit to be with us always. He will care for us and never leave us. Repent and be baptized, every one of you, in the name of Jesus Christ for the forgiveness of your sins; and you will receive the gift of the Holy Spirit."
                    —Adapted from Acts 2:1–12, 30–40

When the crowd gathered at the coming of the Holy Spirit, all of the people could understand the Apostles. This was a sign that the Holy Spirit wanted all people to know that He is there to help them with His grace.

When the Holy Spirit comes to give us grace, He will not come to us in tongues of fire. He will, however, help us act as brighter images of God.

We can think of God the Holy Spirit as our Helper. However, we must remember that God (all three Persons) creates us, saves and teaches us, and helps us. All three Persons work together as one.

Living the Lesson

1. How does God the Holy Spirit help us? (*Through grace given in the sacraments.*)
2. What is grace? (*God's life.*)
3. What does grace help us to do? (*Helps us to act as images of God.*)
4. When the Holy Spirit comes to us, will tongues of fire appear? (*No, but He will help us act as brighter images of God because He is with us.*)

Activity

Student Book, page 28

Fill in the blanks with letters that form words that we can use to describe the Holy Spirit.

```
                        H  E  L  P  S
                     L  O  V  E  S
                     L  I  F  E
               H  O  L  Y
S  A  C  R  A  M  E  N  T  S
                     S  P  I  R  I  T
                     G  I  V  I  N  G
                     G  R  A  C  E
               G  U  I  D  E  S
   P  E  N  T  E  C  O  S  T
```

Life, Holy, Spirit, Helps, Guides, Loves, Grace, Sacraments, Pentecost, Giving

Activity

Crossword puzzle.

Student Book, pages 26–27

ACROSS
1. The second Person of the Blessed Trinity is God the ____. (*Son.*)
2. Jesus is our _____. (*Savior.*)
3 and 4. God the Holy Spirit _____ us to _____ as images of God. (*helps, act.*)
5. God the Holy Spirit is our _____. (*helper.*)
6. The Holy Spirit brings God's life called _____. (*grace.*)
7. Jesus is the _____ image of God the Father. (*perfect.*)
8. God is very _____. (*powerful.*)
9 and 12. The Blessed Trinity is _____ _____ in one God. (*three, persons.*)
10. The three Persons _____ and work as one. (*love.*)
11. Each of us is an _____ of God. (*image.*)

DOWN

1 and 2. Jesus _____ us from _____. (*saved, sin.*)

7. The Holy Spirit first came to the Apostles during _____. (*Pentecost.*)

13. God created the world out of _____. (*nothing.*)

14. God the Father is our _____. (*Creator.*)

15. God is _____. (*wise.*)

16. The first Person of the Blessed Trinity is God the _____. (*Father.*)

17. The third Person of the Blessed Trinity is God the _____ Spirit. (*Holy.*)

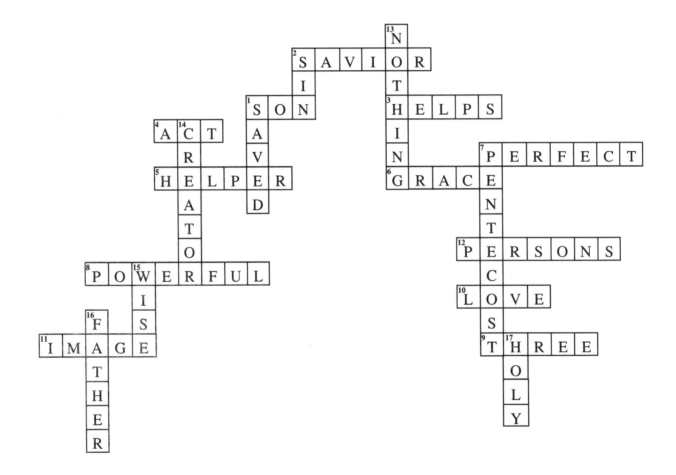

3

Persons Loving as God Loves

1. Lesson Focus

In one God there are three Persons: God the Father, God the Son, and God the Holy Spirit. This mystery is called the Blessed Trinity. Each of the three divine Persons gives Himself totally to the others. Because the three Persons perfectly love one another, they form a communion of Persons.

Created in the image and likeness of God, we all have the same calling in life: to love as God loves. When we love others, we form a kind of family or communion of persons with them. (A communion of persons is formed when two or more persons work together, love one another, and help each other love as God loves; for example, a family or the members of the Church.)

There are three types of communion of persons that we form. The communion of persons of the family is established in marriage. A man and a woman accept the intimate community of life and love and plan to share it with their children. The communion of persons of the work place (which for us is the school) is established when students and teachers work together to achieve the best learning environment for all. Finally, the communion of persons of the Church is founded on the sacrament of Baptism and joins us to another family—God's family.

Note to CCD teachers: Use Parts A, B, C, and D in class. The activities in Parts A and E can be sent home as family projects or used in class as time permits.

2. Concepts of Faith

Student Book, page 36

Things to Remember

What is our calling in life?
To love as God loves.

How do we love as God loves?
By forming groups of persons who work together, love each other, and help each other love as God loves.

3. Lesson Presentation

Part A

Materials needed: bulletin board; photos of the students' families, magazine pictures of students working at school and of people helping each other and praying together at church.

Application

Say to the class, "In one God there are three Persons. Can you name them?" (*God the Father, God the Son, and God the Holy Spirit.*) "What is this mystery called?" (*The Blessed Trinity.*)

"Each of the three divine Persons loves the others totally. Because the three Persons love one another, they form a kind of family. They always love and act as one.

"As images of God, we are called to love as God loves. When we do this, we form families, too. Let's open our books to page 29 and read more about the kinds of families we form."

Student Book, page 29

LOVING AS GOD LOVES WITHIN FAMILIES

Each of the three divine Persons of the Blessed Trinity gives Himself totally to the others. Because the three Persons perfectly love one another, they form a kind of family.

As images of God, we are called to love as God loves. When we love others, we form a kind of family with them.

A kind of family is formed when two or more persons work together, love each other, and help each other love as God loves. There are three kinds of families that we are studying. The first kind of family *is* the family! A family begins when a man and a woman marry. They promise to love each other, work together, and help each other love as God loves.

Ask the class to bring up their pictures of families and place them on the bulletin board.

Student Book, page 29

The second kind of family is the group of persons in the work place. Our work place is school. This kind of family is formed when students and teachers work together, love each other, and help each other love as God loves.

Ask the class to bring up pictures of students working and place them on the bulletin board.

Student Book, page 29

Finally, the sacrament of Baptism joins us to another family—God's family. The people within the Church work together, love each other, and help each other love as God loves.

Ask students to bring up pictures of people praying and working together in church. Say to the class: "Because each of these groups we call families is very important, we are going to look at them one at a time. The first family or group of persons is *the family*!

"When God created Adam and Eve, He said to them, 'Be fruitful and multiply, fill the earth and subdue it.' He was inviting Adam and Eve to form a family, to work together, love each other, and help each other love as God loves.

"On their wedding day, a man and a woman promise to work together, love each other, and help each other love as God loves. They know that they should be kind to one another and do things for each other. When they have children, they should be kind to them and teach them to be kind to others.

"God asks each family member to love the others within the family."

Ask the class, "How can we show our love for our brother or sister?" (*Take the time to listen, talk to him or her, forgive, etc.*)

"Is it always easy to love your sister or brother?" (*No, not always.*)

Say to the class: "Let's make a list of the times when it is difficult to show our love for a brother, a sister, or a parent. Try to think of ways to show our love for them even though it might be difficult. Tell me what you think, and I will write your examples on the blackboard."

Say to the class: "You have shared some very helpful ideas on how to act lovingly toward other family members. Let's use those ideas to help solve these problems as well.

"I will read some problem situations to you. After I have read a problem, please raise your hand and suggest how the problem might be solved."

Note to teachers: The following are common situations within families. The suggested answers are general enough to fit other situations that students may have experienced.

1. Sometimes my sister Amy doesn't want to talk to me. (*Don't bother or tease someone who doesn't want to be bothered. Ask if you can talk together later.*)

2. I sometimes feel like yelling at my sister. (*It isn't kind to yell at someone. It's better to be silent. However, you should make an effort to try to talk kindly and work together with others, even though you don't feel like it. Ask if you can talk together later.*)

3. Your brother Bob does *not* like to be interrupted when he is mowing the lawn! You need your bicycle pump, but it's on a hook in the garage and you can't reach it. Bob is taller than you and could take the pump down for you. What should you do? (*Wait until a person is finished with a chore before asking that person to help you [unless it is an emergency].*)

4. Mike is older than you and teases and pushes you around. (*Tell him that being pushed around bothers you. Remember, the less you say, the greater your chances are of stopping the teasing.*)

5. Mom comes home from work. She is *very* tired and does *not* want to be bothered. You want to show her what you made in school today. What should you do? (*Help her get dinner ready and wait until later to show her your work.*)

Ask the class: "Is it always easy to show your love for your parents?" (*No.*) "What can we do to show our love?" (*Listen, help out, obey, be patient, etc.*) "To love seems like a difficult task. Who will help us if we ask Him?" (*God.*)

Part B

Application

Say to the class, "Let's read the play on page 30 and find out how a loving family works together."

Student Book, page 30

THE BIRTHDAY PARTY

Tommy's birthday is this Saturday. He is very excited! His family plans to have a party for him. Everyone is invited—grandparents, aunts and uncles, and friends from school.

To have a successful party, everyone in the family must work together. This calls for a family meeting. Tommy's mother decided to have the meeting Friday after supper.

Read the following play to find out what happened.

Note to teachers: Assign parts before reading. If time permits, the class could act out the parts. Students without speaking parts could make the scenery.

Student Book, pages 31–33

Cast of characters:
 Narrator
 Tommy Martin, age 9
 Sarah Martin, age 13
 John Martin, age 17
 Mr. Martin (Dad)
 Mrs. Martin (Mom)
 Grandma
 Grandpa

Narrator: It's Friday night. The Martin family is gathered around the kitchen table after supper. All of the dishes have been cleared and washed. Mrs. Martin has a pencil, a list of jobs, and a grocery list.

Mom: We all know that tomorrow is a special day for Tommy. We want to do our best to make it fun for everyone. First, the house needs to be cleaned. I need a volunteer to scrub the floors.

Sarah: I'll do it. I've had a lot of practice. And, when I'm finished, I'll even do the vacuuming!

Dad: Yardwork is my specialty! I'll take care of that. We'll need a lot of food. John, why don't you do the shopping? Mom will give you the list.

John: No problem, Dad! I'll need the car keys.

Dad: Okay, but remember, go to the store and back, with no *additional* passengers!

Mom: I'll give you the list tomorrow morning, John. All of you, remember to clean your bedrooms! Tommy, Grandma and Grandpa will be staying in your room tomorrow. You'll be sleeping in John's room. Sarah, Aunt Terry and Uncle Ed will be staying downstairs. Please make sure the sheets, blankets, and pillows are ready for them. I will look over all rooms after lunch on Saturday. Are there any questions?

Family: No!

Narrator: It is now Saturday morning. Everyone begins to prepare for the party.

Mom: Let's get going on our chores, everyone! John, please take Tommy to the store with you.

Narrator: After Tommy and John have left, Mom, Dad, and Sarah pull out the decorations from behind the sofa.

Mom: We need to get these up before Tommy gets home, so we don't have much time! Dad, you take care of the back yard. Sarah, you take care of the kitchen, and I'll decorate the living room.

Narrator: By lunch time the house was ready. Everyone gathered around the kitchen table.

Mom: Our love for each other was easy to see. Everyone chipped in and helped. No one complained. I guess that's what it means to be members of a family! We all work together, love each other, and help each other love as God loves. I'm so proud of all of you!

Narrator: It's time for the party! The doorbell rings. Sarah answers it.

Grandma: The house looks wonderful, Sarah! How did the family do it all?

Sarah: Everyone in the family helped out. Mom says that we are all members of the family. We work together, love each other, and help each other love as God loves.

Grandma: I agree with your mom.

Grandpa: Now, where is that birthday boy?

Sarah: He's in the kitchen. Go ahead and join him! Mom, Dad, and John are in there, too.

Narrator: The birthday party was a big success! Dad visited with everyone and didn't burn the hamburgers. John didn't tease Tommy at all. Everyone helped Mom with the food. Sarah washed the dishes without being asked, and Tommy was thankful for every gift he received. The Martins showed us what a family should be—a group of persons who work together, love each other, and help each other love as God loves.

———

When members of a family work together and help each other, they are imitating God. They are loving as God loves.

Living the Lesson

1. What was the time before Tommy's party like for the Martin family? (*Everyone wanted to help out. No one complained. The family worked together.*)
2. How should members of a family behave toward each other? (*Love each other, and help each other love as God loves.*)
3. When persons love each other in the right way, whom are they imitating? (*God.*)

Part C

Materials needed: A picture jigsaw puzzle with at least one piece per student.

Note to teachers: If the puzzle has more than the required number of pieces needed for your class, place the extra pieces on a table for the students to pick up when more pieces are needed. Clear a large work space on the floor for the students.

Application

Say to the class: "Because we are all members of the school, together we form the school's family. Let's open our books to page 34 and read more about the second kind of family—the school.

Student Book, page 34

THE SCHOOL'S FAMILY

Our class is like a large family. We need to work together, love each other, and help each other love as God loves. In the classroom we all need to work together so we are all able to learn. Classroom rules help us do this. Can you name some classroom rules?

Note to teachers: The following are some examples of general classroom rules. Use the rules that have been established in your classroom, such as: Be on time. Walk in the classroom and in the hallway. Do not speak when someone else is speaking. Respect school property, your own property, and the property of others.

Say to the class, "We are going to do an activity that will help demonstrate that we all need to work together in our classroom." (*Give each student a puzzle piece.*) "Each of you has been given a puzzle piece. The rest of the pieces are on the table." (*Point to the remaining pieces.*) "When I say 'begin', start putting the puzzle pieces together. The important word is 'together'. You need to work as a group and help each other. When your piece has been used in the puzzle, take another piece from the table until all the pieces are used. Are there any questions? . . . If not, begin."

Note to teachers: Help students with the puzzle if necessary.

When the puzzle is finished, ask the class, "Could the class have finished the puzzle if one of you hadn't given your piece to the group?" (*No.*) "Why not?" (*All of us had puzzle pieces. We would be missing the piece kept by the person who was not participating.*)

Say to the class: "Without working together as a kind of family in the school, we would not be able to finish our puzzle. How do we work together as a kind of family in other classroom activities?" (*Study together, encourage each other, play games, clean up the classroom together, etc.*)

Sometimes you may not feel very important, but what you have to offer the class is important. Each one of us is working hard to make our school the best learning place that it can be. When we work together, we form a kind of family in the school. We work together, love each other, and help each other love as God loves.

Living the Lesson

How can we form a kind of family in school? (*By working together, loving each other, and helping each other love as God loves.*)

Part D

Note to teachers: Have the students take out the baptismal certificate found on page 37 in the student book. Ask the students to have their parents help them complete the forms before Part D is presented. Also, put up a bulletin board or wall display as illustrated below. Use strips of construction paper to form the outline of a church.

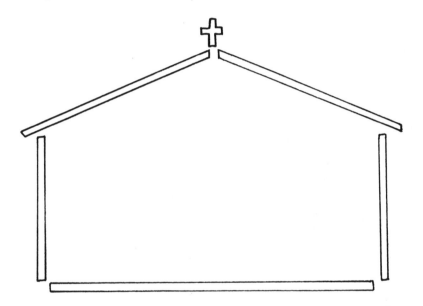

Materials needed:
  Baptismal certificates (student book, page 37).
  Bulletin board—see preceding note to teachers.
  One 3″ x 5″ lined index card per student.
  Pencils, crayons or markers, masking tape.

Application

Say to the class: "Please remove the baptismal certificate that is on page 37 in your book." Ask some of the students to tell the class in what church they were baptized. Ask the class, "Were all of us baptized in the same church?" (*No.*) "Do all of us go to Mass in the same church every week?" (*No.*) "Even though all of us do not go to the same church, we all belong to the same family, God's family. Please keep the baptismal certificates on the corner of your desk until I ask for them in a few minutes."

Say to the class: "The third kind of family we are going to talk about is God's family, the Church. Let's open our books to page 35 and read about God's family, the Church."

Student Book, page 35

GOD'S FAMILY, THE CHURCH

The sacrament of Baptism joins all of us in one family—God's family, the Church. As members of this family, we should work together, love each other, and help each other love as God loves.

There are many ways in which people work together in God's family. Can you think of some of the ways people help out in your church? Many people help out at Mass. Some people are Eucharistic ministers, readers, ushers, altar servers, or choir members. Some people help in other ways, too. Some teach religion classes, and some collect food or clothing to give to the poor.

When you give your time and talents to others, you are showing your love for them. All of the people who are baptized form the family of the Church. They should all work together, love each other, and help each other love as God loves.

Pass out the index cards, one for each student. Divide the class into groups of four. Say to the class, "On each card I would like you to write one way that people help each other in God's family. Remember to help each other in your group. Decorate the cards when they are completed. When your group is finished, bring the cards and your baptismal certificates to me. Are there any questions? . . . If not, then you may begin."

After students are finished, tape the cards and certificates inside the outline of a church on the bulletin board.

Living the Lesson

1. When you were baptized, what family did you join? (*God's family.*)
2. As members of God's family, we should do what? (*Work together, love each other, and help each other love as God loves.*)

Part E

Materials needed:
   Calendar from Appendix—1 per student.
   Page of hearts from Appendix—1 page per student.
   Scissors; crayons or markers.
   Glue; envelopes.

Note to teachers: Display a calendar of the current month. If it is the end of the month, use the next month's calendar instead.

Activity

Duplicate copies of the calendar page and hearts page (provided in the Appendix) so that each student has one calendar and a total of thirty-one hearts. Pass out the calendar, hearts, and an envelope to each student.

Tell the class to look at the calendar in the front of the room. Say to the class, "What month is it?" (*Answer varies according to current month.*) "On what day does this month begin?" (*Again, answer varies.*)

Say to the class: "Each of us is going to make his own calendar. Begin by neatly printing the month at the top." (*Demonstrate.*) "Then, write the numbers that represent the days in this month. Use the calendar in the front of the room to help you.

"When you have finished numbering the days, color and cut out all of the hearts. Place the hearts in the envelope I have given you. Put your name on the envelope.

"When you show your love by helping or working together with the members of your family, your school's family, or God's family, glue a heart on the calendar for that day. Remember, when we work together, love each other, and help each other love as God loves, we are acting as images of God. We are loving as God loves."

Unit 2

WHO WE ARE: IMAGES OF GOD

4

Who Are We?

1. Lesson Focus

Of all the living things God created on earth, only we (human persons) are created in His image and likeness. We can choose what to think. We can choose to love or not to love. When we choose to think like God and to love as God loves, we act as His images. If we are not thinking and loving like God, we can change and begin to act more like Him.

Animals cannot think or freely choose. They can only live their lives looking for food, life, and protection for themselves.

Note to CCD teachers: Use Parts A and B in class. Activities may be sent home as a family project or done in class as time permits.

2. Concepts of Faith

Student Book, page 46

Things to Remember

Who are we?
We are images of God.

How are we different from the rest of God's creations on earth?
We are able to think, to choose, and to love.

3. Lesson Presentation

Part A

Student Book, page 40

VOCABULARY
ability: Being able to act.
decide: To choose.
think: To have in mind; to form an idea in the mind.
understand: To know the meaning of.

Application

Say to the class: "In the story that we are about to read, a boy and a girl made different choices. Please open your books to page 41 and see what choices the boy and girl made."

WHO ARE WE?

Two students, Tim and Joan, came to their new school for their first day of class. Both of them had to find the gym, but neither one knew where it was.

Tim said, "I think we should look for the office first. If we ask the secretaries, they will show us how to get to the gym."

But Joan said, "I think we should stop at the nearest classroom and ask. Looking for the office will take too much time."

Tim said, "Look. Since we each think our idea is the best, why don't you try your way and I'll try mine. I'll meet you in the gym."

"Okay," said Joan, "I'll see you there."

Tim and Joan could think about what to do and could choose what action to take. Like Tim and Joan, we are images of God. We are persons. We can think and choose. We can think and choose to act as images of God.

Say to the class: "When Joan stopped at the nearest classroom, she asked directions. The directions Joan received were hard for her to understand. It took her a long time to reach the gym. Tim was waiting for her when she got there.

"Why did Joan go to the nearest classroom instead of following Tim?" (*She thought her way was faster. She made a different choice.*) "What would you have done?" (*Look at a map of the school; ask other kids; try to find it myself.*)

"As we have learned, God thinks and He makes choices.

"God made us in His image. We are persons. God gave us the ability to think our own thoughts and make our own choices.

"Now, let's pretend that Tim's dog, Spot, followed him to school. How would Spot enter the school?" (*Follow people to an open door; sit and wait by any door until someone comes; or scratch at any door until someone opens it.*) "How would he find Tim?" (*Walk through the school sniffing until he found Tim.*) "What might happen to Spot?" (*Maybe no one would let Spot into the school, or maybe someone would chase Spot out of the school.*)

"Animals, like Spot, cannot think and freely choose. They live their lives by looking for food and protection and by walking until they can see, smell, or feel what they are after."

Living the Lesson

1. What is the only way Spot would be able to enter the school? (*Someone would have to let him in.*)
2. Could Spot choose one door because it was better than the other doors? (*No.*) Why not? (*Dogs cannot think or choose. They take what is given to them or what they see first.*)
3. Can Spot think of more than one way to find Tim? (*No.*) Why not? (*He cannot think. He can only do what all dogs can do: bark, listen for Tim's voice, sniff, wander around the school until Tim finds him or he finds Tim.*)
4. How are Tim and Joan different from Spot? (*Tim and Joan are persons. Spot is an animal.*)
5. What abilities do persons have that animals do not have? (*The abilities to think and choose.*)
6. If Tim needed to get inside the school, what would he have done? (*Try the closest door or go to the front door and open it himself.*)
7. Would Joan have chosen the same door? (*Not necessarily. She might decide to try a different door.*)
8. What makes persons different from each other? (*Looks, things they do, choices they make.*)
9. What do all persons have in common? (*The abilities to think and to choose freely.*)

Activity

Student Book, page 42

Cut out the words below and place them in the proper boxes. Watch out! Some of the boxes will remain blank.

HUNT	THINK	CHOOSE	EAT	SLEEP	LOVE
DRINK	PAINT	CLIMB	LAUGH	RUN	SING
DRIVE	SWIM	KNIT	COLOR	READ	SCREAM

People	**People & Animals**	**Animals**
Drive	*Hunt*	
Think	*Drink*	
Choose	*Scream*	
Knit	*Swim*	
Laugh	*Eat*	
Color	*Climb*	
Read	*Sleep*	
Love	*Run*	
Paint	*Sing*	

Part B

Student Book, page 40

VOCABULARY
image: A copy or reflection of something.
likeness: Similarity; having something in common.
dominion: To be in charge of.
creature: Something or someone made from nothing by God.

Materials needed: Role-playing cards (see Appendix).

Application

Say to the class: "Open your books to page 45. Look at all of the living things in this picture. Name them." (*Plants, fish, animals, man, and woman.*) "Who created the world?" (*God.*) "God created all of the animals, like the ones in the picture. Then He created man and woman in His image and likeness. Let's read page 46 and find out how we were created in God's image."

Student Book, pages 45–46

God created the world and everything in it. God made all kinds of wild animals and creeping things. Then God made man and woman in His image and likeness.

God said, "Let them have dominion over the fish of the sea, the birds of the air, and the cattle, and over all the wild animals and all the creatures that crawl on the ground."

—Genesis 1:24–26

Animals cannot think or freely choose. They can only live their lives looking for food and protection for themselves. They do not determine what to do or not to do in the same way we do.

Of all the living things God created on earth, only we are made in His image and likeness. God thinks and chooses. As images of God, we can think and choose. We can think about how we should act. We can choose to love or not to love. When we think and choose to love as God loves, we act as His images. If we are not thinking and choosing to love as God does, we can change and begin to think and choose as images of God.

Living the Lesson

1. In what way did God create man and woman? (*In His image and likeness.*)
2. How are man and woman made in God's image? (*They can think and choose.*)
3. Are all living creatures created in God's image? (*No.*)
4. Do we always think and choose as images of God? (*No.*)
5. What can we do if we are not thinking and choosing as images of God? (*We can change.*)

Activity

Cut out the role-playing cards found in the Appendix.

Divide the class into four groups. Ask each group to sit in a different corner of the room. Give each group a role-playing card. Ask the students to listen carefully to the directions.

Say to the class: "Each group has been given one role-playing card. When I am finished speaking, share the card with each of the members in your group.

"Your group must decide how to act out each situation on the card. Remember, every group member must participate.

"You will be given ten minutes to practice your skit. Then I will call each group to the front of the classroom, one at a time, to perform its skit. After each skit, I will ask the rest of the class some questions, so make sure you are a polite audience and watch each skit carefully. Are there any questions? . . . If not, you may begin."

Listing of role-playing instructions:

CARD A
Everyone in your group is fishing. Every time a fish is caught, it is thrown *carelessly* onto the shore and forgotten about.

CARD B
One person is standing alone on the playground. The rest of the group is playing baseball. Finally, the players notice the lonely person. The pitcher asks the person to play.

CARD C
Everyone is at school. The whole class should be in their seats, doing their work, but they are not. Instead, they are fooling around.

CARD D
One of you catches a baby bird in a net. All of you like the bird, but you notice that it will not eat. All of you decide to set it free. You remind each other not to touch it. A mother bird will not take care of her baby if it has been touched by people.

Questions to follow each skit:

After skit "A" has been performed, ask the rest of the class: "Were the characters in skit 'A' practicing proper dominion over the animals of the earth?" (*No.*) "Why do you say 'No'?" (*Because they caught the fish and threw them away instead of eating them or letting them go.*)

After skit "B" has been performed, ask the rest of the class: "Were the characters in skit 'B' acting as images of God?" (*Yes.*) "How did they act as images of God?" (*They gave a lonely person a chance to play.*)

After skit "C" has been performed, ask the rest of the class: "Were the characters in skit 'C' acting as images of God?" (*No.*) "Why do you say 'No'?" (*Because they were not doing what they should. They were fooling around instead of sitting quietly.*)

After skit "D" has been performed, ask the rest of the class: "Were the characters in skit 'D' practicing proper dominion over the animals of the earth?" (*Yes.*) "How?" (*They were helping the baby bird live as it should by letting it go.*)

5

God Gives Us the Power to Think

1. Lesson Focus

Because we are images of God, we are persons. Each of us is composed of a body and a personal soul. Our souls are spiritual and give life to our bodies. One of the powers of the soul is the will, which helps us make choices. In order to learn about ourselves, God, others, and the world, we also have the power to know and to think. We call this power the mind. It is also a power of the soul. The mind is where we store the ideas Jesus teaches us. Jesus teaches us that we should pray to Him and that we should remember that He forgives us if we are sorry and if we ask for forgiveness. Jesus also helps us to be His followers. In this lesson we will focus on the power of the mind.

Note to CCD teachers: Use Parts A through D in class. The activities can be sent home to be done as family activities or used in class as time permits.

2. Concepts of Faith

Student Book, page 59

Things to Remember

What are two powers of our souls?
Two powers of our souls are our minds and our wills.

What power do we use to think about and remember what Jesus taught us?
We use the power of our minds.

3. Lesson Presentation

Part A

Student Book, page 47

VOCABULARY
mind: What we think with; where our knowledge is stored.
think: To use one's mind.
store: To keep.

Materials needed: Glue, scissors.

Application

Ask the class: "What might help us remember what we have seen or read about?" (*Take pictures of what we have seen; write down what we have seen or read about; etc.*) "Let's open our books to page 48 and read about the special power God has given us to store information."

Our world is filled with so many fascinating things. Every day we seem to learn something new. In reading we learn new words. With those new words we can read about people we have never met and places we have never seen.

Dogs go to obedience school. But, unlike all of us, they do not use books. Dogs cannot think as we do. Their owners practice with the dogs all of the things the teachers have trained the dogs to do.

God has given us minds to think and to store the special information that we want to keep.

Ask the class: "What are some examples of special information that you have seen, heard, or read about?" (*Friends' phone numbers, birthdays, vacation days, favorite places, foods, school subjects, sports facts, etc.*)

Our minds can be compared to a bedroom closet. At first the closet seems so big. You begin to collect things to fill it. You put so many of your favorite things inside your closet that it becomes overloaded. The closet cannot handle any more, and everything falls out when you open it.

When your closet is cluttered, finding a favorite object becomes very difficult. You dig through all the things you do not need, searching. You throw everything else out of the closet until you've found what you are looking for. You're overjoyed, until you see the pile of objects that need to be placed back into the closet. Oh no, cleaning time!

Carefully, you check through all of the things on the floor and the things left in the closet. You ask yourself, "Which ones do I want to keep? Which ones are not needed anymore?"

After separating your objects into two piles, you begin to place the things you want to keep back into the closet, neatly. What a change! The closet looks great! Things are much easier to find now.

Like our bedroom closet, our minds can become cluttered, too. We continue to learn new things. We need to clear our minds of the things that should not be there and remember only the things that we need to know.

Student Book, pages 50–51

New information comes to us every day. In the morning, when we want to eat breakfast, we look for our favorite cereal. But when we open the cupboard, we see that Mom bought something new. So we decide to give the new cereal a try. We remember how our favorite brand tastes. We find that we still like our favorite brand the best.

At school, during math class, we learn that 2 + 2 + 2 = 6. But our teacher tells us that 2 × 3 = 6, also. So we decide to use 2 × 3 instead of 2 + 2 + 2, because multiplying is quicker.

At home, your little sister is in your room again, making a mess of your model airplanes. You've yelled at her before, but there she is again. You know that yelling is not the way to keep your sister away from your models. You think about how much she likes the models, so you have the idea to make her a model of her own. Maybe that will keep her out of your room.

We keep all these new experiences in our minds and remember them.

Activity

Student Book, pages 52–53

Read the following list of information. From your experiences, think of the things you should keep in your "mind closet". Cut out the items that you should keep and glue them neatly in your "closet" on page 52.

X	Knowledge of God	X	Names of friends
	Unkind words	X	Prayers
X	Birthdays and holidays		Ways to get out of doing work
X	The Ten Commandments	X	Special places you have visited
X	Hobbies	X	Favorite sports
	Dangerous things		Ways to tease someone
	A friend's mistake	X	School subjects

Part B

Student Book, page 47

VOCABULARY
parable: A short story that teaches a religious lesson.

Application

Say to the class: "God knew we needed a good teacher to help us learn about Him and our world. We needed someone to help us think about and decide what we should keep in our 'mind closet' and what we should leave out. One of the reasons God became man was to be that teacher.

"When Jesus, God the Son, was on earth, people did not know what to think about Him and the things He was teaching. Some of the people did not remember His teachings or did not follow Him.

"But Jesus did not give up. He wanted us to remember and think about His teachings. He wanted us to know about God, ourselves, others, and the world. He taught us by telling stories called parables. Each parable has a message for us. After reading each parable, we will think about the parable, find the message Jesus was teaching, and remember this message. The messages will help us follow Jesus. Please open your books to page 55."

Student Book, pages 55–56

THE PARABLE OF THE BUSY JUDGE

There once was a judge who was very busy. A woman whose husband had died kept coming to the judge for help. She had a problem that needed solving. Someone was bothering her. She wanted to know what the judge would do about her problem.

At first, the judge said he was too busy to help the woman. But she kept coming back again and again. She kept disturbing the judge. Finally, he knew he would never get anything done until he listened to her. He listened to her problem and settled it for her once and for all.

—Adapted from Luke 18:1–8

The message in this parable is about God. God is not like the busy judge. God always listens to us. We should turn to God often in prayer, asking Him to help us and thanking Him for all He has given us.

When we pray for something and we do not receive what we prayed for, it is not because God did not hear us or was too busy to help us. It is because God knows what is best for us. We have to learn to trust in God. In our minds we can think about how much God loves us and remember that He will always care for us.

Living the Lesson

1. Who helps us to think about and decide what we should keep in our "mind closet"? (*Jesus.*)
2. What did Jesus tell us about when He was on earth? (*He told us about ourselves, God, others, and the world.*)
3. How did Jesus tell us about these things? (*Through stories called parables.*)
4. What can we think about and remember after reading the story about the busy judge? (*We can think about how much God loves us and remember that He will always care for us.*)

Part C

Student Book, page 47

VOCABULARY

Pharisees: A group who kept all the rules and tried to make other people keep the rules. They were more often concerned with keeping the rules than with loving God.

synagogue: A building where Jewish people pray.

Application

Student Book, page 56

Read the following parable. In this parable the message is about ourselves and others.

THE PROUD MAN AND THE TAX COLLECTOR

Two men went to a synagogue to pray. One of these men was a Pharisee. He kept all the rules completely, no matter what. He was more concerned about rules than about really loving God. The other man was a tax collector. Sometimes he cheated people. No one liked him very much.

The Pharisee stood tall and proud in the front of the synagogue. He made sure everyone could see and hear him. He prayed loudly, saying, "Thank you, God, for not making me like other people, especially not like that tax collector. I fast twice a week, and I give some of my money to the poor." On and on he prayed, bragging and boasting about himself and pointing out what others do wrong.

The tax collector, however, stood quietly in the back. He kept his head bowed low, not even raising his eyes to heaven. When he prayed, he said, "O God, be merciful to me, a sinner."

—Adapted from Luke 18:10–14

The message of this parable is about ourselves and others. God knows what we have done. We should not brag about the good things we do, or feel important because we have helped others. We please God by thanking Him for all He has given us. We should tell God how much we love Him. We need to ask God to help and guide us to be the best images of God we can be. If we have made wrong choices, we should tell God we are sorry and ask Him to help us not to do wrong again.

In our minds we can think about ourselves and others. Do we brag or think we are better than other people? We should remember that all people are made in the image of God and that God loves all people.

Activity

Student Book, page 57

Word Scramble. Think about the following words. Unscramble these words. Write the correct word next to the scrambled word. Remember what you have learned about these words.

1. SEUJS (JESUS)
2. NIHKT (THINK)
3. MBREREME (REMEMBER)
4. IDMN (MIND)
5. RAYP (PRAY)
6. HORTSE (OTHERS)
7. VLSEROSUE (OURSELVES)
8. ODLRW (WORLD)
9. OGD (GOD)
10. EGMAIS (IMAGES)
11. LETCSO (CLOSET)
12. REPASBAL (PARABLES)

Part D

Student Book, page 47

VOCABULARY
servants: Helpers in the house.
in charge: Be responsible for something.

Application

Student Book, page 58

In the following parable the message is about the world.

THE WATCHFUL SERVANTS

A man is going on a trip. He leaves his home and places his servants in charge. All his servants know what their jobs are. They know what work to do while the man is gone. The man asks the servant at the gate to watch the house carefully.

The servants and the man at the gate should do the best that they can at their jobs, even when the owner of the house is away.

—Adapted from Mark 13:34–37

The message in this parable is about the world. Sometimes we are asked to be "in charge" of ourselves. Sometimes we are left alone in the classroom when the teacher has to leave for a few minutes. Sometimes we are left alone at home or in a store. How should we act? Do we always act as we should? There are times when things in the world distract us from acting as we should.

Student Book, page 59

Sometimes our friends might distract us. When the teacher is out of the room, fooling around might look like fun. Sometimes things distract us. At home alone we might want to watch something on TV that we know we are not allowed to watch. In a store, a treat might look too good to pass up, and we might want to take it. We must think and remember what Jesus taught us.

In our minds we can think about how an image of God would act and remember to ask God to help us act as we should.

Living the Lesson

1. Who was left "in charge" when the man went on a trip? (*His servants and the man at the gate.*)
2. What kind of job should the servants and the man at the gate do when the owner is on a trip? (*The best that they can do.*)
3. When we are left "in charge" of ourselves, how should we act? (*As an image of God should.*)

6

God Gives Us the Power to Choose

1. Lesson Focus

Because we are images of God, we are persons. Each of us is composed of a body and a personal soul. Our souls are spiritual and give life to our bodies. One of the powers of the soul is the will. We are able to make choices with our wills. In order to learn about God, ourselves, others, and the world, we also have the power to know and to think. We call this power the mind. Thinking is also a power of the soul. In this lesson we will focus on the power of the will.

Note to CCD teachers: Use Parts A through D in class. All activities can be sent home as family activities or done in class as time permits.

2. Concepts of Faith

Student Book, page 64

Things to Remember

What are two powers of our souls?
Two powers of our souls are our minds and our wills.

What power of the soul do we use to make choices?
We use our wills to make choices.

3. Lesson Presentation

Part A

Student Book, page 60

VOCABULARY
choose: To decide; to make a choice.
will: A power of the soul with which we make choices.

Materials needed: Radio that can be heard only with earphones (i.e., has no loudspeaker).

Application

Note to teachers: Make sure the radio cannot be heard except through the earphones. Make sure the earphones are *disconnected* from the radio when class begins.

Show the class a portable radio without the earphones attached. Turn on the radio. Ask the class why they cannot hear the radio. (*The students will give you a variety of answers.*)

Say to the class: "This is a headset radio. When no one can hear a radio through its speaker, it is not a radio. *This* radio uses earphones as its speakers. Without the earphones, it is not a radio. Similarly, a person is not a person without a will. Let's open our books to page 61 and read about our wills."

Student Book, page 61

People are special. They are made in the image of God. As images of God we have wills to make choices. People can choose to live in houses, apartments, or tents. They can choose to work various hours—night or day. People can choose to eat anything from pizza to roast duck.

Animals do not have wills and cannot make choices as we do. God made animals to act in certain ways at certain times. Animals cannot choose how to act or what to do. They do the same things at the same times to survive. For example, all bears take shelter in dens, they hibernate all winter, and they eat berries.

Part B

Materials needed: "Choice" cards. Teacher should prepare these ahead of time by writing the choices listed on page 44 on individual 3" × 5" cards.

Student Book, page 61

Each and every day we make choices. Some choices are based on what we like (flavor of ice cream), some are based on what we need (food, clothing), and others are based on what we should do as images of God (following the Ten Commandments).

Activity

Show the class the three stacks of cards. Say to the class: "The first group of cards contains things people might like to do. The second group of cards contains things people might need on a cold winter day. The third stack contains things people might do to act as images of God."

Choose one child from the class to come up. Ask the child to choose from the first stack of cards the activity that child likes best. Ask the child, "Which one of these things would you choose to do?" Have the child read the card to the class.

Ask another child to choose from the second stack of cards. Ask this child, "Which of these things would you choose to have on a cold winter day?" Have the child read the card to the class.

Ask a third child to choose from the third stack. Ask this child, "Which of these things would you choose to do to act as an image of God?" Have the child read the card to the class.

Choices on the "Choice Cards":

Things to Do	**Things We Need**	**Acting as Images of God**
Playing sports	*Boots*	*Praying*
Taking out the garbage	*Mittens, scarf, hat*	*Doing what parents ask*
Watching T.V.	*Hot chocolate*	*Visiting the elderly*
Setting the table	*Warm coat*	*Being kind to someone*
Reading	*Bowl of soup*	*Telling the truth*

Using the names of the three children, ask the class, "What were *N*, *N*, and *N* doing?" (*Choosing.*)

Tell the class: "Because we make choices, we know that we have a will, given to us by God. If God had not given us wills, we could not make choices."

Activity

Student Book, page 61

List five foods that you like to eat; five things you need to feel good and be healthy; and five ways you can act as an image of God.

Foods I Like to Eat	**Things I Need to Be Healthy**	**Ways to Act as an Image of God**
_____	_____	_____
_____	_____	_____
_____	_____	_____
_____	_____	_____
_____	_____	_____

Part C

Application

Say to the class: "Let's open our books to page 62 and read more about making choices."

Student Book, page 62

As human beings, we make choices every day. The power to make choices exists within all of us. We call this power the will.

Below you will find five different situations. What choice would you make in each situation? Why?

1. You are invited to a party at your friend's house. Your friend's parents leave the house. While they are gone, a PG-rated movie is put in the VCR. Your parents have told you not to watch a PG movie without their permission. What should you do?
   a) Stay and watch the movie even though you know you should get your parents' permission first.
   b) Call your parents and ask your parents to come and take you home.

Student Book, page 62

2. Your Dad asks you to rake the yard on a Saturday afternoon, and you agree to do it. As you are raking, some friends ride by on their bikes and ask you to play with them. What should you do?
   a) Stay and rake the leaves as you promised.
   b) Go with your friends and have fun.

3. You are walking down the aisle in a grocery store, and you see an open bag of candy. What should you do?
   a) Tell a person who works in the store what you found.
   b) Take a few pieces of candy, because nobody will ever know.

4. You and your friends are deciding to play a game. You need to choose teams. After teams have been chosen, there is one extra person. What should you do?
   a) Tell that person that he or she cannot play, because the teams will be uneven and unfair.
   b) Make room for the person on one of the teams.

5. You have a test that you need to take in one of your classes. What should you do?
   a) Study so that you do a *super* job on it.
   b) Don't study, because you think it will be easy.

Student Book, page 63

It is a little scary when you have to make an important decision and you do not know which way to turn. Remember, you never make a decision alone. You have Jesus as a guide.

An easy rule to follow when making an important decision is to take these three steps first:

1. Listen to what other people have to say—for example, your parents, teachers, parish priests, and religious sisters.

2. Think about the situation and ask yourself what Jesus would do.

3. Pray to Jesus to help you make the right decision.

Living the Lesson

1. How often do we make choices? (*Each and every day.*)
2. Is it sometimes scary to make an important decision? (*Yes.*)
3. Do we make our decisions alone? (*No.*)
4. Whom do we count on to help us? (*Jesus.*)
5. What are the three steps that we should take when we have an important decision to make? (*Listen, think, pray.*)
6. What are some important decisions that you will have to make? (*Answers will vary.*)

Part D

Application

Student Book, page 63

Because God has given each of us the gift of a free will, we can change our choices if we need or want to.

Sometimes we make the right choice and get hurt. At times we make the wrong choice and get by. We should try to make the right decisions. We should try to choose to do what Jesus would choose to do. This is always the right choice to make whether it makes us feel good or not.

Say to the class: "Look at the choices that you made in the previous situations. Think about those choices. Now I'm going to read you some new information about those same situations. This new information should make the situations clearer. Let's see whether any of you would like to change your choices."

Read the following to the students. Have them indicate their new choices.

1. **(a)** You stay at the party because your friend's parents just went out to pick up pizza and pop for later.
   (b) You call for a ride home, and your Mom and Dad say that they know what movie it is and that it is okay for you to stay and watch it.

2. **(a)** You stay and rake the leaves because Dad has promised to take you to see the movie you have been wanting to see.
   (b) You drop the rake and go with your friends for a while. When you get back, Dad is not pleased because you should have asked before taking a break.

3. **(a)** You decide to tell the store clerks, and they reply that the candy was free samples for everyone.
   (b) You take a few pieces of candy. You are caught by a store clerk. You are told to pay for what you have taken.

4. **(a)** You tell the extra person that he cannot play, and he is not happy. He sadly goes to join another game already in progress.
   (b) You make room for the extra person on one of the teams, and that person has a good time and is successful. All the other players have a good time, also.

5. **(a)** You are worried about the upcoming test, and you decide to study; you pass the test.
   (b) You think that the test will be easy, so you do not take the time to study; you do not pass the test.

> **Student Book, page 64**
>
> Anytime that we need to make a choice, we should ask ourselves: *Would Jesus do this?* If not, we should not do it. If so, then it is something we may do or possibly should do.
>
> Look back over the five situations and ask yourself the question: *Would Jesus do this?*

Living the Lesson

1. On what do we base our choices? (*Our likes, needs, and acting as Jesus would act.*)
2. How do we know what choice to make? (*We follow the example of Jesus.*)
3. Once we make a wrong choice, do we have to stay with that choice? (*No, we can change our choice.*)
4. What does it mean "to change our mind"? (*To make a new choice.*)
5. What do we use as the bases for our choices? (*New knowledge or experience of likes, needs, and acting as Jesus would act.*)
6. What is the question that we should be asking ourselves whenever we have to make a choice? (*Would Jesus do this?*)
7. When going back to the five situations, how many of you made choices based on what you thought Jesus would do? (*Answers will vary.*)

Say to the class: "In the following parable about two sons, one son made a wrong choice, while the other son also made a wrong choice but changed his mind. The son who changed his mind decided to do what Jesus would do. Let's open our books to page 65 and read the story of these two sons."

> **Student Book, page 65**
>
> In the following parable, one son made the wrong choice because it was easier. The other made the wrong choice but decided to do what Jesus would do and changed his mind.
>
> THE PARABLE OF THE TWO SONS
>
> There was a man who had two sons. He came to the first and said, "Son, go out and work in the vineyard today."

Say to the class: "What is a vineyard?" (*A vineyard is a garden where grape vines grow.*)

> **Student Book, page 65**
>
> The son replied, "I will not", but afterward he changed his mind and went and worked in the vineyard.
>
> The man came to his other son and gave the same order. This son replied, "Yes, sir", but he did not go into the vineyard.
> —Adapted from Matthew 21:28–32

Say to the class: "Which son thought about what he had done, changed his mind, and did what Jesus would do?" (*The son who went to work in the vineyard.*)

7

God Gives Us Life

1. Lesson Focus

Because we are images of God, we are persons. Each of us is composed of a body and a personal soul. Our souls are spiritual and give life to our bodies. The soul and the body together make up a living human being. The soul also enables us to share God's life, grace. One of the powers of the soul is the will. We make choices with our wills. In order to learn about God, ourselves, others, and the world, we also have the power to know and to think. We call this power the mind. It also is a power of the soul. The mind is where we store the ideas Jesus teaches us. In this lesson we will focus on the soul.

Note to CCD teachers: Use Parts A, B, and C in class. The story in Part C can be sent home as a family activity or read in class as time permits.

2. Concepts of Faith

Student Book, page 72

Things to Remember

What is the soul?
The soul is the invisible, spiritual, and immortal gift from God that gives us life.

What are two powers of our souls?
Two powers of our souls are our minds and wills.

What power do we use to think about and remember what Jesus taught us?
We use the power of our minds to think about and remember what Jesus taught.

What power do we use to make choices?
We use the power of our wills to make choices.

Student Book, page 66

VOCABULARY
soul: The invisible, spiritual, and immortal gift from God that gives us life.
spiritual: Something you cannot see; not material.
immortal: Living forever.

3. Lesson Presentation

Part A

Application

Say to the class, "Let's open our books to page 67 and read about a great gift that God has given us."

> **Student Book, page 67**
>
> God has given each of us a will to make choices and a mind with which to think. The will and the mind are powers of our souls. The soul is a wonderful gift from God. We cannot see our souls. They are invisible. We each have a soul that gives us life and enables us to share God's life, grace. Our souls live forever.
>
> The human soul and the body together make up a living human being. Our souls give us life. We cannot live without our souls.
>
> Imagine a wagon. It would not be a wagon without the four wheels. If we took the wheels away, the wagon would not roll. It would only drag. In this poor condition, the wagon would not last very long. A wagon without wheels is not a wagon. Without our souls, our bodies would not have life.

Part B

Application

Say to the class: "Let's read more about our souls. Please open your books to page 67."

> **Student Book, page 67**
>
> Our souls are the spiritual and immortal part of us. Our souls will never die. Even though our bodies die, our souls live on forever. They are immortal.
>
> When people die, their bodies are not alive anymore. When people die, their souls leave their bodies. Their bodies are buried in the earth. If the person has acted as an image of God, then the person's soul goes to heaven. The person will live forever with God in heaven. We believe that when Jesus comes again, at the end of time, the bodies and souls of all the people who have died will come together again.

Our souls are immortal. That means our souls will live forever. To help understand how long forever is, think about the number of leaves on one tree. Add that number to the number of leaves on all the other trees in the world. Forever is more days than that. Forever is longer than we can ever imagine. We should always try to act as images of God, so that we can live forever with God in heaven.

Part C

Application

Say to the class: "We have the ability to think and to choose. Thinking and choosing are powers of the soul. Let's open our books and read how we can use these powers to act as images of God."

Thinking with our minds helps us learn things. In order to learn we must listen. One way to learn about God and how to act as an image of God is to listen to what the Bible teaches and to listen to what the Church teaches. Our parents, teachers, and priests tell us what the Bible and the Church teach. We should listen to them and learn.

When we make right choices with our wills, we act as images of God. We make the right choices when we follow Jesus' example. Jesus gives us grace to help us make right choices.

We can think because we have minds. We can make choices because we have wills. If we think about God with our minds and make right choices with our wills, we will live as images of God here on earth and someday live forever with God in heaven.

Living the Lesson

Say to the class: "We should remember that we were created by God, body and soul. God loves us, and He will help us act as images of Himself. Let's read the next story about a man who lived as an image of God."

Read the story below about a saint who used the two most important powers of the soul, thinking and choosing, to show his love for God and others.

ST. THOMAS AQUINAS

Thomas was born a long time ago in the year 1225, in a little village in the country of Italy. He was a very well-behaved and happy little boy. He often thought and wondered about God.

It was the custom, in those days, that, when a boy turned five years old, he was sent away to school to study. When Thomas was five, he was sent to a famous monastery, where he began a life of prayer and study.

At first, Thomas was frightened and lonely, because he had never before been away from home. Eventually, Thomas came to love the monastery, because there he seemed to be closer to God. He believed that he should become a priest or a brother.

During this time in Italy, wars were going on. During the wars, soldiers took over the monastery; so Thomas did not return to school there. But after Thomas grew up, he attended college at the University of Naples. There, Thomas met a well-known priest. This priest belonged to a group of people who tried to live a good life by following the example of St. Dominic. Members of this group of people are called Dominicans. Thomas liked what this priest did. Thomas wanted to become a Dominican, too.

Thomas applied to join the Dominicans and was accepted. Thomas' mother became very angry, because she did not think that living the life of a Dominican was good enough for her son. Thomas did not want to go against his mother's wishes, but he felt it was more important to follow God's call.

While Thomas was on his way to live with the Dominicans, his own brothers came and kidnapped him. They took him back home, where his mother locked him in his room.

Months went by. Thomas remained locked in his room. His sisters brought him food and tried to persuade him not to join the Dominicans. Thomas' brothers tried tempting him to commit sins, but God protected Thomas. Thomas made the right choices. Thomas was helped by thinking often about God.

After a while, Thomas escaped. Then he joined the Dominican priests in Naples. Thomas declared that he did not want to serve anyone other than God. In January 1245, Thomas made his promise to live his life as a Dominican. He began his studies to become a priest. He studied very hard and continued to pray often.

After five years of studying, Thomas was ordained a priest. This was the happiest time of his life. However, during that same year something happened to make Thomas very sad. His two brothers and his mother died. Thomas was so sad that he cried often.

Thomas went on to become a teacher at a college. Even though his life was very busy with studying, teaching, preaching, and helping others, Thomas always found time for prayer.

In 1272, Thomas became very sick. His illness left him quite weak, but he continued to teach and to preach the word of God. Two years later, Thomas became ill again. This time he died.

Some years later, Thomas was declared a saint. We celebrate his feast day on January 28. Thomas gave his life to God and others as a priest and teacher. Thomas used the powers of his soul well. Thomas thought about God often. With God's help, Thomas made the right choices. As a saint he lives with God forever in heaven. St. Thomas Aquinas is a good example for us to follow.

8

All Persons Have Dignity

1. Lesson Focus

We are images of God. We are all persons. As persons, we have dignity. As persons, we are worthy of respect. When we do not act as images of God, we do not lose our dignity, but it is not as clearly visible. When we act according to our dignity, it is more clearly seen that we are acting as images of God.

One person does not have more dignity than another person. People can and do have different abilities, likes, and dislikes, but their dignity remains the same. We all have the same boundless worth and value as images of God. We should be proud of who we are because we are images of God.

Note to CCD teachers: Use Parts A, B, C, and D in class. All activities can be sent home as family activities or done in class as time permits.

2. Concepts of Faith

> Student Book, page 78
>
> *Things to Remember*
>
> **Why do we have dignity?**
> We have dignity because we are images of God.
>
> **Who has dignity?**
> All persons have dignity.

3. Lesson Presentation
Part A

> Student Book, page 73
>
> VOCABULARY
> **dignity:** Worthy of respect.

Materials needed: Cardboard boxes—see following note.

Note to teachers: Later in this lesson, the class will be needing sturdy shoe-box-size boxes—one for every five students. The students should also be asked to bring to class copies of favorite recipes—recipes for breakfast, lunch, dinner, desserts, and snacks.

Application

Say to the class: "We all have dignity. Dignity means that we are worthy of respect. When we act according to our dignity, as images of God, our actions make our dignity easier to see. Our dignity does not come from what we own but from who we are—images of God.

"One day, after school, two boys talked about the differences in their families. When the discussion stopped, they both learned a lesson. Let's read pages 74 and 75 in your book and find out what that lesson was.

Note to teachers: The following selection from the student book can be read aloud by two students, one reading the part of James, the other reading the part of John. Assign the parts before continuing.

Student Book, pages 74–75

We are images of God. We are all persons. As persons, we have dignity. As persons, we are worthy of respect.

One person does not have more dignity than another person. People can and do have different abilities, likes, and dislikes. But their dignity remains the same. As images of God, we all have the same boundless worth and value.

Two boys, James and John, are both third-graders. They are in the same class. Both boys are very good students. They seem to be very much alike. Yet their families are very different. James' family owns many things. John's family does not. This difference bothers John.

JAMES AND JOHN

James: My dad owns ten department stores. He has a chauffeur who drives him to work in a limousine every day.

John: My dad is a carpenter. He makes things in our basement.

James: My mom loves to shop. She has a credit card for every store. She also has a closet full of beautiful clothes.

John: My mom enjoys staying home. She makes all of our meals from scratch and decorates our house with beautiful homemade crafts. She even has time to play ball with me and help me with my homework.

James: My older brother Tim has his own car. Dad pays for the gas and insurance. Tim drives his friends to school every day.

John: My brother Mike helps Dad fix our old station wagon. It's the only car we have. Mike rarely uses it with his friends.

James: I have my own TV, VCR, computer, and telephone.

Student Book, pages 75–76

John: We have a small TV in the family room.

James: You don't have much, do you.

John: No.

James: Wouldn't you rather be rich like me?

John: Well, I guess so, but I love my family. We're all healthy and happy. Things just don't mean that much to us. James, we both deserve respect, not for how much we have, but for who we are—images of God.

James: I guess you're right. As persons, everyone has dignity.

Like all of us, James was born with dignity. When he does not act as an image of God and brags too much, he does not lose his dignity. It is just harder for us to see.

John does not lose his dignity by being envious, either. His dignity is just not clearly seen. Acting as images of God makes their dignity clearer to see.

All persons have dignity, not because of what they own but because of who they are—images of God. All persons should be treated with respect.

Living the Lesson

1. Are the families of James and John different or the same? (*Different.*)
2. Explain how the two families are different. (*James' family has more money. They own a lot of fancy things. John's family is not rich and does not have a lot of things.*)
3. James and John finally recognize that they both have dignity and deserve respect. Why? (*They are both persons. They are both images of God.*)
4. What does the word "dignity" mean? (*Worthy of respect.*)
5. Who has dignity? (*All persons.*)
6. Did the boys lose their dignity when they were bragging and being envious? (*No.*) Why or why not? (*When they did not act as images of God, their dignity was only harder to see.*)
7. When we do not act as images of God, do we lose our dignity? (*No, we still have it, but it is not as clearly seen.*)

Part B

Student Book, page 73

VOCABULARY
traditional: Doing things as they were done in the past.
village: Small town.
thatch: Straw.

Materials needed:
A filmstrip (any suitable subject), a filmstrip projector.
10 index cards, numbered 1 to 10.
1 shoe-box-size box for every five students.
1 cardboard tube for every five students (from an empty roll of paper towels).
1 sheet of 8½" x 11" paper for each student.
Pencils, crayons or markers.
Transparent tape.
Optional: map of the world.

Application

Say to the class: "Please open your books to page 76 and read about a young girl's life in a village in Tonga and her life as a student in the United States."

Student Book, pages 76–77

As persons, we have dignity. All human persons in all of the other parts of the world have dignity, too.

The nation of Tonga is made up of 150 islands. It is located about one thousand miles north of New Zealand.

Most of the people are farmers. They like to live a traditional way of life.

Nuku (*noo-koo*) is a happy nine-year-old girl. She lives in a small house with a thatch roof, along with her two brothers and two sisters. All of the children in Tonga attend school until they are fourteen years old.

In the morning, Nuku's father works in the garden; and in the afternoon, he fishes for tuna and shark. Nuku's mother does the housework and sometimes helps in the garden.

After school, Nuku and her friends enjoy playing hide-and-seek among the trees and swinging on the vines that hang from the branches. Sometimes, they create their own play villages with handmade dolls, houses, and furniture.

In school, they read about life in other places. Some of the children they read about live in big houses, play with store-bought toys, and ride in fancy cars.

The children of Tonga do not have these things. This does not bother Nuku, her family, or her friends. The people of Tonga understand that people are more important than things. They respect each other's dignity. They act as images of God. Their dignity is easy to see.

Many people want to visit Tonga because of the warm friendliness of the people. One tourist, a representative of the United States, invited Nuku to live and attend school in the United States for one year.

Nuku did not want to go, at first. She loved her home. But the chance to visit new people in a new place excited her. She accepted the invitation. At the end of the summer, she left for Minneapolis, Minnesota.

If a map of the world is available, point out locations of the islands of Tonga and the city of Minneapolis.

Living the Lesson

1. Nuku had dignity on Tonga. Will she still have dignity in the United States? (*Yes.*) Why? (*Because she is an image of God.*)
2. What do you think will happen to Nuku in the United States? (*She might miss her family. She might meet new friends. She might tell people about Tonga. Etc.*)

Activity

Show the class what a filmstrip looks like. Place the filmstrip in a projector and show the students how it works.

Say to the class: "Each picture of a filmstrip is called a frame. You are going to make a filmstrip. Instead of photographic film, you will use sheets of paper taped together to make your filmstrip. It will look like a filmstrip with large frames.

"I am going to divide the class into groups, with five people in each group. Each group will make a filmstrip. And each person in every group will be responsible for drawing one frame for that group's filmstrip." (*Divide the class into groups.*)

"In my hand I have five cards with numbers on them. When I come to your group, each of you will draw a card, remember the number, and give the card back to me."

After all of the students have drawn a number, say to the class:

"If your number is one, draw a picture of what you think Nuku's family looks like. If your number is two, draw the village that Nuku lives in. If your number is three, draw Nuku's house. If your number is four, draw Nuku's school. If your number is five, draw Nuku and her friends playing among the trees.

"When you draw your picture, keep the paper horizontal, like this." (*Demonstrate.*) "Color all your pictures. When your group has finished, place the pictures face down in a row on the floor (or large table). Tape the pictures together vertically, in a long line, so that they become frames of a large filmstrip. Then tape the *bottom edge* of your filmstrip onto one of these cardboard tubes, and roll the filmstrip up with the pictures facing the inside.

"If you finish your drawing before others in your group, take the box I've given to your group and cut a square hole in the bottom of it. Then cut two slots, one inch wide and twelve inches long in the opposite sides of the box." (*Show the students the locations on one of the boxes.*)

"After your filmstrip has been placed on its tube, thread the first frame through the slots in the box. When all the groups are ready, you can take turns looking at the filmstrips the other groups have made."

Part C

VOCABULARY
scarce: Rare, hard to find, not common.
responsibility: Duty; job.
self-esteem: Self-respect.

Materials needed:
1 sheet of white 8½″ x 11″ paper for each student.
Crayons or markers.
Transparent tape.
Student-made "filmstrips" and box-viewers (from preceding section).

Application

Say to the class: "Let's continue reading the story of Nuku and her trip to the United States."

After the thrill of the plane ride and the excitement of seeing the large city of Minneapolis for the first time, Nuku finds it hard to get used to life in the United States. Material things seem so important to the people here. Children live in large houses, they ride in fancy cars, and some of them even have their own bedrooms and spending money. It seems to Nuku that children with the most things are the most popular.

At home on Tonga, money is scarce. Nuku wears her clothes until she outgrows them. She does not get new clothes very often. When she does need new clothes, her mother makes them for her. The family house her father built has two rooms for seven people. The family does not need a car. Because they live on a farm in the village, everything they need is within walking distance.

Family life is so important on Tonga. Nuku has responsibilities at home. She cares for her younger brothers and sisters, helps with the housework, and helps prepare meals.

Here in the United States, her self-esteem is very low. She doesn't have all the things that the popular girls have. She doesn't do the things she used to do back home. She has very little pride in herself. She has forgotten who she is and what is important to her.

Nuku knows that she is going to be in Minneapolis for a long time. She must talk to someone about her problem. She asks Susan, the daughter of the family she is living with, to meet her after school in the park so they can be alone to talk.

When they meet in the park, Nuku says to Susan, "I've lost the good feeling I used to have about myself. I don't have all of the things to be popular. I don't do the things I used to do back home. I look different from everyone else; my clothes are different; I even talk differently."

Susan said, "Every person is different on the outside. On the inside, every person is made in the image of God. We should be proud of who we are."

> **Student Book, page 78**
>
> "If everyone is an image of God," said Nuku, "then why do so many of the kids make fun of me and treat me like I'm not?"
>
> Susan said, "Unfortunately, people do not always act as the persons they were created to be. Some people do not treat others as kindly as they should. Some people do not respect the dignity of others."
>
> Nuku said, "I feel as if I don't deserve respect."
>
> "As a person, you have dignity!" said Susan. "You *do* deserve respect! When people treat you unkindly, you need to hold your head high and be proud of who you are! Tell other people about life on Tonga. Tell them that people on Tonga know that persons are more important than things, and that acting as images of God is the most important thing of all."
>
> Nuku said, "Thanks, Susan. You've really been a help. You are a good friend."

Activity

Have the students make additional frames for their "filmstrips". Ask the class to get into the same groups they were in before. Make sure that they have their pencils and crayons and markers with them.

Say to the class: "We are going to add on to our filmstrips. When I come to your group, you each draw a card again, remember the number on the card, and give the card back to me."

After each student has a number, tell the class: "If your number is one, draw Nuku at the Tonga airport. If your number is two, draw Nuku arriving in Minneapolis. If your number is three, draw Nuku's host family (the family she is staying with) and their house. If your number is four, draw Nuku's school in Minneapolis. If your number is five, draw Susan and Nuku. When you are finished, tape your frames together as you did before and attach them to the first set of frames on your filmstrip."

When students are finished, they can look at each group's filmstrip, as before.

Part D

Note to teachers: For the following section, students will need to bring from home a copy of a recipe from one of these categories: breakfast, lunch, dinner, dessert, and snack. Make sure each recipe is on a separate sheet of paper.

Materials needed: pencils, crayons or markers, three-hole or similar paper punch, scissors, yarn, glue, recipes.

Note to teachers: Collected the recipes from the students. Have them stacked in the following groups: breakfast, lunch, dinner, desserts, and snack.

Application

Say to the class: "Everyone has different likes and dislikes. I might want to have a tuna sandwich for lunch, and you might want a pepperoni pizza. I might like what I'm wearing, and you might not.

"We deserve respect no matter what we like or dislike! Our dignity does not depend on what we like or dislike, what we have or do not have. Our dignity comes from the fact that we are created in the image of God. All people deserve our respect no matter what they like or dislike, no matter what they have or do not have.

"When we do not act as images of God, our dignity does not go away. It is just very hard to see. We should act as images of God, be proud of who we are, and allow others to be proud of who they are. Then, our dignity will be much easier to see, and we will remember that other people have dignity, too.

"Let's pretend that X [*use the name of one of the boys in the class*] gets his hair cut *really* short, and that Y [*name another boy in the class*] does not like the way X's hair looks."

Say to the class: "Does Y lose his dignity because he does not like X's haircut?" (*No.*) "Does X lose his dignity because Y doesn't like his hair?" (*No.*) "We don't lose our dignity because we disagree with others or because others disagree with us. We don't lose our dignity at all. We are always images of God. We should try always to remember to act as images of God."

Activity

Before beginning this part of the lesson, make sure the students' recipes have been collected and sorted into the five groups mentioned earlier.

Say to the class: "Please take out your desk covers, scissors, glue, pencils, and crayons or markers.

"Today we are going to make a cookbook of favorite foods. We will be using the recipes you brought from home. First, I am going to divide you into five groups."

Divide the class into five groups; ask the students to bring their supplies with them as they form their groups.

Say to the class: "The first group will be working with the recipes for breakfast. The second group will work with the recipes for lunch. The third group will work with the recipes for dinner. The fourth group will work with the recipes for desserts. And the fifth group will work with the recipes for snacks.

"Look over the recipes your group will be using. Read the recipes. Then decorate the recipe sheets. Remember, every person has different likes and dislikes. Even though we might not think that the food made with every recipe is good to eat, we need to respect the likes of others.

"When everyone is finished, we will make a booklet of the recipe sheets."

Note to teachers: You might be able to make copies of the recipes, so that each student can receive a copy. Have the students design a cover for the booklet. Punch holes in the pages and use yarn to make a binding; or staple the pages together along the binding edge.

Alternate procedure: Make a cover for the booklet. Bind the collection of recipes, as described above. Give the students time to look at the completed booklet. Keep it in the classroom in a place where they can get it and look at it in their free time and copy recipes from it if they wish.

Living the Lesson

1. Is it okay if I don't like some of the recipes in our booklet? (*Yes.*) Why? (*Because everyone has the right to have different likes and dislikes.*)
2. Should I be teased because I am the only one who likes one of the recipes? (*No.*) How should my likes and dislikes be treated? (*With respect.*)
3. Why do we have dignity? (*Because we are images of God.*)
4. Who else has dignity? (*All persons.*) Even if they are very old? (*Yes.*) Even if they are not born yet? (*Yes.*)
5. Do people have dignity even if they are very sick? (*Yes.*) Do people have dignity even if they are handicapped? (*Yes.*)
6. Why do all these people have dignity? (*Because all people are made in the image of God.*)

Unit 3

ACTING AS IMAGES OF GOD

9

How We Should Act

1. Lesson Focus

As we learned in Lesson 6, "God Gives Us the Power to Choose", our free wills give us the power to make our own choices. We should choose to act as images of God.

God became man so that we could see, through His example, how we are to act as images of God. If we follow the example of Christ and act as He would act, we act as images of God and will live someday with God in heaven. When we behave in a manner unlike God, we are making wrong choices. Following Christ sometimes involves resisting temptation.

Note to CCD teachers: Use Parts A, B, and E in class. All other activities can be sent home as family projects or used in class as time permits.

2. Concepts of Faith

Student Book, page 84

Things to Remember

How do we know how we should act?
We come to know how we should act by following the example of Christ and by acting as He would act.

---

3. Lesson Presentation
Part A

Student Book, page 80

VOCABULARY
shepherd: One who takes care of sheep.
advisors: People who give advice or information.
prophet: One who speaks for God.

Materials needed: Image of God cards from Appendix. Optional: map of the Holy Land.

Application

Say to the class: "Long, long ago, the king of Jerusalem, a man by the name of Herod, called together all the religious leaders and teachers of his land. He was very upset. He had heard that a baby, the King of the Jews, had been born. He did not want another king to take his place.

"Herod asked the religious leaders and teachers where the prophet had said the Child was to be born. Who was this baby?" (*Jesus.*) "The religious leaders and teachers told Herod that the Child was to be born in Bethlehem in the province of Judea. They told him that the prophet Micah had written that a leader would come out of Bethlehem. This meant that a leader was to be born in Bethlehem. Who is that leader?" (*Jesus Christ.*) "What does a leader do?" (*Show us how to act.*)

—Adapted from Matthew 2:1–6

Say to the class: "As you heard in the story, Jesus was born to us as a little baby. As we know, Jesus is God the Son. He is *the* leader. One of the reasons He was born into this world is to show us how we should act.

"We are followers of Jesus. We follow His example. As followers of Jesus, we want to act as He would act. We want to act as His images."

Activity

Say to the class: "I will draw the names of five people, one at a time. Each of those five will draw one card and read the card out loud to the class. Each card describes a boy or a girl who is acting or not acting as an image of God. When the card has been read to you, the whole class will discuss and decide what Jesus, God the Son, would do and what an image of God should do." (You will find these cards in the Appendix.)

Part B

Student Book, page 80

VOCABULARY
Scripture: Holy writings about God.
test: Proof of ability or skill.

Application

Say to the class: "Following Christ the King and acting as an image of God is not an easy job. Sometimes it involves resisting temptation.

"Jesus was tempted by the devil, but He did not give in to temptation. Let's read the story about Jesus' temptation, on page 81 of your book."

Student Book, page 81

Following Christ the King and acting as an image of God is not an easy job. Sometimes it involves resisting temptation.

In the following story, Jesus was tempted by the devil but did not give in. He showed us how to resist temptation.

THE TEMPTATION

One day, Jesus went into the desert to fast and pray. He had very little to eat for forty days and forty nights. He was feeling weak. The devil knew that Jesus must be hungry, so he tempted Jesus to turn some stones into bread so that Jesus could have something to eat.

The devil wanted Jesus to show off. He wanted Jesus to use His power as God to change stones into bread. Jesus said, "One does not live by bread alone, but by every word that comes forth from the mouth of God." When Jesus spoke those words, He was telling us that we need more than food to live a good life. We also need God's words of love to guide us.

The devil and Jesus were on the roof of the temple. The devil said, "If you are the Son of God, throw yourself down." The devil then said that God would send His angels to protect Jesus. The devil told Jesus: "With their hands they will support you." In other words, the devil was tempting Jesus to test God. Jesus answered, "You shall not put the Lord, your God, to the test." With those words, Jesus was telling us that we should believe in what God says because God always tells the truth.

Finally, the devil and Jesus were on a very high mountain, and the devil showed Jesus all the kingdoms of the world. The devil told Jesus that all these things would be His if He would fall on His knees and worship the devil. Jesus answered: "Get away, Satan!" Jesus told the devil that persons should worship only God.

The devil left Jesus, and angels came and waited on Him.

—Adapted from Matthew 4:1–11

Resisting temptation as Jesus did is a very good way to practice acting as an image of God. It is a way of following Christ the King.

Living the Lesson

1. Why did Jesus go into the desert alone? (*To fast and pray.*)
2. How long did Jesus spend in the desert? (*Forty days and forty nights.*)
3. Why was Jesus so weak? (*He had little food.*)
4. How did the devil first tempt Jesus? (*He wanted Jesus to show off. He told Jesus that he should turn stones into bread.*)
5. What happened on the roof of the temple? (*The devil told Jesus to throw Himself off the roof. The angels would catch Him.*)
6. Jesus did not throw Himself off. Why not? (*Jesus knew the devil wanted Him to test God to see if God was lying.*)
7. How did the devil tempt Jesus the third and final time? (*He tried to make Jesus worship him.*)

Say to the class: "When you practice throwing a football or playing the piano, you become better at throwing the football or playing the piano. When you practice acting as images of God, you become better at acting as images of God. Jesus did not give in to temptation. Not giving in to temptation is a very good way for us to practice acting as images of God."

Part C

VOCABULARY
govern: To take care of.

Materials needed: Small slips of paper (one for each child); an empty can or bucket; a crown made of paper; a master template from which the children can make their own crowns.

Application

Say to the class: "When we think of a king, we often picture a man sitting on a throne, telling everyone else what to do. The story we are about to read reminds us that a true king does not act that way.

"Please open your books to page 82." (*Ask a student to begin reading.*)

THE KING WHO CHANGED HIS WAYS

There was a king who ruled over a large kingdom. He loved to give orders from his throne in the palace. Every day he would make new rules that were unfair to the people of his kingdom.

For example, one day the king announced: "Bicycles and cars are no longer allowed on the streets. The people of my kingdom must walk backward."

The townspeople were angry when they heard the news. But they knew that they must do what the king commanded. So everyone in town began to walk backward.

Meanwhile, the king was spending time alone in his castle garden, looking at his favorite plants. His servants did not know he was out in the garden, so they locked the castle gates.

The king had no key. He was locked out of his castle! He pounded on the large doors, but no one could hear him. He decided to drive into town to get some help.

At a stop sign, a policeman told him that he was not supposed to be driving in the town by order of the king. The king cried, "But I am the king!" The policeman did not believe him and took away his car.

It didn't take the king long to notice that everyone was walking backward. People shouted at him, "Turn around!" He shouted back, "But I am the king!" No one would believe him.

For two days the king had to stay in town and follow his own silly orders. He hated having to do so.

His servants finally came to town looking for him. He was so glad to see them that he made a promise. "I am going to get rid of these awful rules. I am going to see what rules my people need to lead happy lives. Those are the rules I will make, and I will help the people keep them."

From that day forward, the king was a true king. He made only fair rules and helped the people of his kingdom.

We just read that a true king is someone who knows what is right for his people and does it. Christ was a true king. He knew what was right and He did it. Jesus showed us how to act.

Following Christ the King and acting as an image of God is not an easy job. Sometimes it involves resisting temptation.

In the Bible story "The Temptation", Jesus was tempted by the devil but did not give in. He showed us how to resist temptation.

Resisting temptation as Jesus did is a very good way to practice acting as an image of God. It is a way of following Christ the King.

Say to the class: "As followers of Christ, we should act like Christ the King. We should find out what is right and do it.

"Today we are going to choose a king or a queen for our classroom. We are going to help him or her govern our classroom in the best way possible." (*Pass out small slips of paper, one to each child.*)

"Please write your own name on the paper and fold the paper in half. As I walk around the room, place your slip of paper in this container." (*After all the slips have been collected, draw a name.*)

"Our classroom [king or queen] is N_____. So, N_____, would you please come to the front of the room and sit on your throne?" (*Place a crown on the student's head.*)

"Now, what ideas could we share to help our new ruler? Should the classroom be noisy or quiet? Should the students run or walk? Should the students talk or listen when someone is talking?"

Note to teachers: Guide the children in making the right choices. After each right choice, ask the ruler: "How should we phrase this classroom rule?" Then write the ruler's response on the blackboard.

When all ideas have been given, say to the class: "Let's look at our list of classroom rules and decide if our rules are fair.

"Would it be a pleasant classroom if everyone could shout, run around, and talk while others are talking?" (*No.*) "Why not?" (*We couldn't hear what each other was saying; someone might get hurt; we'd miss out hearing the important announcements.*)

Ask the ruler: "How do we achieve a happy, pleasant classroom?" (*By choosing classroom rules that are good for everybody.*) Ask: "Are our rules fair?" (*Yes.*) "Why?" (*They show respect for ourselves and other people.*) Say: "These classroom rules help us to respect ourselves and others as images of God. Thank, you, N. You may return to your seat." (*Save the crown.*)

Living the Lesson

1. How did Jesus act like a king? (*He knew what was right and did it.*)
2. As followers of Christ the King, how should we act? (*We should find out what is right and do it.*)

Activity

Have the students make crowns for themselves if there is time. Say to the class: "We are making crowns as a reminder that we should act like Christ the King."

Part D

Materials needed:
   Desk cover.
   Pencils, crayons or markers, scissors, glue.
   A small brown-paper bag for each child.
   Small cards for assigned characters from Part E.
   One ready-made paper-bag puppet for demonstration.
   Optional: scraps of construction paper; scraps of yarn; buttons.

Activity

Note to teachers: Change the names of the assigned imaginary characters if the names are the same as the names of your students.

Say to the class: "By using puppets, we are going to show how some people act. Each of you will be given the name of an imaginary person. The name also describes each imaginary person. Try to make your puppet look like the description given by the name.

"To make our puppets, begin by putting a desk cover on your desks. Then take one of these brown-paper bags and your crayons or markers and place them neatly on the desk cover." (*Pass out the names of the imaginary persons and the paper bags. Show the children your ready-made puppet as an example.*)

"When you are finished making your puppet, use the stapler to staple the name of your imaginary person on the inside of the bag."

Say to the class: "Place your own name on the back of your bag." (*Show the students where.*) "Place your hand in the bag. Notice where the folds are. The face goes on the bottom of the bag.

"Draw your puppet's face, arms, and legs with a pencil first." (*See diagram.*)

"Then color your puppet with crayons or markers." (*Have the children decorate their puppets with the optional materials if time permits.*) "Are there any questions? . . . You may begin."

Part E

Materials needed: puppets made in Part D of the lesson; cards containing descriptions of imaginary persons (see list below).

Activity

Say to the class: "Take out your puppets. When I call your puppet's name, come up and get your card. On each of the cards, you will find a description of what kind of person your puppet is like. You will have five minutes to think of something your puppet could say or do to help the rest of the class understand what your puppet-person is like. When the five-minute period is up, I will call you to come to the front of the room with your puppet and make your puppet talk to us or do something to let us know what he or she is like.

"When you are finished, the class will try to answer two questions about your puppet-person: (1) Would you like to be that imaginary person? (2) Why or why not?"

Note to teachers: Demonstrate with your puppet, using the description on one of the extra cards. Some children might need help reading the descriptions.

Say: "Are there any questions? . . . Begin thinking of something your puppet could say or do. Remember to make it short!"

DESCRIPTIONS FOR GIRLS

Kind Karen	*Helpful, thoughtful.*
Lying Lucy	*Dishonest, does not tell the truth.*
Patient Patty	*Calm, waits for others, doesn't get angry.*
Efficient Erica	*Does not waste time, gets the job done.*
Hurtful Harriet	*Dislikes everybody and everything.*
Disrespectful Diane	*No honor, insults others, calls them names.*
Obedient Olive	*Listens to parents and teachers.*
Stealing Sally	*Takes other people's things.*
Jealous Judy	*Does not want to share.*
Trusting Teri	*Has faith in God and in others.*
Lazy Laura	*Does nothing, is never busy.*
Mean Margaret	*Unkind, crabby.*
Brave Becky	*Self-controlled, not afraid.*

DESCRIPTIONS FOR BOYS

Dependable Dan	*On time, there when you need him.*
Boastful Billy	*Brags.*
Courteous Kurt	*Helpful, thoughtful.*
Forgetful Fred	*Ignores the time, doesn't keep his promises.*
Goof-off Gus	*Fools around when he should be working.*
Prayerful Pete	*Prays often.*
Rude Ryan	*Interrupts.*
Envious Ed	*Wants what everyone else has.*
Church-going Charlie	*Goes to Mass often.*
Harmful Howard	*Hurts other people.*
Quiet Quincy	*Does not speak when unkind things are said.*
Crabby Casey	*Bad temper, gets mad easily.*
Honest Otto	*Tells the truth.*
Generous Jack	*Giving, generous.*
Unkind Ulysses	*Cruel, unfriendly.*
Reverent Roy	*Believes in Christ, acts as an image of God.*
Arrogant Arnold	*Brags a lot, is mouthy.*

Say to the class: "Some of these imaginary persons act as Jesus would act, and some do not. How should we act?"

10

Loving God and Others: The Ten Commandments

1. Lesson Focus

As images of God, we are created to act as God acts. The Ten Commandments are the way God acts. If we follow the Ten Commandments, then we are acting the way we were created to act, as images of God.

Note to CCD teachers: Use Parts A and B and the accompanying activities in one class session. Use Parts C, D, and E and the accompanying activities in the next session. If time does not permit doing them during class, the activities can be sent home as family projects.

2. Concepts of Faith

Student Book, page 98

Things to Remember

How do we act as God acts?
We act as God acts by following the Ten Commandments.

3. Lesson Presentation
Part A

Student Book, page 85

VOCABULARY
dreaded: Feared.
bitter: Unpleasant.
mortar: A clay and water mixture used to make bricks.
slavery: Treating people as property.
subjects: Those under the rule of a king.
witness: Person who has seen or heard something.

Materials needed: Optional: map of the world.

Application

Note to teachers: Point out the location of Egypt on a world map when starting this section of the lesson.

Student Book, page 86

Thousands of years ago, before Jesus was born, a special group of people called the Israelites lived in Egypt. The number of Israelite families was large. The Israelites were successful and happy.

The Egyptian Pharaoh (or king) was worried that the Israelites might someday take over Egypt. He encouraged the Egyptian people to do something about them.

The Egyptians were afraid of the Israelites because there were so many of them. So the Egyptians decided to make life unpleasant for them by forcing them to become slaves. As slaves, they had to work with mortar to make bricks and work in the fields.

Say to the class: "What do you think this work was like?" (*Difficult, dirty, hot, sweaty.*)

Student Book, page 86

The Pharaoh commanded all of his subjects, "Throw into the river every boy that is born to the Hebrews [Israelites], but you may let all the girls live." He did this so that the number of Israelite families would be fewer.

—Adapted from Exodus 1:12–14, 22

Say to the class: "What happened to the Israelites?" (*The Pharaoh made them slaves.*) "What else did the Pharaoh do?" (*He made his subjects throw all Hebrew baby boys into the river.*)

Student Book, page 87

THE CALLING OF MOSES

A baby boy was born to a Hebrew woman. The mother saved him from being killed by hiding him from the Pharaoh's men for three months. When she could hide him no longer, she placed him in a basket and hid it among the reeds near the river, hoping that someone would come along and find him and care for him.

Pharaoh's daughter was taking a bath in the river when she saw the basket among the reeds. On opening the basket, she found the baby boy, crying! She kept the baby and cared for him.

When the baby grew older, the Pharaoh's daughter adopted him and called him "Moses", which means "I drew him out of the water".

Say to the class: "Moses survived. Who saved him?" (*His mother, and then the Pharaoh's daughter.*) "What does the name Moses mean?" (*It means "I drew him out of the water".*)

As Moses grew, he witnessed the harsh treatment of the Israelite people by the Egyptians. He wanted to do something about it, but he didn't know what to do.

The Pharaoh heard about Moses' wish and ordered him to be put to death. But Moses escaped to another country.

While in that country, Moses heard God call out to him from a burning bush. When Moses understood that God was speaking to him, he hid his face because he was afraid.

God told Moses that He knew about the suffering people in Egypt. God asked Moses to be the one to lead them out of Egypt to a better place. God also promised to stay with Moses and the Israelites throughout their journey.

Moses did what God asked him to do. The journey was long and hard.

Three months after leaving Egypt, the Israelites arrived at the foot of Mount Sinai. God asked Moses to come to the top of the mountain. Moses climbed the mountain to meet God.

There, at the top of the mountain, God gave Moses the Ten Commandments so that the Israelite people would know how God acts and how they should act as images of God. These commandments were written down on stone tablets and taken down the mountain by Moses to the Israelites below.

—Adapted from Exodus 2:1–4:17, 12:37–20:17

Say to the class: "God gave Moses a special job. What was that job?" (*To lead the Israelites out of Egypt.*) "How do you think they traveled?" (*They walked, or they rode on animals.*) "How long had the people been traveling before God called Moses again?" (*Three months.*) "What did God give to Moses?" (*The Ten Commandments.*)

Part B

VOCABULARY
worship: Respect and honor to God.
conversation: Talking; sharing information.
in vain: Without respect.
true: Genuine; right; correct; the only one.
Sabbath: The Lord's day; the day we go to Mass.

Application

We learned that God gave Moses the Ten Commandments on Mount Sinai. The Ten Commandments tell us how God acts and how we should act as images of God. The first three commandments tell us about God and how we should love Him. (The commandments are based on Exodus 20:2–17 and Deuteronomy 5:6–21.)

1. I am the Lord, your God. You will not have other gods besides Me.

2. You will not take the name of the Lord your God in vain.

3. Remember to keep holy the Sabbath day.

In the first commandment, God is telling us that He is the Creator; the only Being deserving of our worship. God is asking us to love Him and worship only Him.

By the choices we make with our free wills, we can choose to love and worship God through prayer and sacrifice.

When we pray, we talk to God. We should give Him our full attention. A prayer is not only some words we have memorized and repeat when we awake in the morning, before our meals, and before bedtime. Prayer is a conversation with God. We thank Him for what we have, ask Him to watch over us and guide us, tell Him we are sorry for our wrong choices, and praise Him.

A sacrifice is a gift. It is not something we can place in a box and wrap. It is the gift of ourselves. It is giving of ourselves, our time, and our talents.

Sometimes we are asked to do things we do not like to do. It is hard to accept a job willingly without complaining. Doing a job without complaining and without being told is a sacrifice.

God asks us to help others when we can. When your mother needs help with the dishes, you should pitch in and help. When someone falls, we should help the person up and try to make the person feel better. When unkind words are spoken, we should disagree and not repeat them.

Remember, other people are images of God, too. Whatever we do for others, we do for God.

God has done a lot for us. We should love Him most of all, be thankful for what He has given us, and expect nothing in return. Even though we should expect nothing in return from God for our love, God does always love us and care for us.

God is not like a television set. That is, we do not turn Him on when we want something and then turn Him off when we think we have everything we need.

Instead, we should be "tuned in" to God all the time. He likes to hear from us every day. He deserves our respect and praise.

Say to the class: "How do we follow the first commandment?" (*Love God and worship only Him.*)

Student Book, page 90

The second commandment tells us: "You will not take the name of the Lord your God in vain." A name is like a person's title. It stands for that person. The way we use a name indicates what we think of that person.

God's name should always be used with respect. When we use His name with love in prayers and songs, we are giving Him that respect. When we use God's name while angry or to comment on something we do not like, we are not giving Him that respect. We are using God's name "in vain", which means without respect. We are using God's name in the wrong way. We should not use God's name in the wrong way.

Say to the class: "What does it mean to take the name of the Lord your God in vain?" (*It means using God's name in the wrong way.*)

Student Book, page 90

The third commandment tells us: "Remember to keep holy the Sabbath day." The Sabbath day, or the Lord's day, is a day of worship and rest. To keep it holy means to give the day to God.

In order to follow the third commandment, we should remember that Sunday is a day of rest. We should finish most of our work during the week and save Sunday for Mass, fun, and family. When we do not spend time with our families, work too hard, or skip Mass on Sunday, we are not following the third commandment.

Activity

Student Book, pages 90–91

The first three commandments tell us about God and how we, as images of God, should love God. Using the "code" given below, write the first three commandments. Then, under each commandment, write what the commandment means.

Code: Write the letter of the alphabet that comes *before* the one that is given.

I		A	M		T	H	E		L	O	R	D,
J		B	N		U	I	F		M	P	S	E

Y	O	U	R		G	O	D.		Y	O	U
Z	P	V	S		H	P	E.		Z	P	V

W	I	L	L		N	O	T		H	A	V	E
X	J	M	M		O	P	U		I	B	W	F

O	T	H	E	R		G	O	D	S
P	U	I	F	S		H	P	E	T

B	E	S	I	D	E	S		M	E.
C	F	T	J	E	F	T		N	F.

Y	O	U		W	I	L	L		N	O	T
Z	P	V		X	J	M	M		O	P	U

T	A	K	E		T	H	E		N	A	M	E
U	B	L	F		U	I	F		O	B	N	F

O	F		T	H	E		L	O	R	D
P	G		U	I	F		M	P	S	E

Y	O	U	R		G	O	D
Z	P	V	S		H	P	E

I	N		V	A	I	N.
J	O		W	B	J	O.

R	E	M	E	M	B	E	R		T	O
S	F	N	F	N	C	F	S		U	P

K	E	E	P		H	O	L	Y		T	H	E
L	F	F	Q		I	P	M	Z		U	I	F

S	A	B	B	A	T	H		D	A	Y.
T	B	C	C	B	U	I		E	B	Z.

Part C

Student Book, page 85

VOCABULARY
honor: Respect.
errand: Job.
attack: Grab, harm.
dignity: Worth, value.
friendship: Being friends; caring about each other.
trust: To have confidence in someone and to be able to count on that person when
you need help.

Application

Student Book, page 92

In the last seven commandments, God tells us how to love ourselves and others the way He loves us and others. As images of God, we should act the way He acts.

The fourth commandment, "Honor your father and your mother", tells us that God loves parents. He gives them the responsibility to love and care for children.

Love is shown in the care that parents provide, the guiding words that they speak, and the good actions that they perform. Parents express care for their children by providing food, clothing, shelter, education, and spiritual guidance for them.

Loving parents would never ask their children to do something that is not God-like, something that is harmful. They would never keep from their children the food, clothing, shelter, or education that they need. Loving parents would never keep their children from prayer or religious education, either.

This commandment tells all children to do what their parents ask. Children should listen to their parents, come when they are called by their parents, help their parents around the house, and help their parents care for younger brothers and sisters. When children do not listen to their parents and help them when they should, the children are not following the fourth commandment.

Adult children are asked to love and respect their parents, too. This love can be shown by running errands for parents, helping them when they are sick, visiting them, and praying for them.

Say to the children: "Whom do we love when we follow the last seven commandments?" (*Ourselves and others.*) "How do we follow the fourth commandment?" (*By honoring our fathers and mothers.*) "I'm older. How can I help my parents?" (*By running errands, helping them when they are sick, visiting them, and praying for them.*) "How should parents treat their children?" (*With love.*)

Student Book, page 93

The fifth commandment is: "You will not kill." We are asked in the fifth commandment to act with kindness toward everyone. This commandment tells us not to hurt or harm anyone, including ourselves. Remember, God loves and cares for all human life, all persons born and unborn. As images of God, we should do the same.

Caring for ourselves includes eating properly, dressing properly, and watching what we do. Eating too much or too little food, or wearing improper clothing, can make us sick. Pills that we are not supposed to take can make us sick. The body is a special gift—it is part of us as images of God. Treat it with care.

Acting with kindness means we should not hit others or treat them badly. An attack on a human body is an attack on a human person, because the human body is part of us. Every human body has the same dignity and value that our own bodies have. We do not want someone to hit us; therefore, we should not hit someone else.

Say to the class: "How do we follow the fifth commandment?" (*By acting with kindness toward everyone and caring for ourselves.*)

Part D

Student Book, page 85

VOCABULARY
steal: To take something that does not belong to you.
adultery: To try to love in a married way someone we are not married to.

Note to teachers: If divorce or separation comes up in the following discussion, tell the children that a man and a woman make a promise at their wedding to love each other always. This is not easy to do. When the promise is broken, there is hurt. Tell the children that they should always pray for their parents.

Application

Student Book, page 94

In the sixth commandment, "You will not commit adultery", God tells us that people should love one another as God loves them.

A good friendship between two people involves a special kind of love. Both people like each other. They trust each other. They depend on each other.

Marriage is a special kind of friendship and love between a husband and wife. On their wedding day, a man and a woman promise to love each other in a particular way, to trust each other, and to depend on each other for help.

Sometimes it is not easy for a husband and wife to do what they promised. While still married, husbands or wives might decide to find someone else to try to love in this special way. This is called adultery.

We must pray for these people. They are no longer doing what they promised. They are not following the sixth commandment.

Even though none of you are married, you are still asked to follow the sixth command-ment. You should make promises only if you can keep them, and you should love as God loves.

Say to the class: "What is adultery?" (*When a husband or a wife tries to love in a married way someone other than the person he or she married.*)

Student Book, page 94

The sixth commandment also asks us to respect the dignity of other persons' bodies. Sometimes movies or books and magazines show people improperly dressed, using the wrong language, and treating each other poorly. These movies and books are not respecting the dignity of these persons' bodies.

When we do not take care of our bodies by dressing properly, we are not following the sixth commandment. When we watch movies or look at books or magazines that show people who are improperly dressed, we are not following the sixth commandment.

Say to the class: "If a friend of yours finds a video cassette with a movie you should not see, what should you do?" (*Not watch it. Return it.*) "You are not married. How can you follow the sixth commandment?" (*By making promises that we can keep, by loving as God loves, and by respecting the dignity of other persons' bodies.*)

Student Book, page 95

The seventh commandment says: "You will not steal." Stealing means taking something that belongs to someone else. Damaging something you have borrowed or not returning it is wrong, too. Persons who love each other respect each other's property. We should show our love for other people by not stealing.

Say to the class: "Should we look at another student's paper while doing our school work so that we can write down the other person's answers on our paper?" (*No. We should not copy someone else's work, because that would be stealing the other person's work—or cheating.*)

Note to teachers: This would be a good time to discuss copying another's answers. Remind the children that God gave each of them a mind to think and that they should trust in their own answers. They should not steal another person's work by cheating.

Student Book, page 95

When God created the world and us, He invited each of us to take care of some of the things in our world. These things include our personal possessions and anything we use or borrow. In giving us these things, God shows His love for all people. We should love all people as God does, by taking care of the things of the world.

God has given us a beautiful world to enjoy. We are responsible for it and must take care of it. Damaging trees and lakes is destroying gifts from God.

Say to the class: "How do we follow the seventh commandment?" (*By not taking what belongs to others, by not cheating, by respecting each other's property, and by taking care of all things.*)

Note to teachers: There is an exception to this explanation of stealing. If it is a matter of life or death, we are entitled to take what we need in order to survive. This is a very rare situation. Do not discuss it unless a child mentions or asks about it.

Part E

Student Book, page 85

VOCABULARY
truth: Something true or right.
bear false witness: Lie.
covet: To want to take for yourself what others have.

Application

Student Book, page 95

God always tells the truth. As images of God, we should tell the truth, too.

The eighth commandment tells us, "You will not bear false witness against your neighbor." To "bear false witness" means to lie. When we lie to another person or about another person, we do not love the truth. When we lie about another person, we are not respecting that person's dignity as an image of God. We are not loving as God loves.

Sometimes people make mistakes or have bad habits. We should not tell others about these mistakes or habits. If we know that someone is doing something harmful to himself or herself or to someone else, then we should tell someone in charge.

It is not easy being honest. We should stop and think before we speak or act, to make sure that we are being honest.

Note to teachers: If there is a problem in the class with tattling, you may wish to discuss it here.

Say to the class: "From what we have just read about the eighth commandment, can you tell me what God always does?" (*He always tells the truth.*) "What should we do as His images?" (*Always tell the truth.*)

Student Book, page 96

The ninth commandment tells us, "You will not covet your neighbor's wife." To "covet" means to want to take for yourself what others have.

God does not want to control us like robots, because He loves us. We have minds to think and wills to make choices. Sometimes people will choose to be friends, and sometimes they will not.

Just as God does not want to control us, we should not want to control others, either. We are asked to respect the freedom of others and not think of them as objects for our own enjoyment.

We learned from the sixth commandment that friendships are special. We enjoy our friends because we like them, we can trust them, and we can depend on them.

> **Student Book, page 96**
>
> Sometimes we want to be a close friend to someone who is a close friend to someone else. We want that person to be our friend only and no one else's. We want to take that person's friendship for ourselves and not share it with anyone else.
>
> When that happens, we need to remember that everyone has a free will to make choices. We must respect other persons' freedom and not think of any person as an object to be owned.
>
> Married people sometimes notice the gifts and talents of other people and wish they had married someone else. But they must remember to notice the gifts and talents that their husband or wife has. The more husbands and wives praise each other for the gifts they already have, the less they will wish that they had married someone else.

Say to the class: "What does 'covet' mean?" (*To want to take for yourself what others have.*) "God loves us and gives us the freedom to love others. Do we also have the freedom to control others?" (*No.*) "How can we follow the ninth commandment?" (*By not wanting to take another person's friendship for ourselves only.*)

> **Student Book, page 96**
>
> Because He loves us, God does not take and keep for Himself the things that He gave us. As images of God, we should not want to take what belongs to others, either.
>
> The tenth commandment tells us: "You will not covet anything that belongs to your neighbor." This means that we should be happy for others when they own something that we would like to have. We should not be envious or unkind. God has given us the right to own things in this world. We should be satisfied with what we own.

Say to the class: "What does it mean to covet something?" (*To want to take for yourself what others have.*) "Is it okay to be envious of what someone else has?" (*No. We should be happy for that person and share that person's joy.*) "How do we follow the tenth commandment?" (*By being satisfied with what we have.*)

Note to teachers: This presentation of the tenth commandment does not imply that people deprived of the basic necessities of life should not strive to obtain the things they need. This presentation also does not imply that people should not strive to better their situation in life.

Activity

Student Book, pages 97–98

Under each picture, write the number of the commandment that applies to it. Then circle "yes" if the people in the picture are following the commandment. Circle "no" if they are not following the commandment. Finally, write the commandment on the lines beneath the picture.

Commandment # _____

YES   NO

_____

_____

Commandment # _____

YES   NO

_____

_____

Commandment # _____

YES   NO

_____

_____

Commandment # _____

YES   NO

_____

_____

Commandment # _____

YES   NO

_____

_____

Commandment # _____

YES   NO

_____

_____

Commandment # _____

YES   NO

_____

_____

Commandment # _____

YES   NO

_____

_____

Commandment # _____

YES   NO

_____

_____

Commandment # _____

YES   NO

_____

_____

11

We Become What We Do

1. Lesson Focus

Each one of us is a person, created in the image and likeness of God. Each of us has a mind, will, and body. What we choose to do with our minds, wills, and bodies in the present, determines what kind of persons we will become in the future.

When we think about something, choose to do it, and practice performing it, we become better performers of that act. It is easier for us to perform that act. We become what we do.

For example, the more we think about being respectful, choose to be respectful, and practice being respectful, the better we become at being respectful. It is easier for us to be respectful. We become respectful persons.

So we should be very careful about what we think, choose, say, and do, because by each of our conscious and free acts, we are determining what kind of persons we will be in the future.

Note to CCD teachers: Use Parts A, B, and D in class. Parts C and E and all activities can be sent home as family projects, or they can be used in class as time permits.

2. Concepts of Faith

Things to Remember

When we think about something, choose to do it, and practice performing it, what do we become?
We become what we do.

3. Lesson Presentation

Part A

Student Book, page 99

VOCABULARY
unreliable: Not trustworthy.
inconsiderate: Thoughtless.

Materials needed: statement on blackboard (see below); activity cards (see Appendix; suggested answers are listed below).

Say to the class: "The more we practice doing something, the better performers of that act we become. The more like God we act, the more like God we become. Let's open our books to page 100 and read about becoming what we do."

Student Book, page 100

When we think about something, choose to do it, and practice doing it, we become better performers of that act. It is easier for us to do that act.

For example, if we are constantly late, we become unreliable, and it is easier for us to continue being late. If we tell many lies, we become more untruthful, and it becomes easier for us to lie. If we are thoughtless and have no time for other people, we become more inconsiderate, and it is easier for us to act in a thoughtless way. As we can see, our actions and words are very important. We become what we do!

Say to the class: "Today, I'd like you to pretend that you are all at a baseball game. Each of you will be given a card that tells you what position you will play.

"Some of you will be passing out programs, selling food, guarding the gates, checking tickets, or sitting in the stands. Others will be playing positions on our make-believe field."

Note to teachers: See the Appendix for the cards. There may be extra cards. Choose the cards you wish to use.

Say to the class: "Remember, we are *pretending* to play these parts! Please remain where you are seated. When your part is called, stand up and read the card you have. Then, the class will complete this sentence." (*Write the following sentence on the board if you have not already done so. Point to the sentence.*)

> If I continue to act in the way given in the example,
> it would be easier for me to act _____
> and I would become a _____ person.

List of cards, with suggested answers:

Pitcher:	unkindly or cruelly . . . an unkind or cruel person.
Umpire:	in an honest and trustworthy manner . . . an honest and trustworthy person.
Batter #1:	in a careless, thoughtless, and selfish manner . . . a careless, thoughtless, and selfish person.

Batter #2:	*in a boastful, showy, and self-centered manner . . . a boastful, showy, and self-centered person.*
Catcher:	*in a deceitful way . . . a cheat.*
First Baseman:	*in a courteous manner . . . a courteous person.*
Second Baseman:	*in a thoughtful manner . . . a thoughtful person.*
Shortstop:	*thoughtlessly and carelessly . . . a thoughtless and careless person.*
Third Baseman:	*in a considerate manner . . . a considerate person.*
Right Fielder:	*determined . . . a determined person.*
Left Fielder:	*in an unfair manner or cheat . . . an unfair person or a cheater.*
Center Fielder:	*in a thoughtless and unkind manner . . . a thoughtless and unkind person.*
Program Passer:	*disrespectfully . . . a disrespectful person.*
Food Vender:	*in a kind manner . . . a kind person.*
Security Guard:	*in a pushy or bossy manner . . . a pushy or bossy person.*
Ticket Checker:	*in a courteous manner . . . a courteous person.*
Crowd Member:	*in a discourteous and disrespectful manner . . . a discourteous and disrespectful person.*

Part B

Student Book, page 99

VOCABULARY
parable: Short story with a religious lesson.
merchant: A buyer and seller of goods.
valuable: Having great worth or importance.

Application

Say to the class: "We learned from the make-believe baseball game that when we think about something, choose to do it, and practice performing it, we become better performers of that act. It is easier for us to perform that act. We become what we do.

"Today, we are going to read a short play about the good Samaritan and what he did. Pay careful attention to all of the characters and the things they say and do. Please open your books to page 100."

Note to teachers: Assign parts before beginning.

Student Book, pages 100–102

The parable of the Good Samaritan is a good example of how we become what we do. Pay careful attention to all of the characters!

THE GOOD SAMARITAN

Narrator: A merchant from Jerusalem had some business to take care of in Jericho. He left the town early one morning. He thought to himself, "It looks like a beautiful day, and I have so many things to trade, sell, and buy. I should be able to reach Jericho by nightfall." Unfortunately, the merchant did not know that he had company waiting for him farther down the road.

Merchant: (*Some time later.*) I have covered many miles, and I am pleased. I hope the good weather holds up.

Leading Robber: (*Hiding behind a large boulder.*) Look at the things the merchant is carrying! They must be valuable! Let's get them!

Narrator: The robbers jumped on the man and beat him up. They took all of his things and left him almost dead.

Merchant: I feel so weak. I hope that someone will come along and help me before it's too late. Oh, look, a man, just down the road! His hands are folded in prayer. Surely he will help me!

Narrator: The man was praying quietly, his eyes focused only on the road in front of him. But out of the corner of his eye he noticed the wounded merchant.

Praying Man: How sad! The poor man must have been beaten. I'd like to stop, but I'll be late if I do. I must hurry on.

Merchant: It looks like there is no hope for me. But wait! Could that be another person coming down the road?

Narrator: It was another person. The sight of the wounded man caused him to stop suddenly.

Traveler: Oh, my gosh, how terrible! I don't know what to do. I know I should stay, but I'm frightened. I think I'd better be on my way.

Narrator: The merchant was so weak that he could not speak. He would surely die if no one came to help him. But someone did come, a person from Samaria. Unfortunately, the merchant and his countrymen were enemies of the Samaritan people. Would an enemy come to his aid?

Samaritan: How can this be? This man has been out here, all alone, for a long time, and no one has helped him. Here, friend, let me clean and wrap your wounds. I'll place you on my donkey and take you to a nearby inn.

Narrator: The Samaritan placed the merchant in a warm bed at the inn. He paid the innkeeper well and requested one more thing before he left.

Samaritan: Take good care of him, please. I will pay you back in full for any additional expenses when I return.

—Adapted from Luke 10:29–37

Living the Lesson

1. What happened on the road to Jericho? (*A merchant was robbed and beaten.*)
2. If the robbers continued to rob, what kind of people would they become? (*They would become greedy, thoughtless, harmful, and unkind people.*)
3. Who were the people who came along when the merchant lay injured on the road? (*A man praying, a traveler, and a Samaritan.*)
4. Why didn't the first two people help the injured man? (*No time; afraid to get involved.*)
5. Is it always easy to do what we know we should? (*No.*) What sometimes keeps us from doing what we know we should? (*Fear. Peer pressure.*)
6. How did the merchant feel about the Samaritan people before he was injured? (*The Samaritan people were his enemies.*)
7. Do you think the merchant felt differently after the Samaritan helped him? (*Yes. He will probably be more loving.*)
8. Did the Samaritan care who the injured man was when he helped him? (*No.*)
9. What was so surprising about what the Samaritan did? (*He helped a man who was his enemy.*) If the Samaritan continues to act in this way, what kind of person will he become? (*He will become a caring, thoughtful, and considerate person.*)

Part C

> **Student Book, page 99**
>
> VOCABULARY
> **decision:** Choice.

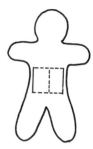

Materials needed:
    Paper dolls (see student book, page 103).
    3″ x 2″ slips of paper—one for each student.
    Pencils, crayons or markers, scissors, glue.
    Scraps of colored paper.
    Buttons.
    Yarn.

Make sure that all materials are available for student use. Then pass out the slips of paper.

Say to the class: "We would like to become better images of God. The more we act as images of God, the better images of God we will become. We become what we do.

"Today, we are going to make paper dolls that will remind us to act the way we should to become the better images of God we want to be. First, cut out your paper dolls. Notice the box in the middle of the paper doll. Cut only on the dotted lines to form a window—like this." (*Demonstrate.*)

"Next, write your name on the back of the paper doll." (*Pass out the 3″ x 2″ slips of paper* at this time.)

"Remember when we pretended to be players and workers and spectators at a ball game? How did the players act?" (*Write all responses on the blackboard—unkind, cruel, honest, trustworthy, careless, thoughtless, selfish, dishonest, thoughtful, considerate, determined, and kind.*)

"On the slip of paper I have given you, write your choice in the center—like this." (*Demonstrate.*)

"Place a small amount of glue on the top and bottom of your slip of paper." (*Demonstrate.*)
"Then, glue the slip of paper on the back of the paper doll." (*Demonstrate.*) "You should be able to read the words you have written through the window on the opposite side.

"Using crayons, markers, scraps of colored paper, yarn, and glue, make your paper dolls look like yourself! Make sure you put back the unused materials when you are finished. Are there any questions? . . . Begin."

Part D

> **Student Book, page 99**
>
> VOCABULARY
> **extraordinary:** Unusual, remarkable.

Materials needed: Optional: map of the world.

Say to the class: "Let's open our books to page 105 and read about a person who became the best image of God she could be."

Sometimes it seems as if only people who do fantastic, extraordinary things can become saints. Yet when we read about saints like Thérèse of Lisieux, we recognize that we can become holy by doing little things well. When we act like a saint, we become more saintly, and it is easier for us to act saintly. We become what we do. We become saints!

THÉRÈSE, THE LITTLE FLOWER

Thérèse Martin was born in Lisieux, France, in 1873. As she grew older, she loved her parents more and more. She would pick wild flowers and bring them to her parents to show her love for them.

When she was fifteen years old, Thérèse became a nun. She remembered picking flowers for her parents as a young girl.

Thérèse compared her everyday actions to those flowers. Every time she scrubbed the floors, set the table, or washed clothes, it was as if she were picking a flower. She would then give this "flower" to God to show her love for Him.

When she died, she was only twenty-four years old. Yet her life was full because she offered all of her everyday actions to God. Thérèse thought about what an image of God should do and chose to do those things over and over again until she became the best image of God she could be. She became a saint.

Like Thérèse, we can think about what an image of God should do in our day-to-day activities. We can chose to do those things well. We can chose to do those things over and over again until we become the best images of God we can be. We become saints!

Living the Lesson

1. What chores did Thérèse have to do? (*Scrub the floors, set the table, and wash the clothes.*)
2. Was there anything special about the things that she did? (*No.*)
3. What did Thérèse compare each of her chores to? (*Each chore was a "flower" for God.*)
4. How did Thérèse become a saint? (*Thérèse thought about what an image of God should do and chose to do those things over and over again until she became the best image of God she could be. She became a saint.*)
5. Could we become saints? (*Yes.*) How? (*In our day-to-day activities, we can think about what an image of God should do. We can choose to do those things well. We can choose to do those things over and over again until we become the best images of God we can be. We become saints!*)

Part E

Materials needed: "Great Players in Life", student book, pages 106–107.

Say to the class: "Carefully remove the 'Great Players in Life' worksheets from your books—pages 106 and 107." (*Wait for the students to remove the worksheets.*) "We learned that when we think about something, choose to do it, and practice performing it, we become better performers of that act. It is easier for us to do that act. We become what we do.

"In this activity, we must decide which actions we prefer. Then, cut out the 'baseballs' that have those actions printed on them and glue them on the 'stadium' page. Are there any questions? . . . Please write your name at the bottom of the 'stadium' page and begin."

Student Book, page 107

Ted makes fun of his teacher when she turns her back.	Even though Ken does not like math, he tries his best and asks for help.	Jane cuts in front of the other children in line.	Fred helps his teacher without being asked.	Mary asks the new girl to jump rope with her.
Jamie chews on the pencil he borrowed and then gives it back.	Eric teases a classmate because of his haircut.	Sue raises her hand before speaking.	Mark helps a classmate clean out his desk.	Harold tells Jim that he can't play ball with the others because Jim isn't good enough.

12

Shaping Ourselves into Followers of Jesus

1. Lesson Focus

Our actions should reflect God's actions, but sometimes our faults get in the way. We do not act as images of God. Jesus is the perfect image of God the Father. If we want to change and become better images of God, we should become followers of Jesus. Our actions should be like His.

Note to CCD teachers: Use Parts A, B, and C. Part D is optional.

2. Concepts of Faith

Student Book, page 120

Things to Remember

How did Jesus act in a difficult situation?
Jesus always acted as the perfect image of God the Father.

How do we become better images of God?
By becoming followers of Jesus.

---

3. Lesson Presentation

Part A

Student Book, page 110

VOCABULARY
fault: Bad habit, weakness.
imperfect: With fault.

Say to the class: "In our last lesson, we learned that we become what we do. When we think about something, choose to do it, and practice performing it, we become better performers of that act. It is easier for us to perform that act. We become what we do. By choosing to follow Jesus and by following Him day by day, we become better followers of Jesus.

"Let's read more about this on page 111 in your books."

Student Book, page 111

Sometimes we share outwardly the thoughts, choices, and feelings we have inside. When we are happy, we smile; when we are sad, we cry; when we want to show other persons that we love them, we give them a hug.

Our actions should reflect God's actions, but sometimes our faults get in the way. We do not act as images of God. Jesus is the perfect image of God the Father. If we want to change and become better images of God, we should become followers of Jesus. Our actions should be like His. Remember to think of Jesus before making decisions. He will help us know what to do, and He will help us make the right choice.

Living the Lesson

1. Give some examples from the reading of how we outwardly show what we think, choose, and feel. (*Happy = smile; sad = cry; love = give.*)
2. Can you think of any more examples of how we show what we think, choose, and feel? (*Answers will vary.*)
3. We want to be followers of Jesus, but sometimes what happens? (*Our faults get in the way.*)
4. If we want to become better images of God, how should we act? (*We should act like Jesus.*)
5. Why do we have to change? (*Because our actions are not always like Jesus' actions.*)
6. Who helps us make the right decisions? (*Jesus.*)
7. Who is the perfect image of God the Father? (*Jesus.*)
8. What should we do when we need to make a decision? (*Think of Jesus. He will help us know what to do, and He will help us make the right choice.*)

Activity

Say to the class: "Notice the picture on page 111. What is happening?" (*Two friends are arguing. Neither one of them will give in. Both of them blame each other.*) Have the students complete the activity.

Student Book, page 111

Write what you think Jesus would do in this difficult situation. If we want to follow Jesus, what should we do in this situation?

"Now, turn to page 112. What we want to do here is think of a difficult situation you or someone your age might face." Have the students complete the activity.

Student Book, page 112

Think of difficult situations that might happen to third graders. Write about one of them here. Tell what Jesus would do in this situation and what we should do as followers of Jesus.

It is often difficult for us to act as images of God. Jesus knows how difficult it is because He is human as well as the perfect image of God the Father. He suffered and died because He acted as the perfect image of God the Father. The Sorrowful Mysteries of the Rosary remind us of the terrible things that happened to Jesus.

When we face a difficult situation, we can think of the Sorrowful Mysteries. We should ask Jesus to help us with the difficult task we must do.

The first Sorrowful Mystery is *The Agony in the Garden*. After the Last Supper, Jesus went with His Apostles to the Garden of Gethsemani to pray. Jesus knew that He was soon going to die on the cross. Jesus was sad. He asked His friends to stay where they were while He went to another spot a little farther away, to pray by Himself. Jesus chose to die on the cross because He loves us. Jesus asked God the Father to give Him the strength He needed to accept the suffering and to die on the cross.

The second Sorrowful Mystery is called *The Scourging at the Pillar*. There were some people who did not like Jesus. They did not believe what Jesus taught. They wanted to hurt Jesus so that the people would stop believing in Him. While Jesus was praying in the garden, a group of these people came and took Jesus away. They took Him to the Roman governor, Pontius Pilate. The people wanted Pilate to put Jesus to death. Pilate thought that if the people saw Jesus punished, they would not want Him to die. Pilate ordered the soldiers to tie Jesus' hands and hurt Him. They hit Jesus with whips. This is called scourging. This whipping hurt Jesus very much.

Those people were very mean to Jesus. Sometimes people are mean to us. We should ask Jesus to help us when people hurt us.

The third Sorrowful Mystery is called *The Crowning with Thorns*. After the men were finished hitting Jesus, they cut branches from a thorn bush. They made a crown out of the branches. They were probably careful not to stick their hands with the sharp thorns. But they did not care about Jesus. They put this crown with its sharp thorns on Jesus' head and pushed it down so that the thorns stuck into Jesus' head. Then they made fun of Jesus and called Him names. Poor Jesus! He suffered all that pain because He loves us.

There are times when people make fun of us or call us names. We should ask Jesus to help us when these things happen to us.

The fourth Sorrowful Mystery is called *The Carrying of the Cross*. The people who did not like Jesus then made a heavy cross out of wood. They gave it to Jesus and made Him carry it a long way to a place called Calvary. Jesus carried the cross willingly, even though it was very heavy. Jesus was so weak after being beaten that He fell down, and the cross fell on top of Him. The people who did not like Jesus were worried that Jesus would not make it to Calvary. So they forced a man named Simon to help Jesus with the heavy cross.

Our difficulties are like crosses, and sometimes they are very heavy for us to carry. But we should remember that Jesus once carried His cross, and that He will help us to carry ours.

The fifth Sorrowful Mystery is called *The Crucifixion*. When Jesus finally made it to the top of the hill of Calvary, the people who did not like Him nailed His hands and feet to the cross. The nails hurt Jesus very much. Instead of being angry, Jesus asked God the Father to forgive the people for what they were doing to Him.

When we are hurt by someone, we should try to forgive the person who has hurt us. We should ask Jesus to help us forgive others.

These are the Sorrowful Mysteries of the Rosary. They help us remember all the terrible things that happened to Jesus before He died. If we want to change and become better images of God, we should become followers of Jesus. Our actions should be like His.

Jesus knows how difficult it is for us to act as images of God. When we are in a difficult situation, we can think of the Sorrowful Mysteries. We should ask Jesus to help us make the right choice.

Part B

Lesson Presentation

Divide the class into groups. Have each group read, discuss, and answer the questions on page 115 of the student book—under the heading "Difficult Situations". After the groups have finished, have one group report their answers to the questions for situation number 1 to the rest of the class. Then have a different group report on situation number 2, and so on until all five situations have been discussed.

DIFFICULT SITUATIONS

1. **You just found out that you have to move to a new town.**
   How would you feel in this difficult situation?
   How would Jesus choose to act in this situation?
   What should we do as followers of Jesus?

2. **You are having an argument with your best friend.**
   How would you feel in this difficult situation?
   How would Jesus choose to act in this situation?
   What should we do as followers of Jesus?

3. **You received a low grade on your report card.**
   How would you feel in this difficult situation?
   How would Jesus choose to act in this situation?
   What should we do as followers of Jesus?

4. **You are being misunderstood by your parents.**
   How would you feel in this difficult situation?
   How would Jesus choose to act in this situation?
   What should we do as followers of Jesus?

5. **You are being blamed unfairly for something.**
   How would you feel in this difficult situation?
   How would Jesus choose to act in this situation?
   What should we do as followers of Jesus?

Part C

Application

Student Book, page 110

VOCABULARY
transform: To change.

Lesson Presentation

Say to the class: "We have talked about some situations that might be difficult for us.

"Now we are going to decide what our response would be in some other difficult situations. Remember that the right choice isn't always the easiest choice, but it is the best.

"Please open your books to page 116."

Student Book, page 116

After reading the situation, choose the action or actions that you would do as a follower of Jesus. Continue with the others in the same way.

Say: "After you have finished, we will discuss the choices you made and the reasons why you made them. Please begin."

Note to teachers: More than one response in each situation can be correct.

Student Book, pages 116–118

DIFFICULT SITUATIONS

● You find out that some of the things your friend has been telling you are not true. Your friend seems to be lying. What would you do?
1. Call your friend a liar.
2. Tell your friend the truth.
3. Tell your friend how important this friendship is to you.

● Your sister seems to dislike everything you say or do. What would you do?
1. Ask your sister what she wants you to say or do.
2. Tell your sister what you like to do.
3. Get mad at your sister.

● You see someone in your class take an object from the teacher's desk. You know that this is not the first time this has happened. What would you do?
1. Tell your teacher privately.
2. Announce what you saw to the class.
3. Ask the student to return the object.

● You wish that you had everything that your next-door neighbor has—a TV, VCR, and telephone in your bedroom. You are envious of what your neighbor has. What would you do?
1. Be satisfied with the things you have.
2. Ask if you could watch TV with your neighbor.
3. Dislike your neighbor.

● Talk about lazy! You have a friend who will not even talk to you any more because your friend is glued to the couch, watching videos. What would you do?
1. Talk to your friend.
2. Stand in front of the TV so that your friend cannot see the videos.
3. Stop being friends with that person.

● You see your friends being mean to the new person in the class. What would you do?
1. Tell your teacher privately.
2. Join your friends in being mean to the new person.
3. Ask the new person to join you on the playground.

● There is one student in your class who is always goofing off. What would you do?
1. Talk to the student about it on the playground.
2. Hit the student.
3. Have everyone else in the class avoid the student.

● You are having a conversation with some of your friends at recess when another person jumps in and disturbs your group. It seems that this person is always interrupting. What would you do?
1. Tell the person to be quiet.
2. Ignore the person.
3. Remind the person that you are talking and ask the person kindly to wait until you are finished.

● While you are playing a game of kickball, one of the players gets angry and throws a temper tantrum because the team is losing. What would you do?
1. Politely tell the player either to play ball or to leave.
2. Help the person understand that winning isn't everything.
3. Kick the person off the team.

● You and a friend are playing at your house. This friend brags that his toys are better than yours. What would you do?
1. Ask your friend to bring his toys to your house next time.
2. Tell your friend to go home.
3. Don't invite your friend back.

Remember: Jesus is the perfect image of God the Father. The more we think about how Jesus acts and the more we choose to act like Him, the better followers of Him we become and the better images of God we become. Following Jesus can be difficult, but He will help us to act as He acts.

Part D

Materials needed: Optional: map of the world.

Application

Note to teachers: If possible, point out the location of Algeria on a world map when starting this section.

Say to the class: "If you will open your books to page 118, we can read about the life of St. Augustine."

SAINT AUGUSTINE

Saint Augustine lived sixteen hundred years ago in what is now Algeria, in North Africa.

When he was a young man, Augustine's heart was filled with disappointment because he could not find happiness. But when he was thirty-two years old, Augustine discovered that following Jesus would make him happy. From then on, Augustine's heart was filled with the desire to serve God and his neighbor. Sometimes it was very difficult for him to fulfill this dream.

Augustine was born November 13, 354 A.D., in Tagaste, North Africa. Augustine had an unhappy childhood, and he was often in trouble. He hated school, got into trouble with his friends, and ignored all that his parents told him. The only thing that Augustine cared about was having a good time. He went from one party to another. He also enjoyed playing tricks on people. He told lies, cheated, and stole things.

Even though Augustine hated school, he was good in his studies. Later he began to like school, and he became a teacher and opened his own school in Rome, Italy. For one reason or another, his school was a failure. His students cheated him out of tuition. He was poor, lonely, and often sick.

Augustine continued to have his problems in life. He searched for happiness, but he could not find it. His mother, Monica (who was later declared a saint), never gave up hope. She continued to pray that her son would find happiness in Jesus.

One day in September in the year 386, Augustine found the courage to make the most important decision of his life—to follow Jesus. Finally his life had begun to change for the better. He had found true happiness. He began to live a life of prayer and service. He became a priest and served at one of the churches in his home town. He became the assistant to a local bishop. Soon afterward, the bishop became ill and died, and Augustine became the bishop there. Augustine asked himself, "Why am I a bishop? Why am I in this world?" He answered his questions with, "Only to live as Jesus did."

Augustine continued to pray and to serve God until the day he died. On August 28, 430, at the age of seventy-six, Bishop Augustine quietly died of a fever, praising God.

Student Book, page 119

Augustine was a great teacher, preacher, and pastor. He thought about the actions of Jesus and chose to follow Him. The more Augustine acted like Jesus, the better follower of Jesus he became and the better image of God he became. Even though following Jesus was often difficult for him, he was able to do it with the help of Jesus. Augustine did many things, but it was only in following Jesus that he found real happiness. We celebrate his feast day on August 28.

Living the Lesson

1. When Augustine was a young man, did he act as an image of God? (*No.*)
2. What were some of the things that Augustine did as a young man? (*He hated school, got into trouble, ignored all that his parents told him, spent too much time at parties, played tricks on people, told lies, cheated, and stole things.*)
3. What was Augustine's mother's name? (*Saint Monica.*)
4. What did Augustine's mother do for him? (*Prayed that her son would find happiness in Jesus.*)
5. Did Augustine ever change his ways? (*Yes.*)
6. In what way did he change? (*He began to follow Jesus.*)
7. What did Augustine do to follow Jesus? (*He prayed and served as a priest and then as a bishop.*)
8. How did Augustine die? (*He came down with a fever.*)
9. Where did Augustine find real happiness? (*In following Jesus.*)
10. When do we celebrate the feast day of St. Augustine? (*August 28.*)

Unit 4

JESUS:
THE PERFECT IMAGE OF GOD

13

Jesus Comes to Us

1. Lesson Focus

Jesus, God the Son and our Savior, came to show us who we are and how we should act as images of God. Jesus also came to return God's love and to help us return God's love.

2. Concepts of Faith

Student Book, page 122

Things to Remember

Why did the Savior, Jesus, come?
To show us who we are and how we should act as images of God, to return God's love, and to help us return God's love.

3. Lesson Presentation

Student Book, page 122

VOCABULARY
Savior: Jesus Christ.
Magi: Wise men.

Materials needed: A bull's-eye target drawn on the blackboard; beanbags or sponges (or similar) for the Activity.

Say to the class: "When Adam and Eve sinned, they lost the close friendship they had with God. But, because God loved them so much, He promised Adam and Eve that someday He would send a Savior. The Savior is Jesus Christ. Jesus came to show us who we are, to show us how we should act as images of God, to return God's love, and to help us return God's love."

Activity

Divide the class into two groups. Ask each group to form a line, starting about eight to ten feet from the target. Have the first person in each group stand, while the others sit quietly.

Toss a coin to see which group goes first. Say to the class: "I'm going to ask each of you a question in turn. After you answer the question, you get to throw one beanbag at the target. If you answer the question correctly, you get to throw another beanbag at the target. The points that you earn will be marked on the blackboard under your team's number. At the end of the game, the points for each team will be totaled, and the team with the most points will be allowed to get a drink of water first."

QUESTIONS

1. What is the name of the king who lived one thousand years before Jesus and was His ancestor? (*David.*)

2. What did Joseph do for a living? (*He was a carpenter.*)

3. Who sent the angel Gabriel to Mary? (*God.*)

4. After the angel visited Mary, whom did Mary visit? (*Elizabeth, or Elizabeth and Zechariah.*)

5. Mary's cousin Elizabeth was expecting a baby also. Who was this baby? (*John the Baptist.*)

6. Elizabeth and Zechariah knew before he was born that their baby was special. How? (*An angel of the Lord appeared to Zechariah and told him John would be great.*)

7. What type of clothes did Mary put on Jesus after He was born? (*Swaddling clothes.*)

8. Who ordered the census to be taken? (*Caesar Augustus.*)

9. Why did Jesus the Savior come? (*To show us who we are and how we should act as images of God, to return God's love, and to help us return God's love.*)

10. What was the name of Jesus' father on earth? (*Joseph.*)

11. What was the name of Jesus' mother? (*Mary.*)

12. Who told Mary that she would have a baby? (*The angel Gabriel.*)

13. What was Mary to name the baby? (*Jesus.*)

14. What was Mary's answer to the angel Gabriel? (*Yes.*)

15. What was the name of the King when Jesus was born? (*King Herod.*)

16. We celebrate Jesus' birthday every year. What day is that? (*Christmas.*)

17. What city did Mary and Joseph live in? (*Nazareth.*)

18. Why did Mary and Joseph go to Bethlehem? (*To be registered and counted in the census.*)

19. Who appeared to Joseph in a dream? (*The angel Gabriel.*)

20. Who is Jesus' Father in heaven? (*God.*)

21. How did Mary and Joseph get from Nazareth to Bethlehem? (*Joseph walked, and Mary probably rode on a donkey.*)

22. Where did Mary and Joseph stay the evening Jesus was born? (*In a stable.*)

23. Why did Mary and Joseph stay in a stable the evening Jesus was born? (*There was no room at any of the inns.*)

24. What type of bed did Jesus sleep in after He was born? (*A manger.*)

25. Who came to visit the baby Jesus? (*Shepherds, Magi.*)

26. How did the shepherds know about Jesus? (*An angel appeared to them and told them the good news.*)

27. How did the Magi find their way to the stable? (*They followed a star.*)

28. Name one of the gifts that the Magi brought to Jesus. (*Gold, frankincense, myrrh.*)

Application

Student Book, page 123

Jesus, Mary, and Joseph lived like any other family in the town of Nazareth. Joseph was a carpenter, and he taught Jesus how to be a carpenter, too. Jesus went to school, did His chores, and was obedient and respectful to His parents. He enjoyed playing with the other children and was kind and helpful to His neighbors. Most of the people in the town enjoyed His company. Almost no one knew that He was the Savior, God the Son.

Jesus grew in size, strength, and wisdom. He worked as a carpenter until He was about thirty years old. Then Jesus began to teach in parables and to perform miracles.

14

Jesus Does Things for Others

1. Lesson Focus

Original sin damaged our minds, wills, and bodies. Because of original sin, it is difficult for us to know who we are and how we should act. Original sin makes it impossible for us to return the love that God has for us. Jesus came to show us who we are and how we should act as images of God, to return God's love, and to help us return God's love. He did this by teaching, loving, and doing things for people.

Jesus was a terrific teacher. He helped people understand who they are by telling short stories called parables.

His love was the greatest of all loves. He died on the cross to show us how to love, to return the Father's love, and to help us return the Father's love by sharing in God's life.

Jesus used self-discipline. In His miracles, He acted lovingly toward others by what He said and did. He used His special powers for others to set an example for all of us.

We should follow the example of Jesus. We cannot perform miracles, but we should use whatever talents and abilities we have to do things for others. We should act lovingly toward others in all that we say and do.

Note to CCD teachers: Use Parts A, B, C, and E. All activities can be sent home as family projects or used in class as time permits.

2. Concepts of Faith

Student Book, page 137

Things to Remember

Why did Jesus come?
To show us who we are and how we should act as images of God, to return God's love, and to help us return God's love.

How did Jesus show us who we are and how we should act?
By teaching, loving, and doing things for people.

3. Lesson Presentation

Part A

VOCABULARY
miracle: An act that shows the power of God, helps people to have faith in what Jesus taught, and helps them to follow Him.
self-discipline: Watching how we act; changing and improving our actions to act lovingly toward others.

Note to parochial-school teachers: For the activity at the end of Part H, ask a kindergarten or first-grade teacher if your students could read stories about miracles to the younger students.

Application

Say to the class, "Let's open our books to page 125 and read about why Jesus came to earth and what He did for us."

Original sin damaged our minds, wills, and bodies. Because of original sin, it is difficult for us to know who we are and how we should act. Original sin makes it impossible for us to return the love that God has for us. Jesus came to show us who we are and how we should act as images of God, to return God's love, and to help us return God's love. He did this by teaching, loving, and doing things for people.

Jesus was a terrific teacher. He helped people understand who they are by telling short stories called parables.

His love was the greatest of all loves. He died on the cross to show us how to love, to return the Father's love, and to help us return the Father's love by sharing in God's life.

As God the Son, Jesus could do many things for people that we cannot do. We call these things miracles, because they can be done only by the power of God.

Jesus performed miracles to show us how to act lovingly toward others by what we say and do. He had the power to do many things for Himself. He could have made His life on earth much easier. But He chose to live as we do and to perform His miracles for others.

Jesus used self-discipline. In His miracles He acted lovingly toward others by what He said and did. Jesus used His special powers for others to set an example for all of us.

We should follow the example of Jesus. We cannot perform miracles, but we can use whatever talents and abilities we have to do things for others. We should act lovingly toward others in all that we say and do.

Student Book, page 126

1. Because of _____, it is difficult for us to know who we are and how we should act. (*Original sin.*)
2. Original sin damaged our _____, _____, and _____. (*Minds, wills, and bodies.*)
3. Original sin made it impossible for us to _____. (*Return the love that God has for us.*)
4. Jesus came to _____. (*Show us who we are and how we should act as images of God, to return God's love, and to help us return God's love.*)
5. Jesus shows us how to act lovingly toward others by _____. (*Doing things for others; performing miracles.*)
6. We can follow the example of Jesus by using our _____ to act lovingly toward others. (*Talents, abilities.*)

Part B

Student Book, page 124

VOCABULARY
disciples: Followers of Jesus.

Application

Say to the class, "Let's open our books to page 126 and read about one of the miracles that Jesus performed for the disciples."

Student Book, pages 126–127

Remember, Jesus came to show us who we are and how we should act as images of God, to return God's love, and to help us return God's love. He did this by teaching, loving, and doing things for others. He often showed His love for His disciples (His special followers and friends) by performing miracles.

The disciples followed Jesus almost everywhere. He often performed miracles in front of them.

After witnessing miracles, the disciples knew that Jesus was special, but they found it difficult to imitate Him.

THE CALMING OF THE STORM

It was late. Jesus had been teaching all day to a large crowd. He was tired. He asked the disciples to take Him by boat to the other side of the Sea of Galilee so that He could get some rest.

The disciples helped Jesus into the boat and rowed away from the shore. The gentle rocking of the boat caused Jesus to fall asleep. Then, a big storm came up. The disciples were afraid. They didn't know what to do, so they gently shook Jesus to try to wake Him.

Student Book, page 127

Jesus woke up. He said to the sea, "Quiet! Be still!" Suddenly, the wind stopped. Everything was calm.

Then he asked them, "Why are you terrified? Do you not yet have faith?" The disciples were amazed. They wondered who Jesus was that He could make the wind and the sea obey Him.

—Adapted from Mark 4:35–41

In this story, Jesus showed His love for others by calming the storm. By His words and actions, He showed His love for the disciples. We cannot perform miracles, but we can use whatever talents and abilities we have to do things for others. We should act lovingly toward others in all that we say and do.

Living the Lesson

Student Book, page 127

1. How did Jesus show us who we are and how we should act as images of God, and how did He return God's love and help us return God's love? (*By teaching, loving, and doing things for others.*)
2. What did Jesus do for other people? (*Perform miracles.*)
3. What is a miracle? (*An act that shows the power of God, helps people to have faith in what Jesus taught, and helps them to follow Him.*)
4. In this story, what miracle did Jesus perform for His disciples? (*Calming the storm.*)

Part C

Student Book, page 124

VOCABULARY
drift: Movement caused by the wind.
doubt: Distrust; disbelief.

Materials needed: Paper; pencils; crayons or markers; scissors.

Application

Student Book, page 128

The disciples followed Jesus for a long time. They watched Jesus perform many miracles. Finally, after seeing another miracle at sea, the disciples knew that they should follow the example of Jesus. They should act lovingly toward others as Jesus acted lovingly toward them. Let us read about that special miracle now.

Student Book, page 128

JESUS WALKS ON THE WATER

One evening, after a long day's work, Jesus wanted to go up on a mountain to pray by Himself. The mountain was close to the sea. Jesus asked His disciples to sail their boat and wait for Him on the other side. Then Jesus went up on the mountain.

When the disciples were a few miles offshore, the wind came up and the boat was being tossed about by the waves. One of the disciples looked up and saw Jesus. The disciple was very frightened. He saw Jesus walking on the water! He told the other disciples to look. They were frightened, too. They thought they were seeing a ghost.

At that moment, Jesus spoke to them. "Take courage; it is I; do not be afraid."

Peter, having doubts, said to Jesus, "If it is you, ask me and I will come to you on the water." Jesus said, "Come."

Peter quickly got out of the boat and walked toward Jesus. Then Peter noticed how strong the wind was, and he became afraid. Peter began to sink. He cried out, "Lord, save me!" Jesus put out His hand and saved Peter from sinking.

—Adapted from Matthew 14:22–33

Living the Lesson

Student Book, page 129

1. What happened to the disciples? (*Their boat was being tossed about by the strong wind and the waves.*)
2. Was Jesus with them? (*No.*)
3. How did Jesus reach the disciples? (*He walked on the water.*)
4. The disciples were afraid. What did Jesus do? (*He calmed their fears.*)
5. When Peter tried to walk on the water and began to sink, what did Jesus do? (*He put out His hand and saved Peter from sinking.*)

Say to the class: "Through His many miracles, Jesus showed the people that He loved and cared for them. As followers of Jesus, we should love and care for our friends, too."

Activity

Have the students each draw, color, and cut out one "follower" of Jesus. When they have finished, tape the art work around the classroom. Tell the students that, as Jesus continued to do things for others by performing miracles, more and more people began to follow Him and listen to Him.

Student Book, page 129

Draw a picture of a loving act that you can do to show that you are a follower of Jesus.

Activity

Student Book, page 130

The Disciples Follow Jesus and Believe

Read all the paragraphs below. Their order is mixed up. In the box in front of each paragraph, give the number in which it took place. (For example, put a "1" in front of the first thing that happened.) (*Correct order: 1, 6, 4, 5, 2, 3.*)

Part D

Application

Say to the class: "Please open your books to page 131 and read about Simon's mother-in-law."

Student Book, page 131

Simon Peter knew that Jesus could help his sick mother-in-law. So he went to ask Jesus for that help.

THE CURE OF SIMON'S MOTHER-IN-LAW

One of Jesus' disciples, Simon, was worried. His mother-in-law was very sick with a fever. He tried everything he could to help her. He decided to ask Jesus for help. Simon, James, and John went to look for Jesus. They found Him working in the temple.

After Jesus had finished His work, He followed the disciples to Simon's house. Jesus walked up to the sick woman and began to speak. The fever left the woman, and she got up and began to wait on Jesus and the disciples.
—Adapted from Luke 4:38–39

In this story, Jesus showed His love for Simon's mother-in-law by curing her. We cannot perform miracles as Jesus did, but we can use whatever talents and abilities we have to do things for others. We should act lovingly toward others in all that we say and do.

Student Book, page 131

1. What did Jesus do for other people? (*Performed miracles.*)
2. Why did Jesus perform miracles? (*To show His love for others.*)
3. How did Jesus show His love for Simon and his mother-in-law? (*He cured Simon's mother-in-law.*)

Part E

Application

Say to the class, "Please open your books to page 132 and continue to read about Jesus' loving care for others."

Student Book, page 132

Jesus continued to help others by performing miracles. Read the following story about the helpless man near the healing waters of the pool of Bethesda. For thirty-eight years, no one had given him the chance to soak his aching bones. Jesus helped the man by performing a miracle.

THE CURE AT BETHESDA

It was the Sabbath Day. Jesus went up to Jerusalem.

In Jerusalem there was a pool called Bethesda, which was near the entrance of the city. A large number of ill, blind, and crippled people were lying by the pool, hoping to be cured. A man sitting by the pool had been ill for thirty-eight years.

Jesus saw the man and said to him, "Do you want to be well?" The man told Jesus that he wanted to be well, but every time he tried to get to the pool, other people would get there before him. There was never any room left for him.

Jesus said to the man, "Rise, take up your mat, and walk." Immediately the man became well, took up his mat, and walked.

—Adapted from John 5:1–9

In this story, Jesus showed His love for the sick man by curing him. We cannot perform miracles, but we can use whatever talents and abilities we have to do things for others. We should act lovingly toward others in all that we say and do.

Living the Lesson

Student Book, page 132

1. Jesus must have loved the sick man very much. How can you tell? (*He cured him of his illness.*)
2. Why do you think Jesus chose that man? There seemed to be many sick people by the pool. (*The man never had been given a chance to soak his aching bones, as the other people had. Jesus cared for him and wanted him to feel better.*)

Part F

Application

Student Book, pages 133–134

Notice in the following stories how people came to Jesus for help. More and more people were recognizing that Jesus loved them. They could tell that He loved them by what He said and did.

A WOMAN WHO NEEDED JESUS' HELP

In the crowd that was following Jesus there was a sick woman. She had been bleeding inside her body for many years. She spent all of her money visiting many different doctors, and none of them could help her. She had heard about Jesus and was moving through the crowd, trying to get close to Him. She thought that, if she could just touch His clothes, she would be cured.

The woman walked up behind Jesus. She touched His cloak. Suddenly, the bleeding stopped. She had been cured.

Jesus could feel the healing power go out from Him, but He didn't know who had touched Him. He asked the crowd, "Who has touched my clothes?"

The woman fell to her knees before Jesus and told Him the whole story. Jesus told her that she had been cured. She could go in peace and be well again.

JAIRUS' DAUGHTER

Jesus was on the shore. A large crowd had gathered around Him. A man named Jairus walked up to Jesus. He fell to his knees and said, "My daughter is at the point of death. Please, come lay your hands on her that she may get well and live."

Jesus went off with Jairus to his home. The large crowd followed closely behind.

Meanwhile, a man from Jairus' house came running. He told Jairus that his daughter had died and that it was no longer necessary for Jairus to bring Jesus to the house.

All that Jesus said was, "Do not be afraid."

Student Book, page 135

When they arrived at the house, Jairus took Jesus inside. People were weeping loudly. Jesus said to them, "Why this commotion and weeping? The child is not dead but asleep."

Many of the people there did not believe Jesus. They said mean things to Him. Jesus told them to leave. He took Jairus and his wife into the room where the child was. Jesus took the child's hand in His and said, "Little girl, I say to you, arise!"

The little girl got up and began to walk around. Jesus told the parents to give her something to eat and to say nothing about what had happened.

—Adapted from Mark 5:21–43

In the first story, the bleeding woman touched Jesus' clothes. She felt His great love for her. The bleeding inside her stopped. She had been cured.

In the second story, Jesus went to see Jairus' daughter. Before He got there, she had died. Again, by His words and actions, Jesus showed His great love for others and cured the little girl of her illness.

We cannot perform miracles as Jesus did, but we can use whatever talents and abilities we have to do things for others. We should act lovingly toward others in all that we say and do.

Living the Lesson

Student Book, page 136

1. What did Jesus do for the woman who needed His help? (*Stopped the bleeding.*)
2. Why did Jesus help her? (*He loved her.*)
3. Jesus helped Jairus' daughter. Why? (*He loved her.*)

Part G

Application

Student Book, pages 133–134

There was a large crowd following Jesus. More people joined the crowd in every town He visited. The people in the crowd saw how Jesus showed His love for others.

When Jesus did things for others, He showed His love for them. By using His special powers for others, He showed us how to use our own talents and abilities for others, too.

The crowd in the following story saw Jesus perform a wonderful miracle for a poor widow and her son.

THE WIDOW'S SON

Jesus was traveling with His disciples to the city of Nain. A large crowd was following them.

As Jesus entered the city, He noticed that a funeral was taking place. A man had died. His body was being taken outside of the city. A woman was following the men who were carrying his body. She was crying. She was the dead man's mother.

When Jesus saw her, He felt sorry for her. He knew that her only son had just died.

He said to her, "Do not weep." Jesus then walked up to her son and touched him. He said to him, "Young man, I tell you, arise!"

The dead man sat up and began to speak, and Jesus gave him to his mother.

—Adapted from Luke 7:11–17

In this story, Jesus showed His love for the widow and her son by bringing the son back to life. We cannot perform miracles as Jesus did, but we can use whatever talents and abilities we have to do things for others. We should act lovingly toward others in all that we say and do.

Living the Lesson

Student Book, page 134

1. What did Jesus do for the widow? (*Brought her son back to life.*)
2. How did the people know that Jesus loved them? (*By what He said and did.*)
3. What do you think the crowd might have done after they saw this miracle? (*They might have imitated Jesus and used their talents and abilities for others.*)

Part H

Application

Student Book, page 136

JESUS AND THE CHILDREN

After Jesus had performed miracles, the crowds that walked with Him were so large that it became impossible for His friends and relatives to get near Him.

People were bringing their children to Jesus to have Him touch them, but the disciples were scolding them for doing so. Jesus said to the disciples, "Let the children come to me; do not prevent them, for the Kingdom of God belongs to such as these. Amen, I say to you, whoever does not accept the Kingdom of God like a child will not enter it." Then Jesus hugged the children, blessed them, and placed His hands upon them.

—Adapted from Mark 10:13–16

In this story, Jesus did not perform a miracle, but He continued to show His love for others. The disciples were afraid that the children would bother Jesus because so many people were around Him all the time. Jesus told them to let the children come to Him. The Kingdom of God belongs to them.

Again, by His words and actions, Jesus showed His love for others. We should use whatever talents and abilities we have to do things for others, too. We should act lovingly toward others in all that we say and do.

Activity

Have the students choose one of the miracles that we have read. Have them read their chosen miracle to a kindergarten or first-grade class. Explain to the younger students that Jesus came to show us how to love. We cannot perform miracles as Jesus did, but we can act lovingly toward others in all that we say and do.

Activity

Student Book, page 138

Match the description to the miracle.

— Jesus said to the sea, "Quiet! Be still!" Suddenly, the wind stopped. Everything was calm. (D)

    a. The Widow's Son

— The disciples drifted to the middle of the sea. Jesus walked out to meet them. (E)

    b. The Cure at Bethesda

— For thirty-eight years, the man had tried to be cured. He talked with Jesus and trusted Him. Jesus cured the man. (B)

    c. Jairus' Daughter

— The sick woman touched Jesus' cloak. Suddenly, she was cured. (F)

    d. The Calming of the Storm

— Jesus walked up to the sick woman and spoke. Her fever was gone and she got up. (G)

    e. Jesus Walks on the Water

— Jesus said to the woman's son, "Young man, I tell you, arise!" The man got up and began to speak. (A)

    f. A Woman Who Needed Jesus' Help

— Jesus went inside the little girl's house with her father and mother. He held the child's hand and said, "Little girl, I say to you, arise!" (C)

    g. The Cure of Simon's Mother-in-Law

15

Jesus Our Teacher

1. Lesson Focus

Original sin damaged our minds, wills, and bodies. Many times we can't find the truth, we don't know how to love, and we do not act as we should. Original sin makes it impossible to return the love that God has for us. Jesus came to show us who we are and how we should act as images of God, to return God's love, and to help us return God's love. He did these things by teaching, loving, and doing things for people.

Original sin left our minds in the dark about the truth. Jesus is the Light and the Truth. With the guiding light of Jesus, we discover the truth about God and ourselves.

Jesus was a terrific teacher! One of the ways that He helped people understand who they were was telling short stories.

In the stories that Jesus told, He talked about familiar, everyday things. The short stories that Jesus told are called parables. These stories always had a special, religious message. The message contained the truth about God and ourselves.

Note to CCD teachers: Use Parts A through C and the activity that follows Part E. All other activities can be sent home as family projects or used in class as time permits.

2. Concepts of Faith

> Student Book, page 156
>
> *Things to Remember*
>
> **What is one of the ways that Jesus teaches us who we are?**
> Through short stories called parables.

Some material in this lesson is adapted from Daphne Rae, *Love until It Hurts* (New York: Harper & Row, Publishers, Inc., 1981).

3. Lesson Presentation

Part A

VOCABULARY

self-discipline: Watching how we act; changing and improving our actions so as to act lovingly toward others.
miracle: An act that shows the power of God, helps people to have faith in what Jesus taught, and helps them to follow Him.
parable: A short story that teaches a religious lesson.

Materials needed: A flashlight.

Application

Standing in the front of the room, hold the flashlight in your hand so the students can see it. Ask one student to turn off the lights in the room. Say to the class:

"Original sin damaged our minds, wills, and bodies. Because of original sin, it is difficult for us to know who we are and how we should act. Original sin makes it impossible for us to return the love that God has for us. Jesus came to show us who we are and how we should act as images of God, to return God's love, and to help us to return God's love.

"Notice how dark it is in the room right now. Can you see the directions I have written on the blackboard in the front of the room?" (*No, not very well.*) "Do you know what you are supposed to do today and how you should do it?" (*No.*) "Why not?" (*You haven't told us yet. We can't see the blackboard.*) "Do you think I should keep the lights off all day while you work?" (*No.*) "Why not?" (*It would be difficult to do what we're supposed to do.*)

"Original sin left our minds in the dark, too. Many times we can't find the truth. Jesus is our teacher. Jesus is the Light and the Truth." (*Turn on the flashlight. Shine it around the room.*) "With the guiding light of Jesus, we can discover the truth about God and ourselves." (*Ask a student to turn the room lights back on.*)

"Please open your books to page 140 and read about how the light of Jesus shows us the truth."

Jesus was a terrific teacher. He helped people understand who they were by telling them short stories called parables.

The parables contained situations that were familiar to the people. When Jesus told these stories, He used everyday experiences of farmers, gardeners, rich people, poor people, travelers, and merchants. Each story always had a special religious message.

Jesus' message is like a light in the dark for us. His message helps lead us to the truth about God and ourselves. By following His message, we also can be a light for others. We can lead others to the truth about God and ourselves.

Student Book, page 140

When we hear a parable, we should do four things:

1. Think about the people in the story and what they did;

2. Look at our own lives and what we do;

3. Think about the truth that Jesus teaches us in the story; and

4. Look again at our own lives and decide whether or not we need to change our way of thinking.

Living the Lesson

Student Book, page 141

1. Original Sin damaged our _____, _____, and _____. (*Minds, wills, bodies.*)
2. Original sin left our minds in the dark. Many times we can't find the _____. (*Truth.*)
3. Jesus is the _____ and the _____. (*Light, Truth.*)
4. With the light of Jesus, we can see the _____ . (*Truth about God and ourselves.*)
5. Jesus was a terrific _____. (*Teacher.*)
6. Jesus taught by using short stories called _____. (*Parables.*)
7. Each story that Jesus told had a special _____. (*Religious message.*)
8. By following the message of Jesus, we can be a _____ for others. (*Light.*)

Part B

Student Book, page 139

VOCABULARY
fig tree: A tree that produces fruits called figs.
barren: Producing little or no fruit.
orchard: A field of fruit trees.
cultivate: To help a plant to grow by loosening the soil around it.
fertilize: To add something to the soil to help a plant to grow.

Materials needed for Activity:
Copies of the "fig tree" hat, one per student (see Appendix).
Markers or crayons.
Scissors.

Materials needed for "The Barren Fig Tree" play (optional):
Poster-board cutouts, painted and decorated, of apple trees, pear trees, banana trees, a small fig tree, cloud, raindrops, and the sun.
Costume for the Gardener (jeans, plaid shirt, hat).
Costume for the Owner (business clothes).

Note to teachers: The following play can be read by the students in the class or performed in front of an audience.

Application

Student Book, pages 142–143

In the following parable, Jesus is telling us that each of us is like a little fig tree. The owner likes the tree very much and watches over it as it grows. Even when the tree does not bear fruit, he does not have it chopped down. He gives it more time to grow.

THE BARREN FIG TREE

Narrator: A long time ago there was an orchard. It had apple trees (*enter Apple Trees*), banana trees (*enter Banana Trees*), pear trees (*enter Pear Trees*), and one little fig tree (*enter Fig Tree*).

When it was time for the trees to produce fruit, the proud owner walked through his orchard to look at all the fruit on the branches of the various trees. (*Enter the Owner of the orchard.*) Sad to say, the owner found no fruit on his little fig tree. (*Owner sadly bows his head.*) He was disappointed.

(*Enter Gardener.*) He saw his gardener working in the orchard and asked him to come and look at the little fig tree. (*Owner waves to Gardener.*) He said to the gardener:

Owner: For three years I have waited for my fig tree to produce fruit. Since it has not produced any fruit, I want you to chop the tree down.

(*Gardener kneels down and begs.*)

Narrator: The gardener begged the owner:

Gardener: Please leave the tree alone for one more year. I promise to cultivate the ground around it and fertilize it. If the tree still does not produce fruit, then I will chop it down.

Narrator: The owner liked his little fig tree very much. He agreed with the gardener to let it grow one more year.

(*The Owner exits. The Gardener stands by the Tree and pretends to rake the soil around it.*)

The gardener worked very hard every day to help the fig tree. (*Enter Sun.*) The sun came out to warm the orchard and help the fig tree to grow. (*Enter Cloud and Raindrops. Cloud stands in front of the Sun, while Raindrops walk around the Fig Tree once. Then Cloud and Raindrops sit down.*) Rain came to water the tree.

After nearly a year had passed, the fig tree still did not bear any fruit. The gardener was sad and tired, so he sat down near the tree to rest. (*Gardener sadly sits, and soon he falls asleep.*)

(*The Fig Tree turns to show branches bearing fruit. The Owner enters. The Gardener stands, his back to the Tree.*)

The gardener stood up when he heard the owner coming toward him. The owner was smiling. The gardener asked:

Gardener: How can you be happy? This is the day that I am to chop down this little fig tree.

(*The Owner points to the Tree.*)

Narrator: The owner said:

Owner: Cut this wonderful tree down? I couldn't do that! It is the most beautiful tree in my orchard!

(*The surprised Gardener turns around to look at the Tree, then happily folds his hands.*)

Narrator: The gardener was overjoyed! He folded his hands and thanked God for the wonderful little fig tree.

(*Actors put down their props and sit down.*)

—Adapted from Luke 13:6–9

We are all images of God. God loves us all very much. He wants us to know this truth about Him and about ourselves.

God the Son became man to teach us the truth. While on earth, Jesus was a very good teacher. He taught people by telling them stories whose religious lesson they could understand.

Each of us is like the fig tree in the parable. God the Father is something like the owner of the little fig tree. The owner liked his tree very much, even though there was no fruit on it. After three years, he was still willing to give the fig tree another chance. He had the gardener—who is like Jesus—cultivate the ground around the tree to help it grow and produce fruit. The tree became very beautiful and did bear fruit.

Sometimes, when we are frustrated, we have a hard time believing that God loves us: schoolwork is hard to do, little brothers and sisters get in the way, big brothers and sisters boss us around, and parents are too tired or busy to help us.

But Jesus tells us the truth. He tells us that we are images of God and that God loves us. So when we stop to clear our minds of those things that frustrate us and think about the truth that Jesus teaches us in the parables, we are reminded that we are images of God and that God loves us very much.

It takes time for us to appreciate this truth. Like the owner of the orchard, God the Father gives us the time that we need to come to an appreciation of this truth. Like the gardener, Jesus helps us to appreciate that we are images of God and that God loves us very much. Once we know this truth, then we, like the fig tree, can produce fruit by sharing this truth with others.

Living the Lesson

1. At first, what was wrong with the fig tree? (*It was not producing fruit.*)
2. Did the owner chop it down? (*No.*) Why not? (*He wished to give it a chance to produce fruit.*)
3. How is God the Father like the owner of the little fig tree? (*The owner liked the fig tree and did not give up on it. God the Father loves us and does not give up on us.*)
4. Whom is the gardener like? (*Jesus.*)
5. What did the gardener do? (*He prepared the ground so that the tree could grow and produce fruit.*)
6. Do you think the gardener helped the tree? (*Yes.*)
7. In this parable, what is the truth that Jesus teaches us? (*We are images of God, and God loves us very much.*)
8. How can we show others that we believe this truth? (*By following the teaching of Jesus.*)

Activity

Pass out patterns for the "fig tree" hats. Remind the students that each of them is like the little fig tree. They should make sure that they learn the truth from Jesus, who is like the gardener.

Have the students trace, color, and cut out the hats. When the hats have been decorated and cut out, have the students try on the hat bands. Measure for a good fit and staple the ends of the bands together.

Part C

Application

Note to teachers: A large map of the world (optional) will be useful for this part of the lesson.

Student Book, pages 144–145

All of us are rich in so many different ways. We are healthy or we are skillful in sports, reading, math, spelling, mowing the lawn, or collecting baseball cards! What we know, or have, or can do should be shared. When we share our thoughts, our goods, and our talents, we are sharing our love. We are following the teaching of Jesus that God loves every person and that we should love others as He loves them.

Everyone should follow the teaching of Jesus and treat others as they should be treated, as images of God. Some people do not treat others as images of God. They do not believe the truth that God loves us and that we should love others as God loves us.

In the following parable, the rich man did not believe the truth that each person is an image of God and is loved by God. He did not think that he should love other persons as God loves them. He did not treat them fairly.

THE RICH MAN AND LAZARUS

There was a rich man whose everyday meals were a feast! He dressed up in fancy clothes for every meal. His table was covered with fine tablecloths and dishes. His servants waited on him and brought him delicious meals.

Every day, while the rich man was eating, a poor man named Lazarus sat on the rich man's doorstep, hoping for some table scraps. Lazarus was given some leftovers of food, but he was never invited inside for a good meal.

When the poor man died, he was taken to heaven, because he knew the truth, believed the truth, and showed others that he believed the truth. When the rich man died, he did not go to heaven. He had had many good things in his life, but he had not shared them.

The rich man did not remember Jesus' teaching that everyone is an image of God, that God loves us, and that we should love others as God loves us.
—Adapted from Luke 16:19–25

Lazarus was an image of God, and he tried to live as an image of God. Lazarus knew the truth, believed the truth, and showed others that he believed the truth. We should be like him.

We should not be like the rich man. We should remember the teaching of Jesus that everyone is an image of God and is loved by God. We should love everyone as God does. We want to follow the teaching of Jesus.

Living the Lesson

1. What was mealtime like for the rich man? (*He dressed in fine clothes, his table was set with fine dishes, he was waited on by servants, and he could have whatever he wished.*)
2. Did the rich man share what he had with anyone? (*No.*)
3. What kind of man was the rich man? (*Selfish.*)

Note to teachers: If possible, show the students where Calcutta, India, is on a world map, as part of your introduction to the story of Mother Teresa.

Mother Teresa (of Calcutta) follows the teaching of Jesus by treating others as images of God. She believes the truth that God loves each person and that we should love others as He loves them and us. By her life she has shown that she believes this truth: she shares her love by helping others in any way she can.

MOTHER TERESA OF CALCUTTA

As a young woman, Mother Teresa lived in India as a member of the Loretto nuns. She dedicated her life entirely to God. She chose to do so because she knew that God loved her. She wished to show her love in return. But, as she prayed and worked with the Loretto nuns, she knew in her heart that she was not sharing all of the love she had to give.

So one day she left the Loretto nuns. She was determined to "walk with God". As God's image, she wished to share His love where she was most needed—with the poorest of the poor.

She had only five rupees in her pocket, which is about the same as five dollars. Where could she go with so little money?

Say to the class: "What do you think Mother Teresa could do with the five dollars?" (*Eat lunch. Give the money to the poor. Buy food to bring to the poor. Give the money to the Church.*) "Where would she live?" (*In a convent, with her family, with others who wished to help her.*)

A person cannot buy very much with five dollars. Mother Teresa knew that. She decided that, because she was going to work with the poor people, she was going to live with them, too.

Mother Teresa went to the slums of Calcutta. Slums are parts of large cities. The very poorest people live in the slums. They have very few jobs, the buildings are in very poor condition, and there is a shortage of running water. In the slums, almost everything and everyone is dirty, and many people are sick because they do not have enough to eat or water to clean themselves with.

It hurt Mother Teresa to see so many people sad and in pain. Many of them were starving, diseased, or sick. She began to help by finding water for the people and by nursing the sores of those who had diseases. She cooked rice for the starving, so that they would have at least one meal a day.

The people saw that Mother Teresa loved them, and her efforts to help them made them feel better. They shared their love with her as she shared her love with them. She knew and lived the truth that Jesus taught: God loves every person very much, and, as images of God, we should love God in return. We should treat everyone as an image of God and love others as God loves them.

Mother Teresa knew that the poor people of the slums needed a place to go for help. She knew also that she herself could not reach everyone who needed her care. She decided to find others who would be willing to share their love as she did. She talked to others and asked for their help. Soon many others came to help her. She was able to start a new religious group of people who dedicated themselves to helping the neediest. This group is called the Missionaries of Charity.

Missionaries are persons who dedicate themselves to a religious life so that they can go to other countries (or to other parts of their own country) to love and serve God by helping others. Helping others "for charity" means helping them for the love of God.

The people who joined Mother Teresa's Missionaries of Charity included men and women who came from all over the world to spend their lives helping the poor.

With the gifts of money, food, and supplies they received from others, the Missionaries of Charity started homes where abandoned children could live and where the dying could be cared for. They set up medical clinics staffed by doctors and nurses to care for the sick. They set up food stations and cooked large pots of rice to feed the hungry. The Missionaries of Charity have done much to improve the lives of people living in the slums.

Mother Teresa and her Missionaries of Charity know the truth: we should treat others as images of God. They know that God loves every person and that we should love others as God does. They believe these truths, and they show others that they believe by loving them as images of God.

Activity

Over a period of time, have the children collect canned or boxed foods for the poor and needy. The food collected can be donated to a local charitable group.

Living the Lesson

1. How does Mother Teresa follow the teaching of Jesus? (*By believing the truths that Jesus taught: that we are images of God, that God loves us, and that we should love others as God loves them.*)
2. What has Mother Teresa done to show that she followed the teaching of Jesus? (*She treated other persons as images of God and loved them as God loves them.*)

Part D

VOCABULARY
patient: Willing to wait.
banquet: A fancy meal or dinner party for a large number of people.
humble: Remembering that we are all images of God; that one person is not more important than another.
lame: Weak; having arms or legs that cannot be used normally.

Materials needed: Two decorated coffee cans, one labeled "First" and the other "Last".

Application

So many times, we want to be first in everything—first in line, first one up to bat, first one to finish schoolwork. But first is not always best. Trying to be first can sometimes cause us to think mean thoughts, or to make wrong choices, or to act in an unkind way.

In the parable that follows, the truth that Jesus teaches us is that as images of God we should be humble. To be humble is to remember that we are *all* images of God. One person is not more important than another. We should not try to be first in order to make ourselves seem more important than others.

We should respect the dignity of other people. If you do your best on a test and receive an "A", while someone else does her best on the same test and receives a "C", do not brag about your grade. Instead, praise the other person for trying her best. We cannot all be good at everything.

THE LOWEST SEAT

Jesus went to a wedding banquet. He was watching people choose where they were going to sit at the long table. He told His followers that, when they are invited to a special banquet, they should not choose to sit in the places of honor. Other guests may have been chosen to sit there. Then the host would have to ask those who had chosen to sit in the places of honor to move to the seats farther down the table, so that the other guests could sit in the places of honor. It would be quite embarrassing to have to move to a lower place.

Jesus suggested to His followers that they choose to go to the lower seats first. Then it might happen that the host will come to them and invite them to sit at a higher place. "For everyone who exalts himself will be humbled, but the one who humbles himself will be exalted."

Say to the class: "To exalt yourself means to make yourself more important than others, to place yourself above others. For example, when a bully shoves ahead of others in a line and says, 'Me first!', he is exalting himself.

"To be humble means to recognize that we are all images of God, that we are all important, and that no one person is more important than any other person. The bully is embarrassed when the teacher tells him to go to the end of the line. We can be humble by remembering that we are all images of God. We should not try to make ourselves seem more important than others by being pushy or first. We can also be humble by not bragging."

Then Jesus suggested that, next time, the host should invite to his banquet the poor, the crippled, the blind, and the lame, instead of inviting relatives and friends.

These needy people probably would not be able to invite him for a feast in return. But the host would be blessed indeed. He would be acting as an image of God. He would be treating everyone, especially those in need, as images of God. He would be recognizing that the poor are important persons, too.

—Adapted from Luke 14:7–14

Living the Lesson

1. What is the truth that Jesus teaches us in this parable? (*As images of God, we should be humble.*)
2. What does it mean to be humble? (*To remember that we are all images of God, and that one person is not more important than another.*)
3. How can we show others that we believe this teaching of Jesus? (*Try not to be pushy, not to be first all the time, not to brag.*)
4. How could the guests at the dinner party in the parable show others they believe this truth? (*By sitting in the lower seats.*)
5. How could the host of the dinner party show others he believes this truth? (*By inviting people who might not be able to extend him a similar invitation.*)

Activity

Write each student's name on two small slips of paper. Place the slips in two decorated coffee cans—one can labeled "First", the other labeled "Last". Each day, draw one name from each can. The student whose name is drawn from the "First" container will be first in line for lunch and for some other daily activities. The student whose name is drawn from the "Last" container will be last for the same occasions. (If the same name is drawn from both containers, draw again from the "Last" container.) Continue until all names have been drawn.

Part E

VOCABULARY
talent: A gift from God; the ability to do something well.

Note to teachers: Assign ahead of time the parts for the skit dramatizing the parable of the talents. The students will perform the skit while you read the script. Make sure the students have a chance to read the parable to prepare their parts and plan their actions. Also, if props and costumes will be used, allow time for preparing them. All the students can remain in their seats, listening and following along in their books; and the students playing parts can come forward at the appropriate time.

The cast of characters includes: a master, three servants, a landowner, a buyer, and an artist.

Everyone has talents. Talents are gifts from God. They are the abilities that help us do certain things well. We should thank God every day for the abilities we have, rather than complain about abilities we don't have.

We also should *use* our talents. If talents are not used, they become like a bicycle left outdoors in the rain and the cold. If a bicycle is not used and not kept in a dry, protected place, it becomes rusty and difficult to ride. In the same way, if we don't use our talents, they can become very hard for us to use.

When something is very hard for us to do, we are tempted to stop thinking about it, to stop choosing to do it, and to act in a lazy way by taking an easy way out.

Jesus reminds us in the following parable that our talents are special. If we use our talents, they make us stronger persons, bring joy to ourselves and to others, and are a help to others. We should be thankful for our abilities and not let our talents get "rusty".

THE SILVER PIECES

(*A man is standing by a table with his suitcase on the floor. There is money on the table.*)

A man was going on a long trip. He wanted to make sure that everything he owned was taken care of, including his money. So, before he left, he called his servants to his office.

(*The man gestures with his hand. Three servants enter.*)

"I am going on a long trip", he told his servants. "I want each of you to take care of my money while I am away."

(*The servants look surprised as the man hands each of them a part of his money.*)

He gave each of the servants silver pieces to take care of. He made sure that each person could manage the amount of money that he was given. "Remember," he said to them, "I am trusting you with the money I have given you. Use it as I would use it."

(*The master exits, carrying his suitcase. The servants exit. After a moment, the first servant and a landowner enter. They look at a map. The first servant gives the landowner five silver coins. He then shows the audience a picture of the land he has just purchased. The landowner exits.*)

The first servant received from his master five silver coins. He traded the five coins for a parcel of land. And then he sold the land for twice the amount he had paid for it.

(*Enter a buyer, who wishes to buy the land. The first servant holds up a price tag for twice the amount he had paid for it. The buyer gives the servant ten silver coins. The servant smiles and shows the audience a picture of the land with a "Sold" sign across it. The servant and the buyer exit.*)

(The second servant and an artist, carrying a painting, enter. The artist shows the painting to the servant. The servant gives the artist two silver coins, and the artist hands him the painting. The artist exits.)

The second servant received two silver pieces. He traded the money for a painting, and then sold it for twice the amount he had paid for it.

(Enter the buyer, who wishes to buy the painting. He gives the servant four silver coins for the painting. They shake hands and exit. The third servant enters and begins digging near the foot of a tree.)

But the third servant, who received one piece of silver, went off and dug a hole in the ground and buried his master's money because he was too lazy to try to put it to good use.

(The servant places the silver coin in the ground, buries it, and exits. The master returns, puts his suitcase down, and summons his three servants.)

Finally, the master returned home from his journey. He called his servants to his side and said to them: "So, tell me, my faithful servants, what have you done with my money?"

(The first servant steps forward and proudly hands his master ten silver coins.)

The first servant presented his master with the ten pieces of silver. With pride he said, "I bought land with your money. When the value of the land went up, I sold the land and got twice as much money as I had paid for it."

(The first servant steps back. The master smiles. The second servant steps forward.)

The second servant came forward and handed his master four silver coins. Happily, he explained, "I bought a painting for the two pieces of silver you gave me. Later, I met a buyer who wanted the painting and willingly paid me twice the amount I had paid for it."

(The master smiles again, as the second servant steps back. The third servant comes before his master, his head hung low.)

The servant who had received one silver piece stepped forward slowly. He knew that his master would not praise what he had done. He said to his master: "I was too lazy to try to do anything with the silver coin you gave me, so I buried it in the ground. Here it is."

(The third servant hands his master one silver coin and steps back. The master shakes his head.)

The master said to the third servant: "I am very disappointed in you. I would not have given you the money if I hadn't thought you could handle it well. Joy comes from using what you are given, not from burying it in the ground. Because you did not use the money I gave you, you will lose it."

(The master exits. The first and second servants follow happily after him. The third servant exits sadly.)

—Adapted from Matthew 25:14–29

Say to the class: "Does the master in this story remind you of anyone?" (*God.*) "With whom can we compare the three servants?" (*Us.*) "The master gave the servants silver coins. What does God give us?" (*Talents.*)

Student Book, page 152

In this parable, the truth that Jesus is teaching us is that we should use the talents God has given each of us, and use them as well as the first two servants used the money their master had given them. God knows how much each person can handle. He doesn't frustrate us by expecting too little or too much from us. He expects us to use our talents. We frustrate ourselves when we don't use the talents we have been given or when we try to do things that are beyond our ability.

Say to the class: "Can all of us play baseball really well?" (*No.*) "That's right. Some of us might be great hitters and fast runners, but some of us are not. Do all of us have to play baseball?" (*No.*) "What are some things that a person can do well besides playing baseball?" (*Play the piano, put puzzles together, write stories, and so on.*) "Does it matter how many talents you have?" (*No.*) "That's true! The important thing to remember is that we should use and develop our talents, because otherwise they will become 'rusty' and useless, and we will lose them."

Student Book, page 152

The master was equally happy with the two servants who used their talents. God is happy, too, when we use whatever talents we have. Remember the truth that Jesus teaches us: use the talents you have been given!

Living the Lesson

1. Which men used the money that their master had given them? (*The first two servants.*)
2. How did they use their money? (*They used their money wisely, to make more money.*)
3. Why didn't the third servant use the money he was given? (*He was lazy.*)
4. In this parable, what is the truth that Jesus teaches? (*We should use the talents that God has given us.*)
5. How can we show others that we believe this truth? (*By using our talents.*)

Say to the class: "Sometimes, because we are tired, we do not use our talents. That is okay. However, we should not be lazy.

"Using our talents takes time. Sometimes using our talents is hard or boring. For example, some of you have a talent for the game of baseball. You know the game very well, but it is hard to use your talent to teach the game to your younger brother or sister, or even to your mom! They might not understand the rules of the game right away. But because you know the game and can play it well, you can help others to understand it a little.

"Think of Jesus. He knew that He was God the Son. He had the power to do everything the easy way. Instead, He chose to use His talents as a teacher and patiently teach us the truth."

Note to teachers: The following activity should be done before moving on to Part F.

Activity

Materials needed:

Coins (from student book, page 153).
A bulletin board with the banner "The Riches of Room ____".
A "bank building" to mount on the bulletin board.

Student Book, page 153

Write one talent on each of the "coins". Then cut out the coins. Write your name on the back of each coin.

Collect the coins. Later, when students are not in the room, hide the coins in various places around the room.

Part F

Student Book, page 139

VOCABULARY
merchant: A buyer or seller of goods for a profit; a storekeeper.

Application

Divide the class into teams of two or three. Say to the class: "Today we are going on a Treasure Hunt. I have hidden all of the coins with your talents written on them in various places in this room. None of the coins are in anyone's personal belongings, such as desks or bookbags or coats.

"You have ten minutes to hunt for as many coins as possible. At the end of the ten minutes, we will count the number of coins each team has found. You will search with your team. If a team member is not considerate of others, that team will have to take a two-minute time out. When I say time is up, return to your seats. Are there any questions? . . . Begin!"

When the Treasure Hunt is over, ask the students to meet with their team members and count the team's coins. Find out which team has the most coins.

Say to the class: "Today, team *x* found the most coins. They are the winners. But as long as we use our talents well and think before we act, we are all 'winners' in God's sight. It does not matter how many talents we have. Were all the coins easy to find?" (*No.*)

Tell the students to place the coins on the bulletin board labeled "The Riches of Room ____", using pins. When they have finished, say:

"One treasure that we should do everything to find is the Kingdom of God! Let's open our books to page 155 and read about this treasure."

Treasures are great! They can make us happy. Sometimes we have to search very hard to find them.

The Kingdom of God is the greatest treasure that we can find. God's Kingdom includes everyone who acts as an image of God and shares God's life.

Every day, we find clues that lead us to the treasure. Some of the clues are in the parables of Jesus, which teach us about God and ourselves.

The parables teach us that we are images of God, that God loves us very much, and that we should love others as God loves them and us. The parables also teach us to be humble and to use our talents wisely.

The more people listen to the parables and act as God's images, the more people there will be in God's Kingdom. Jesus tells us about God's Kingdom in the following parables.

THE TREASURE AND THE PEARL

The Kingdom of God is like a treasure buried in a field. A man finds it. He is so excited that he hides it just to be able to dig it up and find it again. The treasure gives him so much joy that he sells everything he has and buys that field.

The Kingdom of God is also like a merchant searching for fine pearls. While searching, he finds a perfect pearl worth a lot of money. He wants that pearl more than anything else in the whole world. So he sells everything he has so that he can buy it.
—Adapted from Matthew 13:44–46

We are looking for God's Kingdom. We are just like the man hunting for treasure or the merchant searching for pearls. The treasure represents everyone who acts as an image of God and shares God's life both here on earth and in heaven. The perfect pearl represents the same thing as the treasure.

We should be like the man who found the treasure and like the man who found the perfect pearl in the parables. If we are not following the teaching of Jesus in some way, we should "sell" our old way of life and choose to follow the teachings of Jesus. It is not always easy to make such a change.

In these two stories, Jesus presents us with the truth that the Kingdom of God is worth every effort to find it and be part of it.

The more people there are who act as images of God and share God's life, the larger the Kingdom of God will be. By following the teaching of Jesus, we can do our part to increase the Kingdom of God. The Kingdom of God is going to be much larger than we can ever imagine.

Living the Lesson

1. In these parables, what is the truth that Jesus teaches us? (*It is worth doing everything we can to find the Kingdom of God and to be part of it.*)
2. How can we show others we believe this truth? (*By acting as God's images.*)
3. What is one of the "clues" that lead us to heaven? (*The parables, or the story teachings, of Jesus.*)
4. The treasure hunter sold everything for the treasure. The merchant sold everything for the perfect pearl. If we wish to find the Kingdom of God, what should we do? (*Look at our own lives. Think about the truths that Jesus teaches, and do everything we can to follow His teaching.*)
5. How large will the Kingdom of God be? (*Much larger than we can imagine.*)

16

Jesus Returns God's Love

1. Lesson Focus

Original sin damaged our minds, wills, and bodies. Because of original sin, it is difficult for us to know who we are and how we should act. Original sin makes it impossible for us to return the love that God has for us. Jesus came to show us who we are and how we should act as images of God, to return God's love, and to help us return God's love. He did this by teaching, loving, and doing things for people.

Jesus' death on the cross was the greatest of all loves. By dying on the cross, Jesus loved God the Father by doing the Father's will. Jesus also loved us by dying on the cross, because His death on the cross saved us from our sins and restored the friendship with God that was lost for us by Adam and Eve. By His death on the cross, Jesus shows us how we should act. He shows us that we should love God and others.

In addition, by dying on the cross, Jesus returned God's love and helps us to return God's love. By His death on the cross, Jesus made it possible for us to share grace, God's life. With grace, we are able to return God's love.

Note to CCD teachers: Use all Parts, A through D.

2. Concepts of Faith

> Student Book, page 164
>
> ### *Things to Remember*
>
> **Why did Jesus die on the cross?**
> To show us how we should act as images of God, to return God's love, and to help us return God's love.

3. Lesson Presentation

Part A

Say to the class: "Original sin damaged our minds, wills, and bodies. Because of original sin, it is difficult for us to know who we are and how we should act. Original sin makes it impossible for us to return the love that God has for us. Jesus came to show us who we are and how we should act as images of God, to return God's love, and to help us return God's love. He did this by teaching, loving, and doing things for people.

"Jesus' death on the cross was the greatest of all loves. By dying on the cross, Jesus loved God the Father by doing the Father's will. Jesus also loved us by dying on the cross, because His death on the cross saved us from our sins and restored the friendship with God that was lost for us by Adam and Eve. By His death on the cross, Jesus shows us how we should act. He shows us that we should love God and others. In addition, by dying on the cross, Jesus returned God's love and helps us to return God's love. By His death on the cross, Jesus made it possible for us to share grace, God's life. With grace, we are able to return God's love.

"Jesus prepared the people for His death and Resurrection from the dead. He told them, 'The hour has come for the Son of Man to be glorified' (John 12:23). When He said these words, Jesus was talking about His death on the cross.

"Jesus prepared His disciples in a special way for His death and Resurrection. Let's open our books to page 158 and find out what happened."

Student Book, page 158

As Jesus was walking with His disciples one day, He told them that He was going to suffer greatly. He told them that He would be killed, but that after three days He would rise from the dead. By telling His disciples this, He was preparing them for His death and Resurrection. Jesus died on the cross to show us how to act, to return God the Father's love, and to help us to return God's love.

—Adapted from Mark 8:31

Part B

Student Book, page 157

VOCABULARY
betray: To do something against a person who trusts you.

Application

Student Book, page 159

Some people did not believe in Jesus and did not follow Him. They wanted to arrest Him and kill Him. But they had to find someone who would help them have Jesus arrested.

One of the Apostles, Judas Iscariot, was willing to help. Those who wanted Jesus arrested promised to give Judas money for his help. Judas promised to find a time to have Jesus arrested.

Ask the class: "Do you think the people who did not like Jesus liked the Apostles?" (*No.*) "Why do you suppose that Judas wanted to help these people hurt Jesus?" (*Maybe he wanted the money. Maybe he was envious of the good that Jesus was doing.*)

The Passover was coming soon. The Passover is celebrated each year by the Jewish people to thank God for freeing them from the Egyptians. Judas thought he might find a time to have Jesus arrested during this celebration.

Ask the class: "What does the feast of the Passover celebrate?" (*The freeing of the Israelites from the Egyptians.*)

The disciples asked Jesus, "Where do you want us to go and prepare for you to eat the Passover?" Jesus said, "Go into the city and a man will meet you, carrying a jar of water. Follow him. Wherever he enters, say to the master of the house, 'The Teacher says, "Where is my guest room where I may eat the Passover with my disciples?"' Then he will show you a large upper room furnished and ready. Make the preparations for us there."

The disciples went off. When they reached the city, everything happened just as Jesus had told them. They prepared the Passover supper.

When evening came, Jesus entered the room with the twelve Apostles. They sat down at the table and prepared to eat. Jesus said, "I say to you, one of you will betray me, one who is eating with me." One by one, the Apostles said, "Surely, not I!"

Ask the class, "What does it mean to betray someone?" (*To do something against a person who trusts you.*)

Later, while they were all eating, Jesus took bread and said the blessing, broke it, and gave it to them, and said, "Take it; this is my body." Then he took a cup, gave thanks, and gave it to them, and they all drank from it. He said to them, "This is my blood of the covenant, which will be shed for many."

This special meal that Jesus shared with the Apostles is called the Last Supper. It was the first Mass.

—Adapted from Mark 14:1–4; 10–25

Say to the class: "Jesus ate with His Apostles. He trusted them and cared about them. Judas ate with Jesus, too, pretending to be trustworthy. What did he plan to do, however?" (*Help the people who did not like Jesus to arrest Him.*)

Part C

Application

> Student Book, page 162
>
> Jesus was about to suffer many terrible things. But Jesus willingly accepted all His sufferings and offered His sufferings to God the Father to save us from our sins. By doing so, He shows us how we should act, He returned the Father's love, and He helps us to return God's love.
>
> After the Last Supper, Jesus was betrayed by Judas, one of His disciples.

Ask the class, "Who was the disciple who betrayed Jesus?" (*Judas.*)

Discuss being betrayed by a friend. Say: "Have you ever told a friend a secret, only to have your friend tell others so that they all could make fun of you? How did you feel? How do you think Jesus felt when He was betrayed?"

> Student Book, page 162
>
> Then Jesus was arrested and led away. Some soldiers beat Jesus and made fun of Him. Jesus was then given a large wooden cross to carry. He had to carry the cross to a place outside the city. When Jesus got to the place, called Calvary, the soldiers nailed Jesus to the cross. Jesus prayed that His Father would forgive the soldiers. Then Jesus died.

Part D

Application

Say to the class: "We've learned that Jesus has suffered and died, but that isn't the end of the story. Please open your books to page 163, to read about what happened next."

> Student Book, page 163
>
> Some women came to the tomb where the body of Jesus was buried. They brought spices that they had prepared. They expected to find a huge stone covering the entrance to Jesus' tomb. But when they arrived at the tomb, they found the stone at the entrance of the tomb had been rolled back. When they entered the tomb, they found that Jesus' body was gone. They wondered what had happened to Jesus. While they were standing there, two men in dazzling white garments appeared. They asked, "Why do you seek the living one among the dead? He is not here, but he has been raised. Remember what he said to you while he was still in Galilee, that the Son of Man must be handed over to sinners and be crucified, and rise on the third day." When they heard this, the women remembered Jesus' words.
>
> As the women left the tomb, they met the Apostles. The women told the Apostles what had happened to them. It seemed so fantastic that the Apostles refused to believe them. Peter, however, ran to the tomb. He bent down and saw nothing but the linens that had been used to wrap Jesus' body. Peter left in amazement.
>
> —Adapted from Luke 24:1–12

Jesus' death on the cross was the greatest act of love ever. By dying on the cross, Jesus showed us how to act. He showed us that we are to love God and others. By dying on the cross, Jesus also returned God's love and helps us to return God's love. By His death on the cross, Jesus restored the friendship between God and us, and He made it possible for us to share God's life. With God's life, we are able to return God's love.

Unit 5

THE CHURCH:
THE PERSON OF CHRIST

17

Mary

1. Lesson Focus

God the Father asked a young girl named Mary to be the Mother of His Son, Jesus. Mary was conceived without original sin. From the very first moment of her life in her mother's womb, Mary was full of grace, God's life.

Mary never sinned. She chose to love God all her life. When Mary's life on earth was over, Jesus brought Mary, body and soul, to be with Him forever in heaven. Mary is the Queen of heaven and earth. She is our Mother.

Note to CCD teachers: Use all the Parts in class.

2. Concepts of Faith

Student Book, page 166

Things to Remember

How did Mary become the Mother of Jesus?
Through the power of the Holy Spirit.

---

3. Lesson Presentation

Part A

Student Book, page 166

VOCABULARY
Immaculate Conception: From the very first moment of Mary's life, she was without original sin.

Student Book, page 167

A very long time ago, God the Father chose to send His Son, Jesus, to live with us on earth. Jesus would show us who we are and how we should act. He would return God's love and help us to return God's love.

According to Tradition, living in the town of Nazareth was an elderly couple named Ann and Joachim. They had prayed for years to God, asking Him to send them a child. God gave them a daughter, whom they named Mary.

From the very first moment of her life, even before she was born, Mary was without original sin. In other words, from the very first moment of her life, Mary shared God's life, grace. This special privilege given to Mary by God is called her Immaculate Conception. She was given this gift because she was to be the Mother of Jesus.

Living the Lesson

1. Why did God send Jesus to earth? (*To show us who we are and how we should act, to return God's love, and to help us return God's love.*)
2. According to tradition, what are the names of Mary's parents? (*Ann and Joachim.*)
3. Mary was full of grace. What does "full of grace" mean? (*She was without original sin from the first moment of her life. She had God's life.*)
4. What do we call this privilege given to Mary? (*Her Immaculate Conception.*)

Part B

Student Book, page 166

VOCABULARY
Annunciation: The visit of the angel Gabriel to Mary, asking her to be the Mother of Jesus.

Application

Say to the class: "When Mary was growing up, she did not know that she would become the Mother of God. When she was about fourteen years old, God sent the angel Gabriel to give Mary a very important message. We call the visit of Gabriel to Mary the Annunciation. Let's open our books to page 168 and read about what happened that day."

THE ANNUNCIATION, THE VISITATION,
AND THE NATIVITY

One day, God the Father sent a messenger, the angel Gabriel, to the house where Mary lived. The angel said, "Hail, favored one! The Lord is with you." Mary was afraid. She did not understand the angel's greeting and wondered what it meant. Then the angel said to her, "Do not be afraid, Mary, for you have found favor with God." The angel went on to explain to Mary that God was asking her to be the mother of a son and to name the baby Jesus. He would be the Savior. Mary did not understand and asked how she could be a mother. The angel told her that it would happen through the power of the Holy Spirit, and that nothing is impossible for God. Mary said, "Behold, I am the handmaid of the Lord. May it be done to me according to your word." With this answer, Mary was saying that she would do whatever God asked. We call this the Annunciation.

The angel told Mary that her cousin Elizabeth was going to have a baby, too. Then the angel left her. After the angel left, Mary decided to go to visit Elizabeth and to share all the good news. We call the visit of Mary to Elizabeth the Visitation.

—Adapted from Luke 1:26–38

Living the Lesson

1. Who was the messenger God the Father sent to Mary? (*The angel Gabriel.*)
2. What did the angel Gabriel ask Mary to do? (*Be the Mother of the Savior.*)
3. What was Mary to name the baby? (*Jesus.*)
4. How did Mary become the Mother of Jesus? (*Through the power of the Holy Spirit.*)
5. Did Mary accept the angel Gabriel's message? (*Yes.*) What did she say to the angel? (*"Behold, I am the handmaid of the Lord. May it be done to me according to your word."*)

Part C

Application

After Mary returned home from visiting Elizabeth, Mary and Joseph were married. Then they found out that they had to travel to the town of Bethlehem to be counted in a census. We all know what happened when Mary and Joseph reached Bethlehem. Jesus was born! We call Jesus' birth the Nativity.

Let's turn to page 169 and read about the love between Jesus and His Mother, Mary.

Student Book, page 169

Jesus loved His Mother very much, and Mary loved Jesus. Because Mary loved Jesus so much, she stayed near Him during all His suffering. When Jesus was crucified, Mary stood at the foot of the cross with the Apostle John. Jesus said to His Mother, "Woman, behold, your son." Then Jesus spoke to John. "Behold, your mother" (John 19:26–27). In this way Jesus made Mary our Mother.

Jesus loved Mary so much that He did a very special thing for her. When Mary's life on earth was over, Jesus brought Mary, body and soul, to reign with Him forever in heaven. We call this event the Assumption of Mary. Mary is our Mother in heaven, and she helps us by her prayers. We should honor and love Mary.

Part D

Application

Student Book, pages 170–171

The Church celebrates many feast days for Mary.

January 1	Mary as the Mother of God (Mary's "Mother's Day")
March 25	The Annunciation
May 31	The Visitation
August 15	The Assumption
August 22	The Queenship of Mary
September 8	Mary's Birthday
September 15	Mary as Our Lady of Sorrows (remembering the suffering Mary endured)
October 7	Mary as Our Lady of the Rosary
November 21	The Presentation of Mary
December 8	The Immaculate Conception
December 12	Mary as Our Lady of Guadalupe

Mary is the Queen of heaven and earth. She is our Mother in heaven. She helps us by her prayers. In return, we should pray to her for her help. One way we can honor Mary is by praying the Rosary. Mary gave us the Rosary to help us pray and bring us closer to Jesus. By praying the Rosary, we love and honor Mary, our Mother.

Review the Joyful, Sorrowful, and Glorious Mysteries of the Rosary with the children. Review how to say the Rosary, and then say one decade of the Rosary every class period for five classes.

18

God's Family All over the World

1. Lesson Focus

Out of love for God the Father and all of us, Jesus died on the cross. On the third day He rose from the dead. He is now in heaven. But Jesus did not abandon us. Jesus asked His Apostles to teach all people the things that He had taught them through the parables, to help all people celebrate the sacraments and receive God's life, and to show all people how to use their talents to benefit others.

Jesus asked the Apostles to carry on His work. He made them the first bishops. He said that He would send the Holy Spirit to guide them. The Apostles, in return, ordained other men and made them deacons, priests, and bishops so that they, too, could carry on Jesus' work. Together, these men, along with all the other baptized, formed the Church.

Today, we still have bishops and the Pope to help bring the "Good News" to us. Like the Apostles, and with the guidance of the Holy Spirit, the Pope, along with the bishops in union with him, teaches us the things that Jesus had taught through the parables, they help us celebrate the sacraments and receive God's life, and they show us how to use our talents to benefit others.

The Catholic Church is all the baptized members working together—including deacons, priests, bishops, and the Pope—who make it God's family. As members of God's family, it is our duty to continue the mission of Jesus and bring the "Good News of Salvation" to all the world.

God's family is very large. It includes Christian people all over the world. It includes our immediate family, our parish, the diocese, and all Catholic people. All the Catholic people form the universal Church. Together, we can continue the work of Jesus.

Note to CCD teachers: Use Parts C, D, and E in class. Parts A and B and all the activities can be sent home as family projects or used in class as time permits.

2. Concepts of Faith

Student Book, page 180

Things to Remember

What did Jesus tell the Apostles to do?
To teach all people the things that He had taught them through the parables, to help all people celebrate the sacraments and receive God's life, and to show all people how to use their talents to benefit others.

Who does the work of the Church today?
Pope, bishops, priests, deacons, and all members of the Church.

3. Lesson Presentation

Part A

Student Book, page 172

VOCABULARY
miracle: An act that shows the power of God; it helps people have faith in what Jesus taught and to follow Him.
self-discipline: Watching how we act; changing and improving our actions to act lovingly toward others.

Application

Say to the class, "Let's open our books to page 173 and read about what Jesus asked of the Apostles."

Student Book, page 173

When Jesus was on earth, He taught people the truth about God the Father. He also taught them the truth about who they were and how they should act. One of the ways He did this was through the parables.

Out of love for God the Father and all of us, Jesus died on the cross. By loving God the Father and others, He showed us how to love. Also, by dying on the cross, Jesus returned God's love. Through His death on the cross, Jesus gives us the strength to love God, too. Jesus has risen and is now in heaven. But Jesus did not abandon us. He left us the sacraments. The sacraments are physical signs, given to us by Jesus, through which Jesus meets us and gives us His grace.

Jesus used self-discipline. He had the power to do many things for Himself. He could have made His life on earth much easier. Instead, He chose to live His life as we do and to perform miracles for others. He used His special powers for others to show us how to use our talents to benefit others.

Student Book, pages 173–174

Jesus commanded the Apostles to teach all people the things that He had taught them through the parables, to help all people celebrate the sacraments and receive God's life, and to show all people how to use their talents to benefit others.

JESUS ASKS PETER A QUESTION

One day, after the Resurrection of Jesus, Peter, one of the Apostles, decided to go fishing. Some of the other Apostles thought it was a great idea and asked Peter if they could join him.

After fishing all night, they had caught nothing. They were very disappointed. There was a man standing on the shore, watching them.

The Apostles did not know that it was Jesus standing on the shore, watching them. He asked them, "Children, have you caught anything to eat?" They answered, "No."

Jesus then told them to cast the net over the other side of the boat. The Apostles did what Jesus told them to do. They caught so many fish that they could not pull the net in! Then they knew that the man on the shore was Jesus.

Jesus said to them, "Come, have breakfast." After breakfast, Jesus asked Simon Peter, "Simon, son of John, do you love me?" Peter answered, "Yes, Lord, you know that I love you." Jesus said to Peter, "Feed my lambs." Then Jesus asked Peter again, "Simon, son of John, do you love me?" Peter again answered, "Yes, Lord, you know that I love you." Jesus replied, "Tend my sheep." He asked Peter a third time, "Simon, son of John, do you love me?" Peter was disappointed that Jesus had to ask a *third* time, so he said to Jesus, "Lord, you know everything; you know that I love you." Jesus said to Peter, "Feed my sheep."

—Adapted from John 21:1–17

This story shows how Jesus asked Peter to teach people the things that Jesus had taught him through the parables, to help all people celebrate the sacraments and receive God's life, and to show all people how to use their talents to benefit others.

Jesus asked all His Apostles to carry on His work in a special way. Jesus blessed the Apostles and told them that He would send the Holy Spirit to help guide them.

Part B

Student Book, page 172

VOCABULARY
communion of persons: A group of two or more persons who work together, love each other, and help each other love as God loves.
diocese: The people and the parishes under the care of a bishop.
parish: A local church community.
universal Church: The Church throughout the world; all the people from all the dioceses continuing the work of Jesus together.

Application

Say to the class: "The Apostles are not here today to teach us what Jesus taught. The Apostles are not here to celebrate the sacraments and to show us how to use our talents to benefit others. How can the work of Jesus continue without them? Let's open our books to page 175 and find out."

Student Book, page 175

JESUS VISITS THE APOSTLES

A short time after Jesus had risen from the dead, the Apostles met in a locked room. They missed Jesus very much. They needed to talk to each other and comfort each other. They were talking about what Jesus had told them. Jesus had told them that He loved them and that He would always be with them.

While they were still talking, Jesus suddenly appeared before them! He "stood in their midst and said to them, 'Peace be with you.' "

When Jesus had said this, He showed them the wounds in His hands and His side. The Apostles rejoiced when they recognized Jesus!

"Jesus said to them again, 'Peace be with you. As the Father has sent me, so I send you.' " By saying that He was sending His Apostles, Jesus was asking them to teach all people the things that He had taught them through the parables, to help all people celebrate the sacraments and receive God's life, and to show all people how to use their talents to benefit others. And when Jesus had said this, He breathed on them and said to them, "Receive the Holy Spirit."
—Adapted from Luke 24:36; John 20:19–23

Student Book, page 176

The power of the Holy Spirit is stronger than we can ever imagine! The Apostle Paul could feel the Holy Spirit's power in him. Especially when it was hard to teach what Jesus taught, Paul knew the Holy Spirit was there, guiding him.

Not all people wanted to listen to Paul. Some people even put him in prison! But Paul did not give up. His courage was still strong.

While in prison, he wrote a letter to his friend Timothy.

PAUL'S LETTER

Paul wrote that he was very grateful to God for everything that God had given him. Paul also wrote that he could hardly wait to see Timothy again.

Paul reminded Timothy that his grandmother and his mother had great faith in Jesus. Paul believed that their faith lived in his good friend, too.

So Paul told Timothy not to worry about him, a prisoner for the Lord. Instead, Paul recalled how he had blessed Timothy and made him a bishop. As a bishop, Timothy would teach all people the things that Jesus had taught him through the parables, help all people celebrate the sacraments and receive God's life, and show all people how to use their talents to benefit others.
—Adapted from 2 Timothy 1:1–8

Besides Timothy, the Apostles blessed other men so that they too could teach all people the things that Jesus had taught them through the parables, help all people celebrate the sacraments and receive God's life, and show all people how to use their talents to benefit others. Together, these men, along with the other baptized, were the first members of the Church. Today, we have the bishops and the Pope to teach us the things that Jesus taught through the parables, to help us celebrate the sacraments and receive God's life, and to show us how to use our talents to benefit others.

It is all the baptized members of the Church working together—including deacons, priests, bishops, and the Pope—who make up the Church, God's family.

God's family is very large. It includes Christian people all over the world. It includes our immediate family, our parish, the diocese, and the Catholic people all over the world. Together, all the Catholic people form the universal Church.

Part C

VOCABULARY
foreman: A leader of a group of workers.

Materials needed: 4 cardboard cutout pieces of a little schoolhouse (see Appendix).

Note to teachers: Before class, practice assembling the little schoolhouse, and then take it apart. Choose seven students to put the pieces of the schoolhouse together. Give the students the pieces before class begins.

Application:

Say to the class: "A building does not just build itself. Construction involves many people. First, someone has to design the building. Other people must prepare the material. Still others must put the building together under the direction of a foreman.

"Today we are going to build our own little schoolhouse. I'll be the foreman. You'll be my crew.

"The designer plans the building, the owner buys the materials, and the foreman tells the builders where to put the building materials and how to put the building together. Without the foreman, the building might not turn out the way it should. Without the designer, builders, and owner there would be no building at all."

Call the students with the pieces of the little schoolhouse to the front of the room one at a time, in this order: walls, roof, and chimney. Help the students place the tabs in the slips provided. When the schoolhouse is finished, ask the class, "Could you have finished the little schoolhouse in the same way without me?" (*No. We wouldn't have the right plans. Our design would have been different.*) "Builders need leaders or a foreman to tell them what they should do and where everything goes."

Ask the class, "Could we have finished the schoolhouse correctly if one of the builders had been absent?" (*No. It would have parts missing. It would fall apart.*)

"The foreman is the leader. He leads his crew. Jesus is a leader, too. He is the leader of the Church. We are members of the Church. Like the crew who follow the foreman, we must follow Jesus and work together to continue the work of Jesus here on earth.

"In order to build a building, we need an owner, a designer, builders, and a foreman. All of these people must work together for the building to be built properly. In the Church, we have bishops and the Pope, along with all the rest of the baptized. The bishops and the Pope teach all people what Jesus had taught them through the parables, they help all people celebrate the sacraments and receive God's life, and they show all people how to use their talents to benefit others. All the baptized Catholics, including the bishops and the Pope, form the Church. All should follow Jesus and work together to continue the work of Jesus here on earth."

Part D

Materials needed: 4 stacking cups, each slightly larger than the one before.

Application

Say to the class: "A school has an important mission—to teach young people how to live successfully in their community. This mission involves many people. Of course, we cannot have a school without students. The leaders of a school also have to know what subjects will be taught, who will teach those subjects, what books and materials will be used, and what everyone must do in order for the school to be a success.

"A principal helps to make sure that all the people in a school know what their jobs are. A school could not succeed without its leader, the principal. The principal decides what subjects will be taught, what the janitors should fix, and who will coach which sport."

Ask the class, "What would happen to the students if some of the teachers decided not to teach what the principal asked them to?" (*The students might not learn everything they need to know.*) "What would happen to the school building if the janitors refused to fix what was broken?" (*The school building could fall apart.*) "What would happen to the school sports activities if the coaches refuse to coach?" (*There would be no sports activities.*)

Say to the class: "The principal helps everyone make the school successful, just as the foreman helped the builders make the little schoolhouse.

"Our school is not just a building. It is the people inside the building that make the school successful. The Catholic Church is not just buildings, either. In the Catholic Church all the baptized members should work together."

Student Book, page 177

As members of the Church, we are to do all that we can to continue Jesus' mission of bringing the "Good News of Salvation" to all the world. As members of the Church, we should follow the Pope and the bishops. The Pope and the bishops teach all people what Jesus taught them through the parables, they help all people celebrate the sacraments and receive God's life, and they show all people how to use their talents to benefit others. By following the Pope and the bishops, we find out who we are and how we should act, we receive God's life in the sacraments, and we come to know how to use our talents to benefit others.

Say to the class: "Bringing the 'Good News of Salvation' to all the world sounds like a very big job. But remember, God's family is a very *big* family! It includes: our immediate family with whom we live [*show the class the smallest cup*], our parish [*show the class the cup that is slightly larger than the first one*], the diocese [*show the class the next larger cup*], and all the baptized people in the world [*show the class the largest cup*].

"Our Church is a universal Church. If we all work together as a communion of persons and follow Jesus [*place the cups inside each other and hold them up*], we *can* continue the mission of Jesus."

Living the Lesson

1. Can a building crew build a schoolhouse by themselves? (*No. They need a foreman to lead them.*)
2. What does the foreman do? (*Show the builders where to put everything.*)
3. Can a foreman build a schoolhouse alone? (*No. A foreman needs the help of the crew to put all of the pieces together.*)
4. What does a principal do? (*Makes sure that all the people in the school know what their jobs are.*)
5. Would the school be very successful without the principal? (*No.*)
6. Jesus is a leader, too. What does He lead? (*The Church.*)

Activity

Student Book, pages 177–178

Pretend that you are a reporter for Christ. As a reporter, it is your job to spread the "Good News". Before you can spread the Good News, you have to look at what Jesus taught us. Think about your favorite parable. Think about the people in the story and what they did. Look at what people do today. Then think about the truth that Jesus teaches us in that parable and how that truth applies to us today. Retell the story in your own words on the next page.

Part E

Materials needed:
A globe.
1 gallon of white glue; a bucket or pan for every two students.
For each student: a paint shirt; desk cover; scissors; glue; markers or crayons; a balloon; about 25 strips of newspaper; string to hang the balloon.

Note to teachers: Before class begins, mix one cup of glue with one cup of water in each bucket or pan.

Application

Say to the class: "To continue the mission of Jesus, we must first begin with our own family. Please open your books to page 179 and find out more about continuing the work of Jesus."

At Mass, during the Gospel, we hear the parables that Jesus taught. The parables tell us the truth about God the Father and ourselves. Priests and teachers help us understand the truth.

We need to share the truth with the members of our family. Reading the Bible, praying together, and discussing what we have learned are ways we can better understand who we are.

Jesus showed His great love by dying on the cross. We can show our love for God the Father by receiving the sacraments and reminding the other members of our family to receive the sacraments, too.

Jesus served others by performing miracles. We can serve others by using our talents; even to help our brothers and sisters when we don't feel like it.

When we gather together as a parish community, we form a much larger family. There are more people helping each other.

Teachers, priests, and other members of the Church can help explain parables that we do not understand. Sacraments are times of great celebration. Together, the parish community can feel the excitement and joy of receiving God's life.

Some families are poor and cannot help themselves. These families need the help of the *parish family*. Members of the parish can put their talents together to help people in need.

The churches in our diocese and all of the Catholic people all over the world form the universal Church. *Together* we can help each other to understand the truth within the parables, to receive the sacraments, and to use our talents to serve others. Whether in the family, the parish, the diocese, or the universal Church, we do all of these things by following our leaders, the Pope and the bishops. They teach all people the things that Jesus taught them through the parables, help all people celebrate the sacraments and receive God's life, and show all people how to use their talents to benefit others.

Activity

This project will take approximately two hours.

First hour: Ask the students to put on a paint shirt and place desk covers on their desks or tables. (If students will be working at their desks, place two desks together.)

Give each student about 25 strips of newspaper (some will need more, some less) and one balloon. Place one bucket or pan of paste on each pair of desks.

Say to the class: "Today we are going to make our own globes. The globe represents our world. When we look at the globe [*hold up a globe for the class to see*], we notice that it is one continuous circle. All the continents are connected by water.

"All the churches of the world are connected by one mission: to continue the work of Jesus in our families, our parishes, the diocese, and the universal Church.

"As we make our own globes, think about our mission: to find out who we are through the parables, to receive God's life in the sacraments, and to use our talents to serve others.

"Now blow up your balloons and tie a knot at the end." (*Demonstrate and assist.*) "Dip one strip of newspaper at a time into the glue mixture. Place the strip of newspaper between two fingers and gently slide some of the excess glue off of the strip." (*Demonstrate.*) "Wrap the strip around the balloon." (*Demonstrate.*) "Continue wrapping glue-coated strips around the balloon until it is completely covered. Write your name on a small strip of newspaper. Dip the strip in glue, remove the excess, and place it on your balloon. Place your balloon on the newspapers to dry." (*Tell students where to put the globes to dry.*)

Second hour: When the globes are dry, pop the balloon by sticking a pin into the globes. Then ask the students to take out pencils, scissors, glue, and markers or crayons. Then ask the class: "What do we need to do to continue the work of Jesus?" (*Find out who we are through the parables, receive God's life in the sacraments, and use our talents to benefit others.*) "Who will help us do the work of Jesus?" (*Our own families, our parish, the churches in our diocese, and all of the Catholic people all over the world.*) "How do the Pope and the bishops help us continue the work of Jesus?" (*They teach us the things that Jesus taught them through the parables, they help us celebrate the sacraments and receive God's life, and they show us how to use our talents to benefit others.*)

Say to the class: "Open your books to page 181. Notice the four boxes, each with a label: 'My Family', 'My Parish', 'The Bishop and His Diocese', and 'The Pope'. To remind all people that our Church is a universal Church and that we must work together, we are going to place four pictures on our globe. The first picture is of our own individual families.

"The first box is labeled 'My Family'. Write the last name or names of your family on the blank line. Draw a picture of your family inside the box, and color the picture.

"The second box is labeled 'My Parish'. Write the name of our [your] parish on the line. Draw a picture of our [your] parish church and color it.

"The third box is labeled 'The Bishop and His Diocese'. Write the name of our bishop on the line, and color the picture in the box.

"The fourth box is labeled 'The Pope'. Write the name of the Pope in the blank line, and then color the picture in the box.

"When you are done with the four pictures, cut out the four boxes and glue them neatly onto your globes. Place the globes back onto the newspaper to dry. I will come around to tie on a piece of string so that we can hang the globes up."

19

Serving Others in
the Church Community

1. Lesson Focus

Jesus commanded the Apostles to carry on His work. He wanted them to teach all people the things that He had taught them through the parables, to help all people celebrate the sacraments and receive God's life, and to show all people how to use their talents to benefit others by taking care of their physical and material needs.

Like the Apostles, we are to continue the work of Jesus, too. As members of the Church, we should look at the world through the very eyes of Christ. We should see those things that should be done to meet the physical and material needs of others. We should try to meet those needs together with other members of the Church.

To have a Church community that helps others, we must first begin with our own families. Serving everyone within our own families includes using our own talents and having the courage to do *what* we can *when* we can.

However, we belong to more than one community. There are many people outside our families who need our help and support, too.

The next place to look for ways to serve others is within our own local church communities. Our parishes help others both inside the Church and out.

Priests primarily help all people celebrate the sacraments and receive God's life. But priests, deacons, and volunteers also work together to form groups that prepare the church for Mass, assist during Mass, and donate food, clothing, shelter, time, talents, and money to meet the spiritual and physical needs of others.

Parishes try very hard to help and guide their people. But sometimes parishes do not know how to answer certain questions or to solve certain problems. Sometimes there isn't enough food, clothing, shelter, time, or money for the needy.

The priest or parishioners can then turn to the dioceses for help. A diocese is the people and the parishes under the care of a bishop or archbishop. (An archbishop may have auxiliary bishops to help him.)

The bishop primarily teaches all people what Jesus taught through the parables. The bishop also pulls the efforts of many talented people together to help others in need of guidance, food, clothing, and shelter.

The Pope, a very special bishop, is the leader of the universal Church. His primary role is to help bring the "Good News" to all the people of the world by meeting with the bishops in Rome to share ideas and by writing letters to other bishops to help them teach the people. He also creates groups and organizations to help all people, and he travels to different countries.

Note to CCD teachers: Use all the Parts, A through D, in class. The activities can be sent home as family projects or used in class as time permits.

2. Concepts of Faith

Student Book, page 194

Things to Remember

How do we use our talents to benefit others?
We see what should be done to meet the physical and material needs of others and, together with other members of the Church, try to meet those needs.

3. Lesson Presentation

Part A—Our Own Families

Student Book, page 183

VOCABULARY
parish: A local church community.
diocese: The people and the parishes under the care of a bishop.

Materials needed:
    1 small slip of paper (approximately 2" x 2") per student.
    1 hat or empty coffee can.
    10 slips of paper with family needs or problems (see Appendix).
    Picture of a shepherd (see Appendix).

Note to teachers: For the activity in this Part, divide the class into groups of five. Each group represents a family. All families are different, so there can be any number of boys and girls in the groups. Write the numbers "1" through "5" on separate pieces of paper five times each. Place the papers in a hat or coffee can for drawing. Plan on having a place in the room for each group to talk about and to practice the role-playing that will be done.

Application

Say to the class: "Pope John Paul said, 'The Church looks at the world through the very eyes of Christ.' While on earth, Jesus was always looking for ways to help His people. He chose to use His powers to perform miracles to benefit others all the time, even when He could have used His powers for Himself.

"When Jesus asked the Apostles to carry on His work, He wanted them to look for ways to help people. He wanted them to use their talents to meet the physical and material needs of others.

"Like the Apostles and the deacons who helped them, we are to continue the work of Jesus, too. As members of the Church, we should look at the world through the very eyes of Christ. We should see what physical and material needs others have and try to meet those needs together.

"So many people need help. They may be sick, hungry, lonely, homeless, or frustrated. We want to use our talents to help these people, but some of us are only in the third grade. Some of us do not have important jobs or cannot drive a car. Some of us have little money."

Ask the class, "How, then, can we help?" (*By working together as a community. Get the church to help us. Ask our parents.*) "Let's open our books to page 184 and find out how we can begin to help others."

Student Book, page 184

To have a successful church community as the Apostles did, we must first begin with our own families. Each family is a small community all by itself. Family members should pray, receive the sacraments, and serve others together.

Serving everyone within our family sounds like a big job. But Jesus does not expect us to try to take care of all problems and needs right away by ourselves. He just wants us to use our own talents and help a little bit at a time. Even helping someone smile can be a *big* help.

This prayer reminds us to do *what* we can *when* we can, and to get help with the rest:

> God, grant me the serenity [peaceful ability]
> to accept the things I cannot change,
> courage to change the things I can,
> and wisdom to know the difference.

We have talents that are helpful to every member of our families! Of course, there are things that we cannot do, but there are *many* things that we *can* do to meet the physical and material needs of others. We need only the courage and the patience to try them.

Living the Lesson

Student Book, page 185

1. How can we "look at the world through the very eyes of Christ"? (*See what needs to be done for others and do it.*)
2. Where do we begin to help others? (*Within our own families.*)
3. How do we serve others within our own families? (*By having the courage to use our own talents and abilities and to help whenever possible.*)
4. Think about the things that you do to help meet the physical and material needs of the members of your family and write them down. (*Answers will vary.*)

Possible student answers to the last question include: *clean room, set the table, do the dishes, watch little brothers or sisters, get the mail, mow the lawn, shovel the sidewalks, help younger siblings with homework, clean up the yard and the house, do the weeding, write letters to relatives far away, talk to relatives on the telephone, read to others in the family, play games together, run errands when someone is sick, help with a paper route.*

Activity

Say to the class: "We are going to do some role-playing. I am going to divide you into groups of five. As I walk around, please pull a number out of the hat. The number that you receive is the number of the group that you will be in."

Then have the children draw the numbers. Put all the children who have drawn a "1" together in one group. Put all of the children who have drawn a "2" together in another group, and do the same for the remaining numbers. Then say to the class: "Listen carefully when I call your group number and tell each group where to sit."

Tell the class: "Each group represents a family. Each group must decide what the names of the family members are and what each one's place is in the family—mom, dad, brother, sister, grandma, grandpa, and so on. You will be given a family need or problem. Your group must decide how each member of your family will help to solve the problem. When your group is called, show the rest of us, in a short skit, what the need or problem is and how you helped solve it. I will give you ten minutes to discuss the problem and practice the skit."

Give one slip with a need or problem to each group. Answer any questions that the students may have. Then tell them when to begin practicing. After ten minutes, tell the groups to stop and have the students sit down. Then call up the groups, one by one, to present their problem-solving skits.

Part B—The Parish Family

Application

Jesus was always looking for ways to benefit others by using His powers to take care of their physical and material needs. Pope John Paul II said, "The Church looks at the world through the very eyes of Christ."

Because all baptized Catholics are members of the Church, *we* should look at the *world* the way that Jesus did. We should look for ways to help people *everywhere* and then use our talents to benefit others by meeting their physical and material needs.

Caring for the members of our own family community is a good place to start. But we belong to more than one community, and there are many people outside our family who need our help and support, too.

The next place to look for ways to serve others is within our own local church community. Our local church community or parish helps others both inside the church building and out.

When we go to Mass, we see many people volunteering their time and talents to make sure that everything necessary for the celebration of Mass is prepared.

Ask the class, "Can you tell me what some of these volunteers do before, during, and after Mass?" (*Donate flowers to decorate the church, decorate the church, help plan for special Masses, prepare the bulletins, clean the church, and prepare the altar and the gift table.*) "How should we treat the people and things within the church?" (*With respect. Handle books carefully. Put kneelers down gently. Do not scratch names or messages in the wood of the pews. Do not bother, hit, or tease others.*)

Ask the class, "What things can you do to help meet the physical and materials needs of unhappy people whom you know?" (*Talk to them if they want to talk, help them with their yard work or chores, bake cookies and give them some, send them a card.*)

Student Book, page 187

Health, food, and friendship are three things that people need. When people are sick or dying, they often need to be shown that other people care. Many parishes have members who will visit the sick at home or in the hospital. Parishes also have groups of people with the same health problems who meet together for support. They also have groups for concerned family members of those who are ill.

Ask the class, "How can you meet the physical and materials needs of someone you know who is sick or dying?" (*Visit the sick person, send a card, make a meal or bake a cake or cookies for him or her.*)

Student Book, page 187

Many people are hungry and cannot afford a weekly trip to the grocery store. Church members donate food and place it on shelves in a special place. Needy people can go to the "Food Shelves" and select what they need for their families.

Some people cannot walk or drive to local "Food Shelves". Volunteer drivers for "Meals on Wheels" bring the food to the needy.

Ask the class, "How can you help the needy?" (*By donating food or money to the "Food Shelves".*)

Student Book, page 187

Friends help us to enjoy life. Your parish can help you see friends more often or meet new people if you are lonely.

Many parishes have a social hour after one of the Masses that includes coffee, doughnuts, and juice. It's a great time to relax and enjoy each other's company.

Other social groups and events in a parish might include: a festival, a home and school association, an usher's club, a senior citizen's group, a women's club, a youth group, a young adults' club, a Cub Scout pack, a Boy Scout troop, and a Campfire group. With such a list, there are many to choose from!

Ask the class, "What can you do to keep or start good friendships?" (*Invite people over, share time, talents, and things with others, be honest, share secrets.*)

Living the Lesson

1. What is a parish? (*A local church community.*)
2. What are some of the things that a parish does to help meet the physical and material needs of the members of its community? (*Decorate the church, plan for special Masses, prepare the bulletins, clean the church, prepare the altar and gift table, and help with "Meals on Wheels" and other organizations that help the needy.*)

Part C—The Diocese

Application

Student Book, pages 188–190

While Jesus was on earth, He helped many people by performing miracles. The following story gives one example.

JESUS FEEDS A CROWD

One day, Jesus quietly took the Apostles to a town called Bethsaida. He wanted to meet with them privately, away from the crowds that had been following Him.

The crowds, however, heard about the meeting and followed Jesus anyway. Jesus accepted their company. He spoke to them about the Kingdom of God and healed those who needed to be cured.

As nighttime approached, the Apostles became worried. There were about five thousand people following Jesus. All of them needed food to eat and a place to sleep. The Apostles went to Jesus and said, "Dismiss the crowd so that they can go to surrounding villages and farms and find lodging and provisions."

Jesus said to the Apostles, "Give them some food yourselves."

They replied, "Five loaves and two fish are all we have, unless we ourselves go and buy food for all these people."

Jesus told the Apostles to ask the people to sit in groups of about fifty. Then He took the loaves and fish, blessed them, broke them, and gave them to the Apostles to pass out to the large crowd.

The people ate until they were full. When the leftovers were picked up, they filled twelve baskets.

—Adapted from Luke 9:10–17

Today, Jesus has many followers in families, parishes, dioceses, and the whole world. He wants all of these people to be fed and clothed and to have shelter too.

Our local parish community tries very hard to help people who need food, clothing, and shelter. But sometimes the parish does not know how to answer certain questions or how to solve certain problems. Sometimes there isn't enough food, clothing, shelter, time, or money for the needy. The priest or parishioners can then turn to the diocese for help. A diocese is the people and the parishes under the care of a bishop.

Ask the class, "Who is the bishop of our diocese?" (*Bishop or Archbishop* _____.)

Student Book, page 190

Bishops primarily teach all people what Jesus taught through the parables. But bishops also put the efforts of many people together to help others in need of guidance, food, clothing, and shelter.

The bishop is like a shepherd, and we are the sheep of his flock. The shepherd meets the physical and materials needs of the sheep. The bishop meets the physical and material needs of the people.

The bishop of a diocese has many talented people working for him. These people have volunteers who are available to help anyone from any of the parishes in that diocese.

Living the Lesson

1. When Jesus was on earth, how did he help the needy? (*By performing miracles.*)
2. What do the bishop and the members of the diocese do to meet the physical and material needs of others? (*The bishop has many talented people working for him, and these people have volunteers who are available to help anyone from any of the parishes of that diocese.*)

Part D—The Universal Church

Materials needed: It would be helpful to have a map showing the location of the city of Rome.

Application

Student Book, page 191

The Pope, a very special bishop, is the leader of the universal Church. He helps to bring the "Good News" to all the people of the world by meeting with the bishops in Rome to share ideas, by writing letters to other bishops to help them teach the people, by creating groups and organizations to help all people, and by traveling to different countries.

Ask the class, "Can you tell me the name of our Pope?" (*Pope* _____.)

If you have a map, ask, "Can you find Rome, the city in which the Pope lives, on the map?" (*Have a student show the class where Rome is on the map.*)

To help us understand what the baptized do in the Church, let's take a look at organized baseball. In organized baseball, everyone uses his talents to benefit others. Players on a baseball team use their physical talents to help each other play a good game. Coaches help meet the physical and material needs of the players by giving them equipment to use and coaching on how to improve their skills. Team owners hire the coaches, pay them, make team rules, and provide a stadium to play in.

Several teams together form a league. A commissioner, or leader of a league, organizes the teams. He helps all players to know when it's time for their teams to play, to understand the rules of the game and to play fairly, to celebrate championships, and to use their talents to benefit all the teams.

Say to the class: "Four important kinds of people in baseball were mentioned. Can you name them?"

Ask, "What does each person or group of persons do?" Write the responses on the blackboard.

Players: Use their physical talents to help each other play a good game.

Coaches: Help to meet the physical and material needs of the players by giving them equipment to use and coaching on how to improve their skills.

Team Owners: Hire coaches, pay them, make team rules, and provide a stadium to play in.

Commissioner: Organizes the teams and helps all players to know when it's time for their team to play, to understand the rules of the game, to play fairly, to celebrate championships, and to use their talents to benefit all teams.

The Church is something like organized baseball. Everyone uses his talents to benefit others. Within the Church, all of the baptized try to use their talents to benefit others by meeting their physical and material needs. Priests primarily help all people celebrate the sacraments and receive God's life. But priests, deacons, and volunteers also work together to form groups that prepare the church for Mass, assist during Mass, and donate food, clothing, shelter, time, talents, and money to care for the physical health, happiness, and well-being of others.

Write the responses to the following questions on the blackboard. Ask the class: "Can you name some of the people who form the universal Church? What do these people do as members of the universal Church?"

Baptized Catholics: Read and listen to the parables, receive the sacraments, and try to use their talents to meet the physical and material needs of others.

Priests and deacons: Work together to form groups that prepare the church for Mass, assist during Mass, and donate food, clothing, shelter, time, talents, and money to meet the spiritual, physical, and material needs of others.

Bishops: Teach what Jesus taught through the parables and pull the efforts of many talented people together to help others in need of guidance, food, clothing, and shelter.

The Pope: The leader of the universal Church brings the "Good News" to the people of the world by meeting with the bishops in Rome to share ideas and writing letters to bishops to help them teach the people. He also creates groups and organizations to help all people, and he travels to different countries.

Living the Lesson

> **Student Book, pages 193–194**
>
> 1. How can we help everyone within our own families? (*By using our own talents and doing whatever we can, when we can, for others.*)
> 2. What do parishes do to help meet the physical and material needs of others? (*Priests and deacons show parishioners how to use their talents to benefit others. Parishioners clean and prepare the church, assist before and during Mass, donate food, clothing, shelter, time, and money to care for the health and happiness of others.*)
> 3. How does the diocese meet the physical and material needs of others? (*Bishops and the talented people who work for them, together with volunteers, help those who are in need of guidance, food, clothing, and shelter.*)
> 4. Who is a very special bishop, the leader of the universal Church, and the successor of Peter? (*The Pope.*)
> 5. How does the universal Church help meet the physical and material needs of others? (*The Pope creates groups and organizations to help all people.*)
> 6. How does the Pope know when there are problems that need his help in the parishes and dioceses around the world? (*He has meetings in Rome with the bishops, he sends letters to other bishops around the world, he leads helpful organizations, and he travels to different countries.*)

Activity

Ask the students to tear out pages 195, 197, and 199 from their books. Then have the students color and cut out each "building".

When you are certain that all the students have cut out the "family house", ask them to stop what they are doing and watch carefully.

Say to the class: "The universal Church is made up of families, parishes, and dioceses. Take the 'family house' that you have just cut out and fold it in half on the dotted line." (*Demonstrate.*) "Notice the two tabs sticking out on the sides. Fold them back, one at a time, and glue them to the back of the house." (*Demonstrate.*) "When you have finished coloring and cutting out your 'parish church', 'cathedral', and 'universal church', put them together in the same way."

Show the class your completed buildings. Allow the students time to finish their three buildings.

When the students are ready, say: "Now place the house inside the parish church, the parish church inside the cathedral, and the cathedral inside the universal Church. This is a reminder to us that we should do our best to help meet the physical and material needs of our families, our parish, and other people.

20

The Gift of God's Life, Grace

1. Lesson Focus

Original sin damaged Adam and Eve's minds, wills, and bodies. After they sinned, it was no longer easy for them to know the truth, choose to love, and act as images of God. They also lost God's life—grace. As descendants of Adam and Eve, we have inherited original sin and its effects.

Jesus, our Savior, made up for original sin and all other sins. Jesus repaired our relationship with God and returned the Father's love by dying on the cross. Jesus helps us to return the Father's love by giving us God's life, grace.

Jesus' death on the cross was the greatest of all loves. He loved from the heart. He did not love because someone told Him to do it. He made the choice to give Himself to God the Father and others through His death. He wanted to do the Father's will and give us a chance to share in God's life, grace.

If we are to love as God loves, we must share in God's life. Grace is God's life. Grace takes away original sin. Through grace, we can overcome some of the effects of original sin. Grace enlightens our minds, strengthens our wills, and helps us use self-discipline in the things we do and say. Grace also enables us to live in heaven forever with God.

Note to CCD teachers: Use all the parts, A through D, in class.

2. Concepts of Faith

Student Book, page 222

Things to Remember

What is grace?
Grace is God's life.

What does grace do for us?
Grace helps us to act as images of God and makes it possible for us to live forever with God in heaven.

3. Lesson Presentation

Part A

Original sin damaged Adam and Eve's minds, wills, and bodies. After they sinned, their minds were darkened. From then on, it was not easy for them to know the truth. They did not even tell God the truth. Adam told God that it was Eve's fault that he sinned. Eve told God that it was the serpent's fault that she sinned. After they sinned, Adam and Eve still had the free will to choose to love each other as they should, but it was difficult for them to share that love because of original sin. It was difficult for them to act as images of God. They were tempted to think, say, and do things that they knew were wrong. Adam and Eve lost grace, God's life, because they sinned.

Although Adam and Eve did not return God's love, God did not stop loving Adam and Eve. He continued to love and care for them, but the love between Adam and Eve and God was weakened.

As descendants of Adam and Eve, we have inherited original sin and its effects. We are born without God's life. Original sin damaged our minds, wills, and bodies, too. Jesus our Savior made up for original sin and all other sins. Jesus repaired our relationship with God and returned the Father's love. He helps us to return the Father's love.

Jesus' death on the cross was the greatest act of love ever. He loved from the heart. He did not love because someone told Him to do it. He made the choice to give Himself to God the Father and others through His death. He wanted to do the Father's will and give us a chance to share in God's life, grace.

If we are to love as God loves, we must share in God's life. Grace is God's life. Grace helps us to say "yes" to God. Grace enlightens our minds to know the truth. Grace strengthens our wills so we can choose to love. Grace helps us to govern our bodies. Grace helps us to use self-discipline in the things we do and say.

By dying on the cross, Jesus gave us a chance to receive grace. We do not have to die on a cross to show our love. We can choose to receive the sacraments and receive the grace that Jesus meant for us to have.

Living the Lesson

1. What damaged the minds, wills, and bodies of Adam and Eve? (*Original sin.*)
2. How were their minds damaged? (*It was not easy for them to know the truth.*)
3. How were their wills damaged? (*It was not easy for them to choose what was right.*)
4. How were their bodies damaged? (*It was difficult for them to act as images of God.*)
5. Although Adam and Eve did not return God's love, what did God continue to do? (*He continued to love and care for them; but the love between Adam and Eve and God was weakened.*)
6. Who repaired our relationship with God? (*Jesus.*)
7. What did Jesus do to repair our relationship with God? (*He died on the cross.*)
8. Jesus' death on the cross was the greatest of all loves. Give three reasons why. (*He did not love because someone told Him to do it; He did the Father's will; He gave us a chance to share in God's life, grace.*)
9. What is grace? (*God's life.*)
10. What does grace do for us? (*Grace enlightens our minds, strengthens our wills, and helps us use self-discipline in the things we do and say. It enables us to live in heaven forever with God.*)

Part B

Materials needed: Geometric shapes, groups "A" and "B", from the student book; scissors.

Student Book, pages 203–205

"A"

anger—*circle*
disrespect—*triangle*
showing prejudice—*octagon*
selfishness—*hexagon*
dishonesty—*square*
disobedience—*rectangle*
self-centered—*cylinder*
not acting as an image of God—*cone*

"B"

love—*circle*
respect—*rectangle*
fairness—*cylinder*
caring—*cylinder*
honesty—*cone*
obedience—*rectangle*
self-giving—*cone*
acting as an image of God—*square*

Note to teachers: Please cut out your sets of "A" and "B" geometric shapes from the Appendix before class begins.

Application

Say to the class: "Because of original sin, our bodies are broken. It is very difficult to have self-discipline. We do not always act as images of God should act. By ourselves, we do not have the strength to do what is right. Alone we cannot put ourselves back together again. We need grace to give us the strength to use self-discipline in the things we say and do.

"Please remove page 203 from your books. Notice that this page has several geometric shapes. Neatly cut out each of the shapes and put them on your desk. Throw the leftover scraps of paper away in this bag, and wait quietly for more directions.

"Read the labels that are written on each of the shapes. Without grace, we find it hard to do these things. If we don't have grace, our bodies remain broken. Only in heaven will our bodies be completely mended. But grace begins to put us back together while we are here on earth, so that we can act as we should.

"Now, let's see if you can put these shapes together to form the shape of a person."

Give the class five minutes to work with their geometric shapes. You should work with your set of shapes, too, to show the students that what you have asked them to do cannot be done.

Ask the class: "Was anyone successful in forming the shape of a person out of the smaller shapes?" (*No.*) "Why not?" (*The shapes could not be connected together.*)

Say to the class: "Please remove page 205 from your books. Notice that this page has another set of geometric shapes. Neatly cut out each of the shapes and put them on your desk. Throw the leftover scraps away and wait quietly for more directions.

"Read the labels that are written on each of the shapes. If we have grace, these things are easier for us to do. With grace, we have the self-discipline to act as images of God. Let's see now if you can put these shapes together to form the shape of a person."

Give the class five minutes to work with their shapes. You should work with your shapes, too, to show the students that what you have asked them to do can be done.

Ask the class: "Was anyone successful in forming a person out of the shapes?" (*Yes.*) "Why could you do it this time?" (*The shapes could be connected together.*)

"As each of you can see from this demonstration, the gift of grace is a very important part of our lives. Grace helps us to act as images of God with our whole person."

Part C

Application

Say to the class: "Please take your book and turn to page 207. This page has drawings of seven leaves. Notice that each leaf has the name of a sacrament printed on it. Now, remove this page from your book.

"Also, you will see that page 209 has a picture of a tree on it. Please remove this page from your book, too.

"On page 211 of your books, let's read about the seven sacraments that Jesus gave us."

Student Book, page 211

Before Jesus died on the cross, He knew what He was going to do. He knew that He was going to die on the cross to give us a chance to receive grace, God's life.

Jesus knew that without God's life, we would be easily tempted. Sometimes, we would not have the self-discipline to choose to do what is right for ourselves and others. We would say and do wrong things. We would be like the tree pictured on page 209. The tree is alive, but it isn't as alive as it should be, because it has no leaves. Without grace, we are still alive, but that is about all. We are not living as we should be, as images of God.

Because of Jesus' death on the cross, every human person is given the chance to receive grace. What a wonderful gift: the chance to receive God's life, to receive God's help in all that we think, do, and say, and to come closer to Him. Grace helps us to live as images of God.

There are seven special ways that we can receive grace. These seven special ways are called sacraments. A sacrament is a physical sign, given to us by Christ, in which we meet Christ and He gives us His grace. The seven sacraments are: Baptism, Confirmation, Holy Eucharist, Reconciliation, Matrimony, Holy Orders, and Anointing of the Sick.

In the sacrament of Baptism, God gives us His life, grace, for the first time. Grace washes away original sin, makes us members of the Church, and makes it possible for us to live someday with God in heaven.

Tell the class: "Cut out the leaf labeled 'Baptism' and glue it onto the tree."

In the sacrament of Confirmation, the Holy Spirit comes to us and makes it possible for us to love God and others in a grown-up way. The Holy Spirit gives us the strength to be more and more like Jesus and think, say, and do the things we should.

Tell the class: "Cut out the leaf labeled 'Confirmation' and glue it onto the tree."

In the sacrament of the Holy Eucharist, Jesus feeds us with His Body and Blood. He makes us one with Him and with each other. We know that Jesus returned His Father's love by dying on the cross. Jesus' sacrifice of love on the cross is presented again for us in the Holy Eucharist. In this sacrament, Jesus stays with us in the tabernacles in our churches.

Tell the class: "Cut out the leaf labeled 'Holy Eucharist' and glue it onto the tree."

In the sacrament of Reconciliation, our sins are forgiven. God's life becomes stronger in us. We are ready to do penance and to help others.

Tell the class: "Cut out the leaf labeled 'Reconciliation' and glue it onto the tree."

In the sacrament of Matrimony, a man and a woman promise to love and care for each other for the rest of their lives. They promise to act more and more like Jesus, in a loving and caring way.

Tell the class: "Cut out the leaf labeled 'Matrimony' and glue it onto the tree."

Student Book, page 213

In the sacrament of Holy Orders, a man is ordained a deacon, priest, or bishop. He can then act for Christ in a special way.

Tell the class: "Cut out the leaf labeled 'Holy Orders' and glue it onto the tree."

Student Book, page 213

In the sacrament of the Anointing of the Sick, through the anointing by the priest, Jesus gives comfort, strength, and peace to the sick, the elderly, and the dying.

Tell the class: "Cut out the leaf labeled 'Anointing of the Sick' and glue it onto the tree."

Student Book, page 213

When the tree has leaves, it is as alive as it can be. It is the same with us. With the grace we receive through the sacraments, we have the strength to live as we should, as images of God. We are as alive as we can be.

Student Book, page 214

Write the names of the sacraments underneath the descriptions that follow:

1. A man and a woman promise to love each other for the rest of their lives. (*Matrimony.*)
2. Jesus feeds us with His Body and Blood and makes us one with Him. (*Holy Eucharist.*)
3. A man is ordained and acts for Jesus in a special way. (*Holy Orders.*)
4. The priest blesses the sick, the elderly, and the dying, and Jesus gives comfort, strength, and peace. (*Anointing of the Sick.*)
5. God gives us His life for the first time and washes away original sin. (*Baptism.*)
6. The Holy Spirit gives us the strength to be more and more like Jesus. (*Confirmation.*)
7. Our sins are forgiven. God's life within us becomes stronger. (*Reconciliation.*)

Part D

Application

Say to the class: "As we know, because Jesus died on the cross, every human person is given the chance to receive grace. Grace is such a wonderful gift! It is God's life. It is God's help in all we think, do, and say. Grace helps us to be very close to God.

"We have just talked about the seven special ways in which we can receive grace. Those seven special ways are called the sacraments. A sacrament is a physical sign given to us by Christ so that we can meet Him and receive His grace."

There are other ways in which we can receive the gift of grace, too. We can receive grace through prayer, through sacrifices we make for others, through our helpful deeds, and through following the Ten Commandments.

When we pray, we turn our minds and hearts to God. We talk to Him, just as we would talk to a friend. But we should remember that God is more than a friend to us. He is our Creator, Savior, and Helper. When we talk to Him, we should always be respectful. We can show God how much we love and adore Him by praying special prayers that we know. We can also think of Him often during the day and talk to Him in our own way.

Write a short prayer to God, using your own words:

_____

_____

_____

When we make sacrifices, we are following Jesus. To "sacrifice" means going without something you like, or doing something that is hard for you to do, so that others are helped.

Jesus asks us to make some sacrifices. He showed us His sacrifice—His death on the cross. He shows us how to accept suffering and offer it to God the Father. By making sacrifices, we are strengthened by God's grace.

Living the Lesson

1. Whom do we follow when we make sacrifices? (*Jesus.*)
2. What is a sacrifice? (*Going without something you like, or doing something that is hard for you, so that others are helped.*)
3. Did Jesus tell us that sacrifices are important? (*Yes.*)
4. How did He show us His sacrifice? (*By dying on the cross.*)
5. Why should we want to sacrifice? (*So that God's life, grace, can be strengthened in us.*)
6. Think of a time when you made a sacrifice, and write your thoughts down. You can share these thoughts with the class.

Doing a kind or helpful deed is a way of showing that we are images of God. There are many things that we can do to show that we are images of God. We can do things at home for our family. We can do kind deeds at school for our teachers and classmates. We can do kind deeds for ourselves. We all are capable of doing some kind deed each and every day. Each kind deed strengthens God's life in us.

Under each of the following headings, write three ways in which you can be kind or helpful.

Home/Family	School	Yourself	Others
1.	1.	1.	1.
2.	2.	2.	2.
3.	3.	3.	3.

A long time ago, God appeared to Moses. God gave him the Ten Commandments. The commandments tell us how God acts and how we should act as images of God. If we follow the commandments, we will be acting as images of God. Following the commandments strengthens God's life in us.

With a partner, look up the Ten Commandments and explain them in your own words.

Part E

Application

Say to the class: "Jesus died on the cross so that everybody could have the chance to receive grace. Jesus did not pick only blonds, or only redheads, or only boys, or only fast runners, or only math wizards, or only teachers to receive His life. He made it possible for everybody to receive grace.

"Please remove page 219 from your book. This page has a paper-doll figure. You can make this figure look like a person of any age and occupation and from any country. Remember, Jesus came for every person. He gives us all a chance to receive His life, grace.

"When you are finished drawing and coloring, cut out your paper-doll figure and bring it to the front of the room."

Note to teachers: Tape the paper dolls around the room, joining them at the hands.

Say: "Jesus wants all people to share in His life of grace. Zacchaeus was a person who wanted the chance to receive grace. But because he was a rich tax-collector, nobody wanted to help him." (*Explain that a tax collector collects money from the people for the government.*) "Let's read about what happened to him when he got the chance to meet Jesus. Please open your books to page 221."

Zacchaeus, a rich tax-collector who lived in the town of Jericho, was not a popular man. He always seemed to be collecting money from the people, and they wanted nothing to do with him.

One day, Jesus was passing through Jericho. Zacchaeus heard that Jesus had come to town. He wanted to meet Jesus very much—but so did everybody else. The streets of the town were very crowded, and Zacchaeus was too short to see anything.

He suddenly had a wonderful idea: he climbed a nearby tree and waited for Jesus to pass by.

When Jesus came near the tree that Zacchaeus had climbed, Jesus looked up and said to him, "Zacchaeus, come down quickly, for today I must stay at your house."

Zacchaeus was so happy, but all of the other townspeople complained. They said that Jesus was going to the house of a sinner.

But Zacchaeus promised to give half of what he owned to the poor and to pay back four times what he owed to the people he had cheated.

Jesus then said, "Today salvation has come to this house. The Son of Man has come to seek and to save what was lost."

—Adapted from Luke 19:1–10

Jesus went to the house of Zacchaeus to help save him. Jesus wanted Zacchaeus to have a chance to share in God's life, grace. We are all constantly being called to share in God's life, grace. We can answer that call by celebrating the sacraments frequently, by praying, by offering sacrifices, by doing kind and helpful deeds, and by following the Ten Commandments.

21

The Seven Ways the Church Celebrates: The Sacraments

1. Lesson Focus

When Jesus came to earth He showed us who we are and how we should act. Jesus returned the Father's love by dying on the cross, and He helps us to return the Father's love by giving us grace.

While on earth, Jesus did many wonderful things for the people who came to Him. He taught in parables, performed miracles, forgave sins, and spoke words of peace. But He performed the greatest of all His work when He died on the cross and rose to new life.

Today, Jesus is still at work in the world. He works through the Church. He continues to care for our spiritual needs by means of the seven sacraments that He gave the Church. The sacraments show us the love Jesus has for us and how we should love.

The sacraments are physical signs, given to us by Jesus, through which Jesus meets us and gives us grace. Through the sign of each sacrament Jesus speaks to us, looks at us, touches us, and loves us today.

There are seven sacraments: Baptism, Confirmation, Holy Eucharist, Reconciliation, Matrimony, Holy Orders, and Anointing of the Sick.

In each sacrament Jesus touches us. His touch helps us. He forgives sins. He gives us Himself and helps us to love as He loves. When Jesus loves through the sacraments, He gives us grace, His life. The grace we receive helps us to love Jesus and others. The sacraments put us in touch with Jesus' merciful love given to us on the cross.

Note to CCD teachers: Use all the Parts in class as time permits.

2. Concepts of Faith

Student Book, page 236

Things to Remember

What is a sacrament?
A physical sign, given to us by Jesus, through which Jesus meets us and gives us grace.

How many sacraments are there?
There are seven sacraments.

How does Jesus do His work in the world today?
Through the Church's teachings, sacraments, and other works of love.

---

3. Lesson Presentation

Part A

Student Book, page 223

VOCABULARY
Sacraments of Initiation: The sacraments of Baptism, Confirmation, and Holy Eucharist, which make us full members of the Catholic Church, believing in Jesus and His teachings.

Application

Say to the class: "Even though Jesus died on the cross some two thousand years ago, He is still at work in the world today. Jesus works through the Church. Jesus continues to care for our special needs through the seven sacraments that He gave to the Church. Let's open our books to page 223 and read about what a sacrament is."

Student Book, page 223

A sacrament is a physical sign, given to us by Jesus, through which Jesus meets us and gives us grace. Each sacrament is Jesus' special way of speaking to us, looking at us, touching us, and loving us in our lives today.

Each of the sacraments has a different physical sign. The physical sign is something we can see, touch, hear, taste, or smell. In each sacrament, Jesus touches us through the physical sign. His touch helps us. He forgives sins. He gives us Himself and helps us to love as He loves. When Jesus loves through the sacraments, He gives us grace. The grace we receive helps us to love Jesus and others. The sacraments put us in touch with Jesus' merciful love given to us on the cross.

There are seven special ways that Jesus speaks to us, looks at us, touches us, and loves us in our lives today. The seven sacraments are Baptism, Confirmation, Holy Eucharist, Reconciliation, Matrimony, Holy Orders, and Anointing of the Sick.

The sacraments can be divided into three different groups. The first group includes the three sacraments of Initiation. Baptism, Confirmation, and Holy Eucharist make up this group. Through these three sacraments we become full members of the Catholic Church, believing in Jesus and His teachings. We are called to love God and others as Jesus did. We are invited to worship in prayer and service. We celebrate Jesus' love.

In the second group are the sacrament of Reconciliation and the sacrament of the Anointing of the Sick. Both of these sacraments repair our relationship with God and draw us closer to Him. We can call these sacraments the sacraments of Healing. Through these two sacraments we ask God to bring us closer to Him and help us continue to believe and trust in Him.

The third group of sacraments includes Matrimony and Holy Orders. We can call these two sacraments the sacraments of Vocation. A vocation is a call from God to act as an image of God by loving others in a certain way. Through these two sacraments we answer God's call to the kind of life He asks us to follow.

We should remember that each time we receive one of the sacraments, God's life in us grows stronger. We grow closer to Jesus, and He makes us holier. The whole Church grows in holiness also and gives thanks to God.

Living the Lesson

1. When is Jesus at work? (*Today; all the time.*)
2. Into how many groups can we divide the sacraments? (*Three.*)
3. Name the groups and the sacraments in each group.

Initiation	**Healing**	**Vocation**
Baptism	*Reconciliation*	*Matrimony*
Confirmation	*Anointing of Sick*	*Holy Orders*
Holy Eucharist		

4. What happens each time we receive a sacrament? (*God's life in us grows stronger. We grow closer to Jesus, and He makes us holier.*)
5. What sacraments have you received? (*Baptism, Reconciliation, Holy Eucharist.*)

Note to teachers: The number of sacraments that each student has received may vary. Note which students have not received the sacraments customary for their age in your parish.

Part B

Application

Say to the class: "Before Jesus ascended into heaven, He said that everyone should have a chance to be baptized. He told His Apostles to go and baptize everyone."

Student Book, page 225

BAPTISM

We all need Baptism because of the first sin of Adam and Eve. All people (except Mary and Jesus) are born with original sin, without God's life, grace. Because of original sin, everyone finds it hard to do what is right all the time. All people need God's life, grace, to help them love God here on earth by following the Ten Commandments, and to live with Him someday in heaven.

In Baptism, water is poured on the person to be baptized while the priest or deacon says the name of the one to be baptized and then says, "I baptize you in the name of the Father, and of the Son, and of the Holy Spirit." The water and these words make up the sign of Baptism. When we are baptized we receive grace.

In Baptism, Jesus touches us and helps us, because He takes away original sin. When we are baptized, we receive grace. The grace of Baptism helps us because we no longer have original sin. The grace of Baptism makes us God's children and members of His family, the Church. The grace of Baptism also makes it possible for us to love God and others on earth and to live with Him someday in heaven. The sacraments put us in touch with Jesus' merciful love given to us on the cross.

Living the Lesson

Student Book, page 226

1. We listen to and read the Word of God from the _____.
2. The place in which we hope to share eternal life with God is _____.
3. The person who usually baptizes is a _____.
4. The liquid used to baptize is _____.
5. _____ sin is washed away when we are baptized.
6. The men Jesus told to go and baptize all people were the _____.
7. At Baptism, the priest or deacon asks the parents what _____ they have chosen for their child.

```
                    B   I   B   L   E
                H   E   A   V   E   N
                    P   R   I   E   S   T
            W   A   T   E   R
            O   R   I   G   I   N   A   L
        A   P   O   S   T   L   E   S
            N   A   M   E
```

Say to the class: "Read a story about your patron saint. How did your patron saint act like Jesus? Write a short report about your findings."

Part C

Application

Say to the class: "After Jesus ascended into heaven, He sent the Holy Spirit upon the Apostles at Pentecost. The Holy Spirit came to strengthen their faith and make them witnesses to Jesus. Let's read about how Jesus continues to send the Holy Spirit today."

Student Book, page 227

CONFIRMATION

Today Jesus continues to send the Holy Spirit. The Holy Spirit strengthens our faith and unites us more closely to the Church in the sacrament of Confirmation. The sacrament of Confirmation helps us love God, the Church, and others in a more grown-up way.

In the early Church, the Apostles celebrated the sacrament of Confirmation and gave the Holy Spirit to others. Before the Apostles died, they chose other men, called bishops, to continue their work. The sacrament of Confirmation is usually celebrated by a bishop.

The sign of Confirmation is the oil (chrism) and the words said by the bishop. The bishop lays his hands upon the head of the person receiving the sacrament. Then the bishop traces the shape of the cross on the person's forehead with an oil called chrism. As he does so, he says the name of the person and then the following words, "Be sealed with the Gift of the Holy Spirit." When he says these words, he means that the person is strengthened to witness to Jesus in a grown-up way. In Confirmation, the Holy Spirit gives people the grace to show by their words and actions that they are followers of Jesus.

When the bishop celebrates Confirmation, Jesus touches the person receiving the sacrament and gives the Holy Spirit to the person. He gives us Himself and helps us to love as He loves. When Jesus loves through the sacraments, He gives us grace, His life. The grace we receive in Confirmation helps us to love God and others in a more grown-up way. The sacraments puts us in touch with Jesus' merciful love given to us on the cross.

Living the Lesson

Student Book, page 228

You need not wait for the sacrament of Confirmation in order to be a witness to Jesus. All baptized people should show by their words and actions that they are followers of Jesus.

What are some ways in which you are a witness to Jesus? (*Answers will vary.*)

Part D

Application

175

Lesson 21
*The Seven Ways the Church
Celebrates: The Sacraments*

Student Book, page 229

HOLY EUCHARIST

Just as we need natural food every day to keep our lives healthy and strong, we also need spiritual food to keep God's life in us healthy and strong. Jesus gave us the sacrament of the Holy Eucharist for our spiritual food. The Eucharist is much greater than natural food. When we receive the Holy Eucharist we receive the risen Jesus. He feeds us with Himself. We become one with Him. We are united with all His people who share the same food.

We usually receive the sacrament of the Holy Eucharist for the first time when we are about eight years old. We call this our first Holy Communion. After our first Communion, we should receive this sacrament often. In the sacrament of the Holy Eucharist, the sign is the bread and wine and the words spoken by the priest over the bread and wine. At Mass, during the Consecration, the priest says the words of Jesus, "This is my body" over the bread, and "This is the cup of my blood" over the wine. The bread then becomes the Body of Jesus, and the wine becomes the Blood of Jesus. Through the Consecration of the bread and wine, Jesus' sacrifice on the cross is presented again. Jesus' Body and Blood become our food and drink. At Mass, we can receive Jesus in Holy Communion. Jesus loves us so much that He remains with us in the Holy Eucharist after Mass is over. We can visit Jesus in church. The consecrated Hosts are kept in the tabernacle.

The sacrament of the Holy Eucharist is the greatest of all the sacraments. When we are nourished by Jesus' Body and Blood, we become like Him. He fills us with His love so that we can be more concerned about others. He gives us the grace to help us forgive those who hurt us. His grace helps us to accept sufferings and to make sacrifices.

In this sacrament Jesus touches us. His touch helps us because, in this sacrament, Jesus' sacrifice on the cross is made present for us. His Body and Blood become our food and drink. Further, Jesus remains with us in the tabernacle. He gives us Himself and helps us to love as He loves. He gives us grace, His life. The grace given in the sacrament of the Holy Eucharist helps us live our lives each day as images of God. The sacraments put us in touch with Jesus' merciful love given to us on the cross.

Note to teachers: This would be a good time to take the children to the church and show them where the tabernacle is and where the Eucharist is kept. Pause a moment with the children and pray.

Part E

Application

Student Book, page 230

RECONCILIATION

Almost two thousand years ago, Jesus gave His life to save all people from sin. From the sufferings and death of Jesus we can see how terrible sin is.

The sins we commit hurt God, ourselves, and others. We commit a sin when we know something is wrong to do, and we choose to do it anyway. We know what is right, because God has given us the Ten Commandments. Sin can be committed by thoughts, words, and actions.

There are two types of sin: mortal sin and venial sin. Mortal sin hurts our relationship with God. When we commit a mortal sin, we turn completely away from God. God can help us feel sorry for a mortal sin, and it can be forgiven in the sacrament of Reconciliation. We cannot commit a mortal sin without knowing it. We commit a mortal sin when we do something seriously wrong, we know that it is seriously wrong, and we still go ahead and do it freely and willingly.

Venial sin hurts our relationship with God. It makes it harder for us to love God. It is still a sin, but it is not as serious as a mortal sin. Venial sin also can be forgiven in the sacrament of Reconciliation.

Jesus never sinned. As followers of Jesus we should try to avoid all sin. But if we should fail, Jesus will always forgive us. In the sacrament of Reconciliation, Jesus forgives all sins, mortal and venial, when we are truly sorry and promise to act as better images of God. We should try to receive this sacrament often.

The sign of the sacrament of Reconciliation is the sorrow we have when we say our sins to the priest and the words of forgiveness said by the priest. In this sacrament, Jesus touches us. His touch helps us. He forgives our sins. When Jesus loves through the sacraments, He gives us grace, His life. The grace we receive in the sacrament of Reconciliation helps us to love Jesus and others by helping us not to sin again. The sacraments put us in touch with Jesus' merciful love given to us on the cross.

Living the Lesson

1. When we commit sin, what happens? (*We hurt God, ourselves, and others.*)
2. How do we sin? (*We sin when we know something is wrong to do and choose to do it anyway.*)
3. What is a mortal sin? (*A mortal sin hurts our relationship with God. When we commit a mortal sin, we turn completely away from God.*)
4. When do we commit a mortal sin? (*We commit a mortal sin when we do something seriously wrong, we know it is wrong, and we freely and willingly choose to do it.*)
5. Can you think of any actions that would be seriously wrong? (*Accept any justifiable answers, such as murder and very deliberately missing Mass on Sundays.*)
6. What is a venial sin? (*It is a sin that hurts our relationship with God. It makes it harder for us to love God. It is not as serious as a mortal sin.*)
7. Can you think of any actions that would be classified as venial sins? (*Accept any justifiable answers.*)
8. As followers of Jesus, what should we try to do? (*Try to avoid all sin.*)
9. Do we all sin despite our best efforts? (*Yes.*)

10. What should we do if we sin? (*We should celebrate the sacrament of Reconciliation and receive God's forgiving love.*)
11. How often should we receive this sacrament? (*Often.*)

Part F

Application

Say to the class: "Jesus loved us so much that He gave up His life for us. It was through His death that He gave life to His Church. Jesus helps the baptized grow in His life and love. He wants all members of His Church to be happy and live with Him forever."

Student Book, page 231

MATRIMONY

Jesus loves us so much that He gave the Church the sacrament of Matrimony. In Matrimony, the bride and the groom say "yes" to marrying one another, "yes" to the promises they make to one another. The priest or deacon and two other people are witnesses to the promises the bride and groom make to each other and to God. The bride and groom promise to love and to care for each other for the rest of their lives—in good and bad times, in sickness and in health. Their love should remind people of the great love Jesus has for His Church.

When a man and a woman marry, they become a family. They try to make their love grow. Often their family grows to include children. Children are the greatest gift God gives to married couples. The child should be a reminder to the parents of their love for each other and God's love for both of them. Also, the parents' love for each other shows the child God's love.

In the sacrament of Matrimony, Jesus touches the bride and groom. His touch helps them because it makes it possible for them to love each other the way Jesus loves us. He gives them Himself and helps them to love as He loves. When Jesus loves through the sacraments, He gives us grace, His life. The grace received in the sacrament of Matrimony makes a man and a woman a family. The sacraments put us in touch with Jesus' merciful love given to us on the cross.

Living the Lesson

Invite to your class a couple who have been married a long time. Ask them to discuss what the sacrament of Matrimony means to them.

Part G

Application

HOLY ORDERS

When Jesus lived on earth, He loved the people, taught them, and forgave their sins. At the Last Supper, Jesus celebrated the Holy Eucharist. We remember that Jesus asked His Apostles to carry on His work in a special way. Before the Apostles died, they ordained other men as deacons, priests, and bishops to carry on the work of Jesus. Today this ordination occurs through the sacrament of Holy Orders.

God calls some men to serve Him and to carry on the work of Jesus as deacons, priests, or bishops. After a man is prepared and approved by the Church, he is ordained. He is touched by Jesus in the sacrament of Holy Orders.

The man who is ordained as a deacon receives graces that make him able to celebrate some sacraments (baptisms and witnessing marriages) and to do works of love and charity. Through his works of love and charity, the deacon helps us to know how to love God and others.

The man who is ordained as a priest has already received the sacrament of Holy Orders once, when he became a deacon. When he is ordained as a priest, he receives the graces that make him able to celebrate all of the sacraments except the sacrament of Holy Orders. The ordained priest acts in the Person of Christ. He proclaims the Word of God and celebrates the Eucharist. He forgives sin and comforts the sick. He receives new members into the Church community. He belongs to the ordained priesthood.

The man who is ordained as a bishop has already received the sacrament of Holy Orders twice, when he became a deacon and when he became a priest. When he is ordained as a bishop, he receives the sacrament of Holy Orders again, in a special way. Through his ordination as a bishop, he is able to celebrate all of the sacraments and to teach as the Apostles taught.

The sacrament of Holy Orders is celebrated by a bishop. The bishop ordains men to carry on the work of Jesus in a specific way. The sign of the sacrament of Holy Orders is the bishop laying his hands upon the head of the man receiving the sacrament and the prayer the bishop says as he does this.

In this sacrament Jesus touches the ordained. His touch helps them because they can carry on His work in a special way. He gives them Himself and helps them to love as He loves. When Jesus loves through the sacraments, He gives us grace, His life. The grace received in Holy Orders helps the ordained man to love Jesus and all members of the Church. The sacraments put us in touch with Jesus' merciful love given to us on the cross.

Living the Lesson

Invite a deacon, priest, or bishop to come and talk to the class about the preparation that he made to be ordained. Before he comes, have the students write down questions that they would like him to answer.

Application

THE ANOINTING OF THE SICK

Jesus loves all people. Through His healing touch, Jesus cured many people when He was on earth. Today people get sick, suffer, and die. Sickness and suffering are a mystery. If Jesus does not cure the sick people of today, He helps them accept their sickness or suffering in the way He accepted His Cross. Even the greatest sufferings can be tolerated when we compare them with the good that is waiting for us in heaven.

When people are very ill, or when elderly people are not in good health, the Church brings Christ's love and support to them in the sacrament of the Anointing of the Sick. Those who receive the sacrament ask for Jesus' comfort. This sacrament helps them to accept their sickness and suffering as Jesus accepted His Cross. It also gives sick people the strength to offer these sufferings to God.

The sacrament of the Anointing of the Sick may be celebrated in a person's home, in a church, in a hospital, or in a nursing home. It can be celebrated during Mass. People may be anointed more than once during their lives. The sign of the sacrament of the Anointing of the Sick is the prayer the priest says and the oil with which he anoints the forehead and hands of a person. In this sacrament, Jesus touches the person, forgives the person's sins, and draws the person closer to God. Sometimes Jesus restores sick and suffering people to health through the sacrament of the Anointing of the Sick.

In this sacrament Jesus touches us. His touch helps us to accept sickness or suffering the way He accepted His Cross. He gives us Himself and helps us to love as He loves. When Jesus loves through the sacraments, He gives us grace, His life. The grace we receive in the sacrament of the Anointing of the Sick helps us to offer our sufferings to God. The sacraments put us in touch with Jesus' merciful love given to us on the Cross.

Living the Lesson (Review)

Although we cannot celebrate the sacrament of the Anointing of the Sick for others, we can do our part to comfort the sick and suffering people. We can do kind and helpful deeds, or we can just listen to what they have to tell us.

As a class, plan to visit a nursing home and spend some time with the people there.

Name That Sacrament

1. The sacrament that joins a man and a woman who promise to love and care for each other for their entire lives.
   The sacrament of _____ (*Matrimony*).

2. The sacrament that cleanses us from original sin, gives us a share in God's life of grace, and makes us members of the Church.
   The sacrament of _____ (*Baptism*).

3. The sacrament in which Jesus forgives our sins. This sacrament brings us closer to God.
   The sacrament of _____ (*Reconciliation*).

4. The sacrament by which the Holy Spirit helps us to love God, the Church, and others in a more grown-up way.
   The sacrament of _____ (*Confirmation*).

5. This is the greatest sacrament because it is the risen Jesus. He feeds us and unites us with Himself and one another.
   The sacrament of _____ (*the Holy Eucharist*).

6. The sacrament that helps people accept their sickness and suffering and offers Jesus' comfort.
   The sacrament of _____ (*the Anointing of the Sick*).

7. The sacrament that makes a man an ordained deacon, priest, or bishop so that he can act for Jesus in a special way.
   The sacrament of _____ (*Holy Orders*).

22

Review of Units 1–5

1. Lesson Focus

The students have learned so much this year! To help them retain what they have learned, this chapter reviews units 1 through 5 using exciting games and activities. If the students have any related questions or concerns, please refer to the unit and lessons being reviewed.

Note to CCD teachers: Use all the Parts in class; or, if that is not possible, send home as family projects whatever Parts were not used in class.

2. Lesson Presentation

Part A—Unit 1

Materials needed: 1 clean coffee can; 3″ x 5″ index cards—one for each student.

Note to teachers: Print the letter "A" on half of the index cards, and "B" on the other half. Place the cards in a clean, empty coffee can for the drawing. Read the directions for playing the game that follows *before* starting the lesson.

The "baseball game" activity can be played inside the classroom or outdoors. If the game is played outdoors, you may choose to let the students run to their bases instead of walking.

You will notice that this game is different from regulation baseball. Instead of having one team "up to bat" and then the other, the members of Team A and Team B take turns. Instead of hitting a ball with a bat, players answer questions. A question answered incorrectly is a "strike". Three strikes make an out.

First, decide where first base, second base, third base, and home plate will be. Then divide the class into two teams by having them draw the index cards from the coffee can. Line the teams up in two separate rows behind or near home plate. Assign a "run counter" for each team. Show the class where the bases are located.

Ask one player from Team A a question. If the player gives a correct answer, he or she moves to first base. If the answer is incorrect, the player moves to the end of the Team A line, and the question is repeated for the player at the head of the Team B line. If the player from Team B answers the question correctly, that player moves to first base; if incorrectly, that player goes to the end of line, and the question is again repeated for the next player on Team A. If four players fail to answer a question correctly, give the correct answer and ask a new question.

It is possible for a player from both teams to be on the same base at the same time. But two players from the *same* team cannot be on the same base at the same time. Players advance as subsequent players from their own team answer questions correctly. You continue to ask questions until one of the teams has 9 strikes (3 outs) and the game ends. The team with the most runs wins.

Application

Say to the class: "We come to know God by studying the things He has made, by reading Bible stories about Him, and by listening to what the Church teaches. When we study, we could say that we 'cover all the bases', that we learn everything we can about God and ourselves.

"To help us remember everything we can about what we have learned in Unit One, we are going to play a baseball game. First, I am going to divide the class into two teams."

Have each student draw a card from the coffee can. Ask the students to sit on the floor, one behind the other, in two straight lines. They should sit behind or near home plate, in the order in which they have selected the team they are on. Team A is in one line, Team B in the other. Tell the students where first base, second base, third base, and home plate are located.

Then say to the class: "I am going to ask the first player from Team A, [student's name], a question. *N* should stand. If *N* can answer the question correctly, he [she] can *walk* to first base. If *N* misses the question, the miss will be called a strike, and he [she] will sit down at the end of the Team A line.

"Then I will ask the first player from Team B, [student's name], a question. With a correct answer, *N* can *walk* to first base. Again, a miss will be called a strike, and *N* will sit down at the end of the Team B line. Notice that there can be two players from different teams on the same base. That's okay in this game! Remember to keep with you the card that says what team you are on.

"Now, if there is a player from Team A on first base and another player from the same team answers a question correctly, the player on first base goes to second base and the other player walks to first base. And so on, all around the bases. When a player gets to home plate in this way, a run is scored.

"The game ends when one of the teams has nine strikes, or three outs. Then we add up the runs for each team. The team with the most runs is the winner. Are there any questions before we begin? . . . Then let's start."

Note to teachers: When the game is over, collect the index cards. You will use them again for the other team games.

Questions for the "Baseball Game"

What does the word *mystery* mean? (*A truth that our minds cannot completely understand.*)

Why is God a mystery to us? (*We cannot completely understand God.*)

How do we learn about God? (*By studying the things He has made, by reading Bible stories about Him, and by listening to what the Church teaches.*)

Did God create the world the way we create things? (*No. God created the world from nothing.*)

What kind of being created the world? (*A wise, powerful, truthful, loving, living being.*)

Who made God? (*No one. He was, is, and always will be.*)

How do we know that God is living? (*It takes a living being to create living things.*)

How can we thank God for everything that He has given us? (*By taking care of the things God has made; by loving and praising Him.*)

Long ago, people did not have radio, TV, newspapers, or telephones. How did they share special events with others? (*They passed them from one person to another through stories.*)

What is the purpose of the Bible? (*The Bible is the collection of books in which God speaks to us and tells us about Himself.*)

What is the Blessed Trinity? (*Three Persons in one God.*)

How can we think of each Person of the Blessed Trinity? (*We can think of God the Father as Creator; we can think of God the Son as Teacher and Savior; and we can think of God the Holy Spirit as Helper.*)

Why do we say that God the Father is powerful? (*He created the world out of nothing.*)

The first man, Adam, was special. Why? (*He was a person, an image of God. He could share God's life. He could think, love, and work.*)

Adam and Eve loved each other as God's images. They formed the first what? (*Family.*)

Who is the second Person of the Blessed Trinity? (*God the Son.*)

Why did God the Son become man? (*To show us who we are and how we should act, to return God's love, and to help us return God's love.*)

What does Jesus teach us and show us about ourselves? (*That we are images of God.*)

How did Jesus free us from sin and return the Father's love? (*By dying on the cross.*)

How does God the Holy Spirit help us? (*Through grace given in the sacraments.*)

What is grace? (*God's life.*)

What does grace help us to do? (*Grace helps us to act as images of God.*)

When you were baptized, what family did you join? (*God's family.*)

As members of God's family, what do we do together? (*We work together, love each other, and help each other to love as God loves.*)

Part B—Unit 2

Materials needed:
    Clean coffee can.
    A 3″ x 5″ index card for each student (half marked "A", half marked "B").
    Slips of paper with questions on them for the "Climbing the Ladder of Grace" activity
        (see Appendix).
    Masking tape.

Note to teachers: Place the slips of paper with questions on them face down on a table in front of a blackboard. Read the following explanation of the game *before* starting this activity.

Shuffle the index cards and place them in the coffee can. Students draw cards to divide the class into two teams, A and B. Print a large "A" and "B" about two feet apart at the top of the blackboard. Have the students sit in two lines or rows near the blackboard.

The object of this game is to build the tallest "ladder" of correctly answered questions. The first player from Team A picks up a slip of paper from the desk or table and reads the question to the first player from Team B. If the Team B player answers correctly, she tapes the slip of paper to the bottom of the blackboard under the letter B. She then picks up another slip of paper and asks the first player from Team A the question written on it. If this player cannot answer or answers incorrectly, the slip is placed face down on the table again. The two players go to the end of their respective lines.

In other words, the teams alternate in choosing a slip of paper and asking the question. When a question is answered correctly, the slip is taped to the blackboard in the answerer's column. As slips are added to a column, a ladder is formed. When a question is answered incorrectly, the slip is returned to the table. When all questions have been asked, the team with the most slips (or "rungs") in their ladder is the winner.

Application

Say to the class: "As we climb the ladder of life, we occasionally slip and miss a step. We make a wrong choice.

"But because we are images of God with minds and free wills, we have the power to change our minds. We can *think* about what Jesus would do and then *choose* to change our actions. Acting as Jesus would act makes us better images of God. As better images of God, we move up the ladder of God's Kingdom. God's life in us is strengthened.

"To help us remember what we have learned in Unit Two, we are going to play a game called 'The Ladder of Grace'. First, I am going to divide the class into two teams."

Divide the class, using the index cards in the coffee can. Ask the students to pick a card and keep it with them. Have each team line up in a column near the blackboard. When the students are settled, give them the directions for the game.

Say: "In this game there are slips of paper with questions printed on them. I have placed the slips face down on this table. When the game starts, the first player from Team A will come to the table and choose one slip, and then read the question on it to the first player from Team B. If the player from Team B answers the question correctly, he tapes the slip of paper to the blackboard. Each slip of paper is like a rung of a ladder. The object of the game is for each team to get as many correct answers as possible so that they can build the tallest ladder. If a player answers incorrectly, the slip of paper is placed face down on the table again. The first two players then go to the end of the line, and the next two players have their turn. Each team will take turns in drawing a question to ask the other team. When all the questions have been asked, the team with the most "rungs" on their ladder will be the winner. If there is a tie, I will ask tie-breaker questions.

"Do you have any questions before we begin the game? . . . Then let's begin."

Questions for Climbing "The Ladder of Grace"

Who are we? (*Images of God.*)

What abilities do persons have that animals do not have? (*Thinking and freely choosing.*)

What makes persons different from each other? (*Looks, things they do, choices they make.*)

What do all persons have in common? (*The ability to think and to choose freely.*)

What power do we use to think about and remember what Jesus taught us? (*The power of our mind.*)

What did Jesus tell us about when He was on earth? (*Ourselves, God, others, and the world.*)

How should we live our lives? (*As followers of Jesus.*)

Why can we choose? (*God has given us a free will.*)

Whom do we count on to help us make decisions? (*Jesus.*)

What are three things we should do when we have an important decision to make? (*Listen, think, and pray.*)

How do we know what choices to make? (*Follow the example of Jesus.*)

Once we make a choice, do we have to stay with that choice? (*No, we can change our choice.*)

What is the question that we should be asking ourselves when we make a choice? (*Would Jesus do this?*)

What gives us the strength to listen and make right choices? (*Grace.*)

Who made us, body and soul? (*God.*)

How will God help us? (*He gives us grace.*)

What is dignity? (*Being worthy of respect.*)

Who has dignity? (*All persons.*)

Why do we have dignity? (*We are images of God.*)

When we do not act as images of God, do we lose our dignity? (*No. We still have it, but it is not so clearly seen.*)

Note to teachers: Use questions from Unit 1 as tie-breakers.

Part C—Unit 3

Application

Say to the class: "Let's open our books to page 237 and review Unit Three, 'Acting as Images of God'."

We learned in Unit 3 that God gave Moses the Ten Commandments on Mount Sinai. The Ten Commandments tell us how God acts and how we should act as images of God.

In the activity below, match the letter in front of the phrase to the rest of the sentence. On the blank line, write the letter of the matching phrase that you choose.

The first three commandments tell us (D) *about God and how we should love Him.*

I am the Lord, your God. (A) *You will not have other gods besides Me.*

In the first commandment, God is asking us (B) *to love and worship only Him.*

You will not take the name (C) *of the Lord your God in vain.*

The second commandment tells us that we should not (E) *use God's name in a wrong way.*

Remember to keep holy (F) *the Sabbath Day.*

The third commandment tells us (L) *to give Sundays and holy days to God.*

The last seven commandments tell us (J) *how to love ourselves and others the way God loves us and others.*

Honor your (K) *Father and your Mother.*

The fourth commandment asks (G) *loving parents to care for their children and loving children to obey their parents.*

The fifth commandment says: You will not (H) *kill.*

We follow the fifth commandment by (I) *taking care of our own bodies and not hurting others.*

You will not commit (N) *adultery.*

The sixth commandment asks us to (O) *make promises we can keep and to respect the dignity of other persons' bodies.*

The seventh commandment says: You will not (T) *steal.*

The seventh commandment asks us not to (S) *take something that belongs to someone else or damage the property of others.*

You will not bear (V) *false witness against your neighbor.*

The eighth commandment tells us that (R) *as images of God, we should tell the truth.*

You will not covet (M) *your neighbor's wife.*

The ninth commandment asks us to (Q) *respect the freedom of others and not think of them as objects to be owned.*

You will not covet anything that belongs (P) *to your neighbor.*

The tenth commandment tells us that we should (U) *be satisfied with what we own.*

Part D—Unit 4

Materials needed:
   Two flat-bottomed lunch bags.
   Masking tape.
   Twenty-two 3″ x 5″ index cards.

Note to teachers: Write "Team A" on one paper bag, "Team B" on the other. Put ten cards in the Team A bag: eight marked with an X, one with a heart, and one with the word "Oops". Put ten cards in the Team B bag: eight marked with a zero (0), one with a heart, and one with the word "Oops". Also, make two extra "Oops" cards, but do not put them in the bags at this time.

Place the bags, the two extra "Oops" cards, and a roll of masking tape on a table in the front of the class. Draw a large tic-tac-toe diagram on the blackboard. Then divide the class into two teams, as before.

Ask a student from each team, one at a time and alternating, a question. If the question is answered correctly, the student can reach into the bag marked with her team name and pull out a card. If the card is an X or 0, she can tape it in one of the squares of the tic-tac-toe diagram. If the card is a heart, the player can put the heart card back in the bag and try again for a letter card. If the card drawn says "Oops", the player puts the card back into the bag and loses a turn. The team that gets a tic-tac-toe string is the winner.

Application

Say to the class: "We learned about Jesus in Unit Four. He knew that He was God the Son. He had the power to do everything the easy way. Instead, He chose to use His talents as a teacher and patiently teach us the truth.

"Jesus patiently teaches us the truth even when we stumble and make the same mistakes. To help us remember what we have learned, we are going to play a game called 'Oops'.

"First, I am going to divide the class into teams." (*Shuffle the index cards, and have students draw a card to form teams. After the teams are arranged as you prefer, collect the cards for use in other activities.*)

Say: "Notice the two paper bags on the table here. One is labeled 'Team A', the other is labeled 'Team B'. Each bag has ten cards in it. Eight of the cards in the Team A bag have an X on them, one has a heart, and one has the word 'Oops'. Eight of the cards in the Team B bag have a zero on them, one has a heart, and one has the word 'Oops'.

"This game is similar to tic-tac-toe. I will ask each player a question. If the question is answered correctly, the player can reach into her team's bag and draw out a card. If the card has an X or a zero, the player can tape the card onto the tic-tac-toe diagram on the blackboard. If the player draws a card with a heart on it, he can put the card back in the bag and draw another card. But if the player draws out the 'Oops' card, he has to place it back in the bag and he loses his turn. Whichever team gets the first tic-tac-toe string is the winner."

If some of the students did not get a chance to answer a question, play the game again. This time, add an extra "Oops" card to each bag.

Questions for the "Oops" Game

Because of this, it is difficult for us to know who we are and how we should act. (*Original sin.*)

Original sin damaged three things. What are they? (*Minds, wills, and bodies.*)

Original sin made it impossible for us to do what? (*Return the love that God has for us.*)

Why did Jesus come to earth? (*To show us who we are, how we should act, to return God's love, and to help us to return God's love.*)

How can we follow the example of Jesus to act lovingly toward others? (*By using our talents and abilities.*)

How did Jesus show us who we are, how we should act, and how to return God's love, and help us to return God's love? (*By teaching, loving, and doing things for others.*)

How did Jesus use His talents to benefit others? (*Performed miracles.*)

What is a miracle? (*An act that shows the power of God, that helps people have faith in what Jesus taught, and that helps them to follow Him.*)

Why did Jesus perform miracles? (*To show His love for others.*)

How did people know that Jesus loved them? (*By what He said and did.*)

How does Jesus teach us? (*Through short stories called parables.*)

What do parables help us understand? (*The truth about God and ourselves.*)

With the light of Jesus, what can we see? (*The truth about God and about ourselves.*)

Jesus was a wonderful what? (*Teacher.*)

What has Mother Teresa done to show others that she believed we should treat others as images of God? (*She has shared her love and helped all people in need whenever she could.*)

What does it mean to be humble? (*To remember that we are all images of God. One person is not more important than another.*)

How can we show others that we believe the truths that Jesus teaches us? (*By using our talents, by acting as images of God, and by recognizing that other people are images of God, too.*)

Part E—Unit 5

Materials needed:

Clean coffee can, with cards for both A and B teams in it.

Cards for "bowling ball" and "bowling pins" (see Appendix for pattern). Teacher will have to duplicate and prepare these cards ahead of time.

Note to teachers: In the game that follows, make sure you use "bowling pins" with answers to match the questions on the "bowling balls" that you choose!

With the class divided into two teams as before, Team A will *sit* on one side of the classroom, and Team B will *stand* on the other side. (It is not necessary to move desks.) Give a "bowling ball" card to each player on Team A (sitting), a "bowling pin" card to each player on Team B (standing). The first player on Team A reads the question on his card, then chooses a player on Team B. The team player reads the answer on her card. If the answer and the question "match", Team A gets one point and the Team B player sits down. If the answer does not match the question, Team B gets one point and the Team B player remains standing.

After all of the questions have been asked, collect the "bowling ball" cards and "bowling pin" cards. Shuffle them. Then give the "bowling ball" cards to Team B and the other cards to Team A. Team B can sit down, while Team A stands. Continue the game as before. After all the questions have been asked again, total the points. The team with the most points wins.

Application

Say to the class: "Jesus asked the Apostles to carry on His work in a special way. The Apostles, in turn, ordained other men and made them deacons, priests, and bishops so that they too could carry on Jesus' work.

"The Catholic Church is the baptized members working together with deacons, priests, bishops, and the Pope.

"God's family is very large. It includes our immediate family, our parish, the diocese, and Catholic people all over the world. All the Catholic people form the universal Church. Together we can continue the work of Jesus.

"Like the Apostles, the Pope and the bishops in union with him teach us the things that Jesus taught through the parables, help us celebrate the sacraments and receive God's life, and show us how to use our talents to benefit others.

"Today, we are going to play a game called 'Bowling for Ways to Benefit Others'. We are going to form two teams again, Team A and Team B." (*After teams are formed by drawing cards, show Team A where to sit and Team B where to stand.*) "Each player on Team A is going to receive a 'bowling ball' card, with a question written on it. Each player on Team B is going to receive a 'bowling pin' card, with an answer written on it." (*Pass out the cards.*)

"The first player from Team A will read the question on her 'bowling ball' card; then she will choose a player on the B Team, who will read the answer on his 'bowling pin' card. If the answer matches the question, Team A gets one point, and the player from the B Team has to sit down. If the answer does not match the question, Team B gets the point and the player from Team B remains standing.

"After all the questions have been asked, I will collect all the cards, shuffle them, and then give the 'bowling ball' cards to Team B and the 'bowling pin' cards to Team A. Team B will sit down and Team A will stand. The game will continue until the questions have been asked a second time. I will keep score; and whichever team has the most points will win."

Questions for "Bowling for Ways to Benefit Others"

What did Jesus command the Apostles to do? (*To teach all people the things He had taught them through the parables, to help all people celebrate the sacraments and receive God's life, and to show all people how to use their talents to benefit others.*)

Who does the work of the Church today? (*The Pope, bishops, priests, and all members of the Church.*)

Where do we begin to help others? (*Within our own families.*)

How do we serve others within our own families? (*By having the courage to use our own talents and abilities to help whenever possible.*)

When Jesus was on earth, how did He help the sick and needy? (*By performing miracles.*)

What do the bishops and the members of the diocese do to benefit others by meeting their physical and material needs? (*The bishop and the talented people who work for him help others who need guidance, food, clothing, and shelter.*)

What do parishes do to meet the physical and material needs of others? (*Priests and deacons show parishioners how to use their talents to benefit others. Parishioners clean and prepare the church, assist before and during Mass, donate food, clothing, shelter, time, and money to care for the health and happiness of others.*)

How does the Pope know when there are problems that need his help in the parishes around the world? (*He has meetings in Rome with the bishops, sends letters to other bishops around the world, leads helpful organizations, and travels around the world.*)

Although Adam and Eve did not return God's love, what did God continue to do? (*God continued to love and care for them, but the love between Adam and Eve and God was weakened.*)

What did Jesus do to repair our relationship with God? (*Died on the cross.*)

Jesus' death on the cross was the greatest of all loves. Why? (*He did the Father's will and gave us a chance to share in God's life, grace.*)

What is grace? (*God's life.*)

What does grace do for us? (*Grace enlightens our minds, strengthens our wills, and helps us to use self-discipline in the things we think, do, and say. It enables us to live forever in heaven with God.*)

In which sacrament do a man and woman promise to love and care for each other for the rest of their lives? (*Matrimony.*)

Jesus feeds us with His Body and Blood and makes us one with Him in which sacrament? (*The Holy Eucharist.*)

In which sacrament does the priest bless the sick, the elderly, and the dying? (*The sacrament of the Anointing of the Sick.*)

In which sacrament does God give us His life for the first time? (*Baptism.*)

In which sacrament does the Holy Spirit give us the strength to love God in a more grown-up way? (*Confirmation.*)

We tell our sins to the priest and receive Jesus' forgiveness in which sacrament? (*Reconciliation.*)

A man is ordained a priest in which sacrament? (*Holy Orders.*)

How does Jesus do His work today? (*Through the teachings of the Church, the sacraments, and other works of love done by the Church.*)

What is a sacrament? (*A physical sign, given to us by Jesus, through which Jesus meets us and gives us His grace.*)

How many sacraments are there? (*Seven.*)

What happens each time we receive a sacrament? (*God's life in us grows stronger.*)

Unit 6

LITURGICAL SEASONS AND HOLIDAYS

23

Advent: Waiting for Jesus

1. Lesson Focus

God loved Adam and Eve very much. They did not return His love. They disobeyed Him. God was offended by what they had done. Their sin caused all people to lose God's life. But God promised to send a Savior. The Savior would return God's love and give everyone the chance to share God's life. It was thousands of years after Adam and Eve that the promised Savior came.

In the meantime, the people who came after Adam and Eve continued to disobey God. These people did not want His love! Because they rejected God's love and care, a flood destroyed the world and everything in it except Noah, his family, and two of every creature. God promised Noah that a flood would never again destroy the earth and the people on it.

Later, God promised Abraham, Isaac, Jacob, Joseph's brothers, and Moses that He would take their descendants to a new land. The new land would give God's people a fresh start. God would help them with this new beginning by giving them the Ten Commandments.

Years passed. A prophet by the name of Samuel was born. When he became an adult, he was chosen to select a new king.

Samuel anointed the shepherd boy David. God promised David that, from his family, the Savior would be born. The Savior, God the Son (Jesus), was born in a stable one thousand years after the time of King David. His first visitors were shepherds.

Jesus was a shepherd, too. But not the kind of shepherd who guards sheep. Jesus loves, guides, and cares for the people who follow Him. He returned God's love and helps us return God's love by giving us a share in God's life, grace.

Note to CCD teachers: Use all the Parts in class. If that is not possible, send home as family projects whatever Parts were not completed in class.

2. Concepts of Faith

Things to Remember

Student Book, page 255

Who was born one thousand years after King David?
Jesus.

---

3. Lesson Presentation

Part A

Student Book, page 240

VOCABULARY
Savior: Jesus Christ, the second Person of the Blessed Trinity, Who became man.
family tree: A list of family members in order of birth that, when finished, looks
    like a tree.
generation: A group of family members who are about the same age.
diagram: Drawing or chart that explains something.

Materials needed: 3″ x 5″ index cards; masking tape.

Note to teachers: Draw a diagram of the Johnson family tree on the blackboard before
class. You can use 3″ x 5″ cards to make a set of "family tree" cards using the names given
on page 243 of the students' books. Use ink colors to match the colors shown there, or
color the cards themselves.

Application

Student Book, page 241

When Adam and Eve sinned, they lost the close friendship they had had with God.
They also hurt their minds, wills, and bodies. God still loved them. But because
they had said "no" to God's love and care, they could not live in the Garden of Eden.

Life was difficult out of the Garden. They had to find food and shelter for themselves
and for their children.

Because He loved them so much, God promised Adam and Eve that He would send
a Savior someday to return God's love and help them return God's love.

Thousands of years passed before the Savior, Jesus Christ, was born to the family
of David.

The family of David was huge! After David, many generations passed before Jesus
came. The Jesse Tree helps us understand when Jesus came and why He came. The
Jesse Tree is a family tree. It includes the names of people from various generations
of Jesus' family on earth. Most of these people lived a long time before Jesus did.

Ask the class, "Before we study the 'Jesse Tree', can anyone tell me what a generation
is?" (*A group of family members who are about the same age.*)

Say to the class, "To help us understand what a generation is, let's read the story 'A Boy Named Jimmy Johnson'. Please open your books to page 242."

A BOY NAMED JIMMY JOHNSON

Every Christmas, all of Jimmy Johnson's relatives celebrate at his house. When everyone has finished eating dinner, Jimmy and his cousins get to do the dishes.

"Mom, we can't possibly be related to all of these people!" said Jimmy. "They must have come to our house because they knew I had to do the dishes."

"Jimmy," said Mom, "Everyone here is related to a Johnson in some way."

"Can you prove it?" asked Jimmy.

"Sure", said Mom. "Stop washing, come over to the table, and sit down. I'll show you."

"This diagram shows part of my family tree", said Mom. "This is my mom and this is my dad."

Place the blue cards with the parents' names on them in the appropriate spots on the blackboard.

"Hey!" said Jimmy. "That's Grandma and Grandpa!"

"You are right!" said Mom. "Now, here I am, and here are my brothers and sisters."

Place the yellow cards in the appropriate spots on the blackboard.

"Some of us are married. These are our spouses. We form one generation because we are all close to the same age."

Again, place yellow cards in the appropriate spots on the blackboard.

"You and my brothers' and sisters' children are from a different generation", said Mom.

Place the red cards in the appropriate spots on the blackboard.

> **Student Book, page 242**
>
> "Can you name someone from your generation, Jimmy?" asked Mom.
>
> "Sure," said Jimmy, "Ann Marie."
>
> "That's right!" said Mom.

Ask the class, "Can you name someone else in Jimmy's generation?" (*Any of the fifteen names in red.*)

> **Student Book, page 242**
>
> "Now count all of the people, Jimmy", said Mom.
>
> "Wow! Thirty! No wonder we have so many dishes to do!" said Jimmy.
>
> By looking at some of Jimmy's family, you can see how large families can get. The Jesse Tree shows us only a part of Jesus' family here on earth. The Jesse Tree gives you some idea of how long people waited for the Savior to come—many, many, many years!

Living the Lesson

1. What is a family tree? (*A list of family members in order of birth. When the list is finished, it looks like a tree and its branches.*)
2. What family tree tells us about Jesus' family on earth? (*The Jesse Tree.*)
3. Who is Jesus Christ? (*God the Son, the Savior.*)

Part B

Materials needed: Jesse Tree and symbol—an apple with a snake wrapped around it (see the Appendix); masking tape.

Note to teachers: Remove the Jesse Tree and the symbols from the Appendix ahead of time. Tape the Jesse Tree to a wall before class.

Application

Ask the class: "What is this?" (*A tree.*) "We are going to turn it into the tree of Jesus' family here on earth. What is that tree called?" (*The Jesse Tree.*)

Say to the class: "It is called the 'Jesse Tree' because Jesse was the father of King David. David was chosen by God to be the father of the family of Jesus. If we study the Jesse Tree, it will help us learn about Jesus' family on earth. Let us begin by looking at the first branch."

Show the class the apple symbol. Say to the class: "This picture reminds us of two people and an important event. Can you name the people and what they did?" (*Adam and Eve and the first sin.*)

"Let's open our books to page 244 and read about Adam and Eve."

ADAM AND EVE

When God created the world, He made all of the plants and the animals first. He liked them very much. But He also wanted to create someone in His own image, someone He could share His love with, someone He could care for. So He created two human persons: Adam and Eve.

Adam and Eve lived in the beautiful Garden of Eden. It had everything they needed: water for drinking and cleaning, and plants and trees with good food to eat.

God loved Adam and Eve very much. He wanted them to have everything they needed. He even gave them His life, grace.

God asked them to stay away from the tree of knowledge of good and evil. "If you eat the fruit from the tree of knowledge of good and evil," God said, "you will not be able to live with Me forever." In addition, by eating from the tree, Adam and Eve would lose grace.

Adam and Eve loved God. They obeyed Him, acted as His images, and stayed away from the tree of knowledge of good and evil until the devil came to visit them. The devil came disguised as a snake. The devil asked Eve, "Is it true you cannot eat any of the fruit in the Garden?"

"No", Eve answered. "We can eat the fruit from all of the trees except one. God said that we should not eat from the tree of knowledge of good and evil. If we eat from the tree of knowledge of good and evil, we cannot live forever with God."

"But that is not true", the devil lied. "God only told you that because He does not want you to be as wise and powerful as He is."

Eve knew the devil was lying. But she picked a piece of fruit from the tree of knowledge of good and evil. First she tasted the fruit, then she took the fruit to Adam.

"Taste this fruit", she said. "It will make us as wise as God. It is from the tree of knowledge of good and evil."

After the first bite, they knew they had done something wrong. They felt ashamed. They heard God coming and they hid.

"Why are you hiding?" God asked.

"Because we heard you coming", they answered. God knew they had disobeyed Him and had eaten from the tree of knowledge of good and evil.

This sin of Adam and Eve was the first sin. It is called "original sin", which means first sin.

Adam and Eve had hurt the special relationship they had with God. They could not live with Him forever. They lost grace, God's life. They hurt their minds, wills, and bodies. They could no longer live in the Garden.

God still loved Adam and Eve. He made clothes for them to wear. He reminded them that they must find food and shelter on their own.

Student Book, page 245

Adam and Eve were sad because they had disobeyed God. But God promised them that He would send a Savior someday. The Savior would show us who we are and how we should act. He would return God's love and help us return God's love.
—Adapted from Genesis 1:11–27, 2:8–9, 16–17; 3:1–23

Say to the class, "Our Jesse Tree begins with Adam and Eve." Ask one of the students to tape the apple symbol on the Jesse Tree.

Living the Lesson

1. Adam and Eve were free to eat from any tree except one. Which one? (*The tree of knowledge of good and evil.*)
2. What would happen to Adam and Eve if they ate from the tree of knowledge of good and evil? (*They could not live forever with God. They would hurt their special relationship with God. They would lose grace. They would hurt their minds, wills, and bodies. They would not be able to live in the Garden.*)
3. What did the devil tell Eve? (*God told you not to eat the fruit of the tree of knowledge of good and evil because He does not want you to be as wise and powerful as He is.*)
4. What happened when Adam and Eve ate the fruit? (*They knew that they had disobeyed God. They hid.*)
5. Why did Adam and Eve hide? (*They heard God coming. They were ashamed because they had disobeyed God.*)
6. What happened to Adam and Eve because they sinned? (*They lost God's life, grace. They hurt their minds, wills, and bodies. They had to leave the Garden of Eden and find food and shelter.*)
7. What did God promise? (*To send a Savior to show us who we are and how we should act, to return God's love, and to help us return God's love.*)

Part C

Student Book, page 240

VOCABULARY
covenant: A promise of love between God and people spoken in words and shown in acts.

Materials needed: Jesse Tree and symbol—an ark (see the Appendix); masking tape.

Note to teachers: If not done already, remove the Jesse Tree and the symbols from the Appendix. Tape the Jesse Tree to a wall.

Application

When you are ready to begin this Part, point to the next branch on the Jesse Tree. Say to the class: "Jesus' family here on earth is growing larger. We've reached the next branch on the Jesse Tree."

NOAH AND THE ARK

Many years passed. The earth was filled with people. Very few of them were acting as images of God. Noah, a kind and gentle man, was acting as an image of God.

One day God called down to Noah and said, "The earth is filled with people who are not acting as images of God. But you, Noah, are not like these people."

God said to Noah, "Soon a flood will cover the earth. Protect yourself and your family. Make an ark [a big boat] out of wood. Cover it inside and out with pitch [pitch is like tar]. Enter the ark and bring with you your wife, your sons, and your sons' wives. You will also bring with you two of every living creature. I will keep you safe in the ark."

Building the ark was not easy, but Noah obeyed God. Together Noah and his family worked very hard.

After Noah entered the ark with his family and two of all God's creatures, it rained for forty days. The flood came upon the earth. The ark floated on top of the water.

Finally, the rains stopped. The earth began to dry up. Then God spoke to Noah and his sons, "My covenant with you and all generations that follow you is this: Never again will there be a flood to destroy the whole earth and every living creature. This rainbow will be a sign of the covenant that I have made with you."
—Adapted from Genesis 6:8, 11, 14, 18; 7:1–9, 12–18; 8:6–14; 9:11–17

Say to the class, "Noah is the second person on the Jesse Tree. His symbol is the ark." Ask a student to tape the symbol on the Jesse Tree.

Living the Lesson

What was the covenant God made with Noah? (*Never again would a flood destroy the whole earth.*)

Part D

Materials needed: Jesse Tree and symbols—tent and camel (found in the Appendix); masking tape; world map (optional).

Application

Point to the next branch on the Jesse Tree. Say to the class: "Jesus' family on earth is growing larger! We've reached the next branch on the Jesse Tree."

Student Book, page 246

GOD'S COVENANT WITH ABRAHAM

After Noah, many years passed. A fine man by the name of Abram married a woman named Sarai. They were very happy.

The Lord then said to Abram, "Leave your country and your family for a new land that I will show you. I will watch over you and I will bless you. Your name will be great, and in you all the families of the earth will be blessed."

So Abram did as the Lord asked. He placed himself under God's care and took his wife Sarai and nephew Lot with him. They came to the land of Canaan.

Show the students where Canaan was on the map, if you are using one.

Student Book, pages 246–247

Abram's nephew Lot was like a brother to him. Both he and Abram owned livestock together. Abram's herdsmen and Lot's herdsmen had a hard time keeping the livestock separated, so they had many fights. Abram did not like the fighting.

So he asked Lot to pick whatever land he wanted, and Abram would take the rest. Lot chose the valley near Sodom, and Abram settled in Canaan.

After Lot left, the Lord appeared to Abram and made this promise: "The land you can see will belong to you and your descendants forever. Your descendants will be great in number, and I will care for them."

After the Lord's promise, God changed Abram's name to Abraham, which means "father of many nations". Sarai's name was changed to Sarah, which means "princess".

—Adapted from Genesis 12:1–5; 13:5–17; 17:4–5, 15

Say to the class: "Abraham is the third person on the Jesse Tree. His symbols are the tent and the camel, because he traveled so much." Ask two students to tape the symbols on the Jesse Tree.

Living the Lesson

1. What did God promise Abram? (*Land, a large family, and His care.*)
2. To what did God change Abram's name? (*Abraham.*) What does his new name mean? (*Father of many nations.*)

Part E

Student Book, page 240

VOCABULARY

sacrifice: An action by which someone or something is offered to God as a sign of love.

Materials needed: Jesse Tree and symbol—an altar (see the Appendix); masking tape.

Application

Point to the next branch on the Jesse Tree. Say to the class: "Jesus' family on earth continues to grow! We've reached the next branch on the Jesse Tree."

Student Book, page 247

THE SACRIFICE OF ABRAHAM

Abraham's wife Sarah thought that she could not have any children. Yet, when she was very old, she gave birth to a son. Abraham named him Isaac.

When Isaac was much older, God gave Abraham a chance to show his love for Him. He said, "Take now your only son whom you love and offer him as a sacrifice." Abraham was sad and worried. If Isaac were dead, he would not be able to inherit the land.

The next morning, Abraham, Isaac, and two of his servants split wood for the sacrifice and took it to the place God had told them.

On the way, Isaac asked Abraham, "My father! Here are the fire and the wood, but where is the lamb for the sacrifice?"

Abraham answered, "God will provide the lamb, my son."

Say to the class, "Abraham meant that God would let him know what to use for the sacrifice."

Student Book, page 247

When they came to the place for the sacrifice, Abraham built an altar.

As Abraham was about to offer the sacrifice, an angel of the Lord called him. "Abraham, Abraham! Do nothing to Isaac. For now I know that you love God."

Then Abraham noticed a ram caught in the bushes. "The Lord really did provide the lamb for the sacrifice!" he thought.

So Abraham offered up a ram instead of his son. God had cared for Abraham and Isaac.

—Adapted from Genesis 21:1–3; 22:1–3, 7–14

Say to the class, "The symbol for Isaac is the altar of sacrifice." Ask a student to tape the symbol to the Jesse Tree.

Living the Lesson

1. What happened when Sarah was very old? (*She had a son.*)
2. What name did Abraham give to his son? (*Isaac.*)
3. What did God ask Abraham to do? (*To offer Isaac as a sacrifice.*)
4. What happened as Abraham was about to offer the sacrifice? (*An angel stopped him.*)
5. What did God give Abraham to offer as a sacrifice in place of Isaac? (*A ram.*)

Part F

Materials needed: Jesse Tree and symbol—a ladder (see the Appendix); masking tape.

Application

Point to the next branch on the Jesse Tree. Say to the class: "Jesus' family on earth is growing larger! We've reached the next branch on the Jesse Tree."

Student Book, page 248

JACOB'S DREAM

Isaac's two sons were Esau and Jacob. Esau loved to hunt, which pleased his father very much. Jacob liked to stay at home.

One night Jacob had a dream. In his dream, a ladder that reached heaven was placed right next to where he was sleeping! Angels were climbing up and down the ladder. God stood above the ladder and said, "The land on which you are sleeping I will give to you and your descendants. I will care for you and your descendants, and in you, Jacob, all of the families of the earth will be blessed."
                    —Adapted from Genesis 25:21–27; 28:11–15

Say to the class, "The symbol for Jacob is the ladder, because it reminds us of his dream and the promise God made. God continues to care for His people." Ask a student to tape the symbol to the Jesse Tree.

Living the Lesson

1. What did God promise Jacob in the dream? (*That He would give Jacob and his descendants the land on which he was sleeping. God also said He would care for Jacob and his descendants and that in Jacob all the families of the earth would be blessed.*)
2. Why is a ladder the symbol for Jacob? (*A ladder appeared in Jacob's dream, and so it reminds us of his dream and the promise God made to him.*)

Part G

Student Book, page 240

VOCABULARY
Pharaoh: The name given to ancient Egypt's rulers.
famine: A long-lasting and severe shortage of food.

Materials needed: Jesse Tree and symbol—a colorful coat (found in the Appendix); masking tape.

Application

Point to the next branch on the Jesse Tree. Say to the class: "Jesus' family on earth continues to grow! We've reached the next branch on the Jesse Tree."

JOSEPH FORGIVES HIS BROTHERS

Jacob's youngest son, Joseph, was tending sheep in the fields with his elder brothers. His brothers were not taking care of the sheep. When Joseph got home, he told his father about them.

Jacob loved Joseph more than the others. He gave Joseph a long and beautiful coat.

Joseph's brothers were jealous of Joseph.

One day, when Joseph was walking down the road to meet his brothers, they saw him coming. They plotted to put him to death. "Let us kill him and throw him into a pit. Then we can say a wild beast did it!"

But one of the brothers, Reuben, told the others not to kill Joseph. Reuben told them to throw Joseph into a pit and leave him there. Reuben planned to come back secretly and rescue Joseph.

When Joseph reached his brothers, they stripped him of the beautiful coat his father had given him. Then they threw him into the empty pit.

But before Reuben could come back to get Joseph, the other brothers sold Joseph to traveling strangers who took him to Egypt. There Joseph became the slave of an Egyptian master.

Joseph was a very good slave. He knew that God was always with him, even when his master decided to put him in jail for something he did not do.

While he was in jail, Joseph used a special gift that God gave him. Joseph told people what their dreams meant. The Pharaoh heard about Joseph's gift and sent for him.

After the Pharaoh told Joseph about two of his dreams, Joseph said, "Both of your dreams mean the same thing. There will be seven years of good harvests and seven years of bad harvests. In the seven years of good harvests, save some of the food for the famine that is to come."

The Pharaoh thanked Joseph by putting him in charge of his palace and the land of Egypt. Joseph was good at his job. He saved enough food for the time of famine. He was kind to the people of Egypt. When his brothers came to Egypt for food, Joseph gave them some. He even forgave his brothers for what they had done to him.

Before he died, Joseph said to his brothers, "God will care for you. He will bring you to the land that He promised to Abraham, Isaac, and Jacob."

Joseph died of old age. He was buried in Egypt.
> —Adapted from Genesis 37:2–4, 18–30; 39:1–6, 11–23;
> 40:1–23; 41:12–49, 56–57; 45:4–14; 50:24–26

Say to the class, "The symbol for Joseph is the beautiful coat." Ask a student to tape the symbol to the Jesse Tree.

1. Why were Joseph's brothers jealous of him? (*Because he was Jacob's favorite.*)
2. Why did the Pharaoh send for Joseph? (*The Pharaoh wanted to know what his dream meant.*)
3. How did the Pharaoh thank Joseph? (*By putting Joseph in charge of the palace and of the land of Egypt.*)
4. What did God promise Joseph's brothers? (*He would bring them to the new land He had promised to Abraham, Isaac, and Jacob.*)

Part H

Materials needed: Jesse Tree and symbol—the stone tablets (found in the Appendix); masking tape.

Application

Point to the next branch on the Jesse Tree. Say to the class: "Jesus' family on earth is growing larger! We've reached the next branch on the Jesse Tree."

Student Book, page 250

MOSES LEADS THE ISRAELITES OUT OF EGYPT

Joseph and his brothers grew up, got married, and had many children. When their children grew up, they had many children. The descendants of Joseph and his brothers are called Israelites. The Israelite community grew larger and larger.

The presence of so many Israelites in Egypt worried the Pharaoh. He did not want these Israelite children to grow up and take over his kingdom. He knew that he had to come up with a plan to make the Israelite families smaller. So he told his workers to take every Israelite baby boy away from his family.

During this time, a baby boy was born to an Israelite woman. The mother hid her baby so that the Pharaoh's men could not take him from her. After three months, when she could hide him no longer, she placed him in a basket by the river, hoping that someone would come along and find him.

The Pharaoh's daughter was taking a bath in the river when her servants saw the basket. They brought the basket to Pharaoh's daughter. She opened it, looked in, and found a baby boy, crying.

The Pharaoh's daughter kept the baby and chose a kind woman to care for him. The woman happened to be the baby's own mother!

Because the Pharaoh's men were still looking for Israelite baby boys, the woman could not tell anyone who she really was. She was afraid that something would happen to her baby.

When the baby grew older, the Pharaoh's daughter adopted him and called him Moses, which means "I drew him out of the water."

After Moses had grown up, he wanted to help the Israelite people who were being poorly treated by the Egyptians. But he didn't know what he could do.

The Pharaoh heard about Moses' wish and ordered that Moses be put to death. But Moses escaped to another country.

While Moses was in this country, God called out to him from a burning bush. When Moses recognized that God was speaking to him, he hid his face, because he was afraid.

Say to the class: "Moses was not taken by the Pharaoh's men. Who saved him?" (*The Pharaoh's daughter.*) "What does the name Moses mean?" (*It means "I drew him out of the water."*)

God told Moses that He knew about the suffering Israelite people in Egypt. God asked Moses to be the one to lead the people out of Egypt to a better place. God also promised to stay with Moses and the Israelites throughout their journey.

Moses did what God asked him to do. He led the Israelite people out of the land of Egypt.

Three months after leaving Egypt, the Israelites arrived at the base of Mount Sinai. God asked Moses to come to the mountain top. Moses answered God by climbing up the mountain to meet God.

God gave Moses the Ten Commandments to tell the Israelite people how to act as images of God. These commandments were written on stone tablets and taken down the mountain by Moses to the Israelites below.

Throughout the journeys of Moses and the Israelites, the Lord stayed with them and cared for them. Moses died before reaching the land that God had promised to Abraham, Isaac, and Jacob.
> —Adapted from Exodus 1:6–10, 15–22; 2:2–11, 15; 3:2–10; 12:31; 19:2–3; 20:2–17; 31:18; 32:15–16; Numbers 10:11; Deuteronomy 32:48–52

Say to the class, "The symbol for Moses is the stone tablet." Ask a student to tape the symbol to the Jesse Tree.

Living the Lesson

1. God gave Moses a special job. What was that job? (*To lead the Israelites out of Egypt.*)
2. How do you think they traveled? (*They walked or rode on animals.*)
3. How long had the people been traveling before they came to Mount Sinai? (*Three months.*)
4. What did God give Moses on Mount Sinai? (*The Ten Commandments.*)

Part I

Student Book, page 240

VOCABULARY
anoint: To bless with oil.

Materials needed: Jesse Tree and symbol—a crown (see the Appendix); masking tape.

Application

Point to the next branch on the Jesse Tree. Say to the class: "Jesus' family on earth continues to grow! We've reached the next branch on the Jesse Tree."

Student Book, pages 251–252

DAVID AND GOLIATH

After the people had entered the promised land, a war broke out between the Israelites and their neighbors, the Philistines.

The last battle of the war was going to be between a huge Philistine soldier called Goliath and any Israelite soldier.

None of the Israelite soldiers wanted to fight in the battle. They were too scared.

No one volunteered to fight Goliath except a young shepherd named David. He brought his slingshot and stones and stood before the giant man.

The giant man laughed at David but told him to step forward. David ran quickly to the battle line and shot a stone from his slingshot. The stone hit Goliath in the middle of the forehead and killed him.

Say to the class, "As you can see after reading about David, a slingshot is not something to be played with. It can be very dangerous."

Student Book, page 252

Saul had David live in the palace with his son, Jonathan. David and Jonathan became best friends.

Saul, however, began to worry. He thought that the people of Israel might want David to be king instead of him. So Saul planned to kill David.

Jonathan heard about the plan and warned David. David escaped not only this threat, but several others.

Yet when David had the chance to kill Saul, he did not do it. Saul had been anointed king; he was blessed by God. David did not want to go against God's blessing.

Student Book, page 252

After Saul died, David became king. God made a special promise to David. He said, "I will make a house for you. When your days on earth are over, I will raise up one of your descendants. He will rule over a kingdom. I will be a father to him, and he will be a son to me. My loving kindness will always be with him."

—Adapted from 1 Samuel 17:1–11, 32–50; 18:1–11;
19:1–2; 24:5–14; 2 Samuel 7:12–15

Ask the class, "What does God's promise mean?" (*Jesus will be a descendant of David. Jesus will begin His Kingdom on earth, and it will continue in heaven. God the Father's loving kindness will be with Jesus always. Jesus will share that loving kindness with us. He will show us how to act as God the Father acts. He will help us return God's love.*)

Say to the class, "The symbol for David is a crown." Ask a student to tape the symbol to the Jesse Tree.

Living the Lesson

1. What peoples were involved in the war? (*The Israelites and the Philistines.*)
2. When it was time for the last battle to take place, none of the Israelite soldiers would fight Goliath. Why? (*All of the soldiers were afraid of Goliath.*)
3. Who fought the battle against Goliath and won? (*David.*)
4. Then what did Saul do for David? (*He asked him to live in the palace.*)
5. Do you think David acted as an image of God? (*Yes.*) How? (*He did as God asked.*)
6. Who is one of David's descendants? (*Jesus.*)

Part J

Student Book, page 240

VOCABULARY
incense: Dried tree-sap that gives off a sweet odor when burned.
swaddling clothes: Clothes that are wrapped tightly.

Materials needed: Jesse Tree and symbol—the baby Jesus in a manger (see the Appendix); masking tape.

Point to the last branch on the Jesse Tree. Say to the class: "Jesus' family on earth has grown quite large! We have reached the last branch on the Jesse Tree."

Student Book, page 253

THE BIRTH OF JESUS

Many generations after David, a man named Zechariah was offering incense in the temple. An angel of the Lord appeared to him. Zechariah was afraid, but the angel said to him, "Do not fear, Zechariah. The Lord has heard your prayers. Your wife Elizabeth is going to have a baby boy. You will name him John. He will be great in the Lord's sight. Many people will return to the Lord because of him."

In a city in Galilee called Nazareth, a man by the name of Joseph had a dream. In this dream, an angel appeared to him. The angel said, "Your wife, Mary, is going to have a baby boy. The Holy Spirit has made this possible. You will name your son Jesus, 'because He will save His people from their sins'."

Joseph's wife, Mary, also heard a message from an angel. The angel Gabriel came to Mary and said, "Hail, favored one! The Lord is with you."

Ask the class, "What does 'Hail' mean?" (*Hello. The angel is greeting Mary or calling to her.*)

Student Book, page 253

Mary was afraid. But the angel said, "Do not be afraid, Mary, for you have found favor with God. You will have a son and name him Jesus."

Ask the class, "What does the angel's message mean?" (*It means that Mary is going to have a baby and call him Jesus.*)

Student Book, pages 253–254

The angel continued, "He will be called the Son of God. The Lord will give Him the throne of David."

Mary asked the angel, "How can this be?"

The angel answered her, "The Holy Spirit will come upon you." The angel also told Mary that even though her cousin Elizabeth was very old, Elizabeth was going to have a baby. The angel said that nothing is impossible for God.

Mary said, "Yes, I will do what the Lord has asked." A few days later, Mary went to the home of her cousin Elizabeth to share the news.

When Mary and Elizabeth greeted each other, Elizabeth was filled with the Holy Spirit. The baby moved inside her. Elizabeth knew what Mary was going to say before Mary told her. Elizabeth said, "Most blessed are you among women, and blessed is the fruit of your womb!"

Ask the class, "What did Elizabeth mean when she said, 'Most blessed is the fruit of your womb'?" (*Blessed is the baby you will have.*)

Mary stayed with Elizabeth for three months. A short time later, Elizabeth's son was born. Elizabeth's husband, Zechariah, was unable to speak because he had not believed the angel Gabriel's message that in his old age he would be the father of a son. After his son was born, Zechariah asked for a tablet, and he wrote that his son should be called John. Then Zechariah could speak.

Zechariah was so happy. He praised and thanked God for his wonderful son.

Everyone in town was surprised that Zechariah could speak as soon as his son was named. They could tell that John was special in God's eyes. They didn't know that John would become John the Baptist when he grew up. He would help prepare the people for their Savior.

At this time, a census was taken to count the number of people in the country. Because Joseph's family was from the town of Bethlehem, he and Mary had to go there to be counted.

It took a long while to travel from Nazareth to Bethlehem. Joseph walked, while Mary probably rode on a donkey.

When they arrived, it was time for Mary's baby to be born. But there was no room at the inn. Joseph had to take Mary to a stable for shelter.

There, Mary gave birth to a baby boy. She wrapped Him in swaddling clothes and laid Him in a manger.

Some shepherds were in a field watching over their sheep. An angel of the Lord suddenly stood before them. They were so afraid.

But the angel said to them, "Do not be afraid; for behold, I proclaim to you good news of great joy that will be for all the people. For today in the city of David a savior has been born for you.

"And this will be a sign for you: you will find an infant wrapped in swaddling clothes and lying in a manger."

When the angel left them, the shepherds decided to look for the baby. It was late at night. The shepherds found Him in a stable nearby.

The baby was so wonderful! The shepherds knelt down in praise before Him. Before returning to their flocks, they told Mary and Joseph what the angel had told them. Mary kept these things in her heart.

The shepherds went back, praising God for what they had just seen and heard.

A long time after Adam and Eve had sinned, the Savior Whom God had promised was born!
　　—Adapted from Luke 1:5–20, 24–44, 56–66; 2:1–20; Matthew 1:17–21

Say to the class: "The symbol for Jesus is the baby in the manger, because He was born in a stable and laid in a manger." Ask a student to tape the symbol to the Jesse Tree.

Living the Lesson

1. Elizabeth had a baby boy named John. Why was he special? (*He became John the Baptist, who helped prepare the people for their Savior.*)
2. What did the angel tell Joseph in his dream? (*Mary was going to have a son by the power of the Holy Spirit. Joseph should name the child Jesus.*)
3. Why did the angel tell Joseph to name his son Jesus? (*Because the name Jesus means "savior", someone who will save people from their sins.*)
4. Jesus was born in a stable. Why? (*There was no room in the inn.*)
5. Some shepherds were the first visitors to the infant Jesus. What does a shepherd do? (*Takes care of sheep.*)

24

Lenten Preparation

1. Lesson Focus

Lent is a time to prepare for the joy and new life of Easter. During this time we remember that Jesus loved God the Father and us so much that He suffered and died on the cross.

In return, we too should show our love for Jesus by sharing in His sacrifice of love. We are able to do this by praying, offering sacrifices, doing kind deeds for others, and celebrating the sacrament of Reconciliation.

There are many different forms of prayer. The Mass, of course, is always the most important prayer. One of the most appropriate prayers during Lent is the Stations of the Cross. This prayer reminds us of the suffering that Jesus accepted because of His great love for God the Father and us.

During Lent we can also offer sacrifices. Sometimes life is difficult. Instead of complaining about how difficult things are, we can offer difficult tasks as sacrifices to God. We can carry our own crosses without complaining as Jesus carried His cross without a complaint. We also make sacrifices when we give up something we like or when we do something good even though it might be something difficult for us to do.

Another way to return Jesus' love is for us to do things for others. Perhaps we can share what we have with those who do not have as much. We can share toys, books, time, kind words, clothes, and money.

Jesus has told us that He will forgive those who want to be forgiven. All we have to do is to be sorry for our sins and to ask for forgiveness. We can ask for forgiveness for our wrong choices by celebrating the sacrament of Reconciliation. Through this sacrament our sins are forgiven, and we receive the grace to act as better images of God. Grace gives us the strength to carry out our promises during Lent: to pray, to offer sacrifices, to do things for others, and to celebrate the sacrament of Reconciliation.

Note to CCD teachers: Use all the Parts in class as time permits.

2. Concepts of Faith

Student Book, page 266

Things to Remember

What is Lent?
Lent is the time during which we prepare ourselves for the joy and new life of Easter. We should remember Jesus' sacrifice of love—His death on the cross.

3. Lesson Presentation
Part A

Materials needed: Newspaper; pot with soil for planting; pitcher of water; calla lily (or other) bulb.

Note to teachers: Place newspaper on the table first. Prepare a pot full of soil. Have a pitcher of water ready. Place the calla lily bulb on the table next to the pot of soil.

Student Book, page 256

The season of Lent is a time of reflection and a time to prepare our hearts for the celebration of the Resurrection of Jesus.

In the past we may have forgotten who we are and made some wrong choices. We may have not loved as images of God should love. God's life in us may have been weakened.

Lent is the time to examine our relationship with God and with those around us. We need to take time to prepare ourselves to celebrate the Resurrection of Jesus and the new life of Easter. This new life is called grace. Grace is God's life. Grace helps us to act like Jesus and to follow His example. Grace also makes it possible for us to live in heaven with Jesus someday.

Say to the class, "Please come and sit on the floor in front of the table." (*You should stand by the table.*)

Ask the class, "How does the weather make you feel?" (*Ready for spring; tired of the cold.*)

Say to the class: "All of creation is getting ready for new life. Everything is growing and changing. Plants begin to bloom. People smile more often. The world is a happier place. It is time to celebrate!"

Hold up the calla lily bulb and ask the class, "Does anyone know what this is?"

Say to the class: "It is a calla lily bulb. The bulb can be compared to all of us." (*Hold the bulb in front of the class.*) "It cannot grow without good soil, water, and sunlight. We cannot grow to be better images of God without grace. We receive grace through prayers, sacrifices, doing good deeds for others, and the sacraments. Let us plant the calla lily bulb, water it, and place it in the sunlight." (*Do the above.*)

Ask the class, "What do you think will happen?" (*The bulb will grow into a plant. The plant will produce flowers.*)

Say to the class: "When we are without grace we are like a bulb or a seed that is not planted. We cannot grow to be better images of God.

"Until the bulb or seed is planted (or rooted), watered, and placed in the sunlight, it will not grow. Unless we pray, offer sacrifices, do things for others, and celebrate the sacraments, we will not grow to be better images of God."

Note to teachers: During Lent, use the growth of the plant to remind the students of their growth as better images of God.

Living the Lesson

1. What is Lent a time for doing? (*Lent is a time for reflecting and preparing our hearts for the celebration of the Resurrection of Jesus.*)
2. Why do we need to reflect and prepare for the Resurrection of Jesus? (*We may have forgotten who we are, have made wrong choices, and not have loved as images of God should love.*)
3. What happens when we do not act as images of God? (*God's life in us is weakened.*)
4. What is grace? (*God's life.*)
5. How does grace help us? (*It helps us to act like Jesus and to follow His example, and it makes it possible for us to live forever in heaven with Jesus someday.*)

Part B

Application

Note to teachers: Bring in a palm branch to show the class, or point out the drawing of palms on page 256 of the student book.

Student Book, pages 256–257

We start our journey on the road to Easter with Ash Wednesday. Ash Wednesday is the beginning of the Lenten season. The name Ash Wednesday comes from the ashes that are placed on our foreheads. The ashes are made by burning blessed palms left over from last year's Palm Sunday. The ashes are placed on our foreheads at the beginning of Lent to remind us of our humble beginnings and common end. We are reminded that nothing on earth lasts—animals, plants, and even people eventually die. But Jesus and His message are everlasting.

When the priest places the ashes on our foreheads, he tells us one of Jesus' messages: "Turn away from sin and be faithful to the gospel", or "Remember, man, you are dust and to dust you will return."

When we hear the priest say these words, we might be sad, because the words remind us that we are sinners. We like to hear good things. We do not like to be reminded of the wrong things we do, but these words can help us turn away from sin and love God more.

Now that we are older we can prepare ourselves to celebrate the Resurrection of Jesus on Easter Sunday. We have the Lenten season to examine our relationship with God and those around us. During each day of Lent, we should turn away from sin and be faithful to the Gospel. We should follow Jesus more closely and turn away from wrong choices.

Student Book, page 257

If we properly prepare our hearts and minds during Lent, then Easter Sunday will truly be a time to celebrate. Christ rose from the dead on Easter, and we will rise to a new strengthened life of grace. Grace will be strengthened within us if we have prayed, offered sacrifices, done things for others, and received the sacraments during Lent.

Someday our journey through life will end. All of us will die. But, by leading good lives as images of God, we hope to rise to a new and better life with God in heaven.

Student Book, pages 260–261

OUR JOURNEY TO GOOD FRIDAY

There is one stone for each of the days from Ash Wednesday to Good Friday. Write the date on each stone. When a day is completed, color a stone.

Part C

Materials needed: Large tree branch with several smaller branches on it; brown or white spray paint; a pot or bucket; rocks; leaf pattern from Appendix; crayons; yarn or string.

Application

Student Book, pages 257–258

Lent is a time to prepare for new life: the Resurrection of Jesus to new life and the new strengthened life of grace, which we can have.

We can receive this new strengthened life of grace from God in four ways:
1. Prayer
2. Sacrifices
3. Kind deeds
4. The celebration of the sacrament of Reconciliation

Note to teachers: The following words are underlined in the next story in the Student Book (pages 258–259). Write the words on the blackboard as you say them.

greets	adoring
cares	love
thanks	thank
asks	ask
promises	resolve

When we pray, we lift our minds and hearts to God. We talk with Him, just as we would talk to a friend. Read the following story about two girls who are good friends and how they talk to one another.

GOOD FRIENDS

Amy and Mary are very good friends. When Amy talks to Mary, she usually greets her first. Then Amy shows Mary how much she cares about her and needs her by the words that she says.

Amy was at Mary's house last Saturday, and she enjoyed herself very much. Seeing Mary at school, Amy thanks Mary for the great time she had at her house. Amy senses that Mary is sad, and so, to help her feel better, she asks Mary to go shopping with her after school.

When the girls are shopping together, Mary becomes aware of how often Amy takes her places to help lift her spirits when she is feeling sad. Mary promises herself that she will try to do the same thing for Amy more often.

God is more than a friend to us. He is our Creator, Savior, and Helper. When we talk with Him, we should always be respectful.

When we begin our conversation with God, we should greet Him by telling Him how wonderful He is. By telling God how great and good He is, we are adoring Him.

God loves us so much. We must remember to tell Him that we love Him, too.

Every day we are reminded of all of the marvelous things that God has given us: family, friends, talents, love, and a world to share. We should thank God for all of His gifts.

We can show how much we love and adore God by praying special prayers that we know. We can also think of Him often during the day and talk to Him in our own way.

After adoring God and sharing our love and thanks, we can ask Him to help us, our families, and all people.

We should be reasonable in what we ask for. If we need the strength to prepare for a hard test, we should ask God for the strength to study, not for an easy "A". We know what we can do. We know what our talents are, and we know what our weaknesses are. Practice and hard work can sometimes change those weaknesses. We cannot expect God to change who we are, but He will help us become better images of Himself.

When you make a promise to a friend, you should keep that promise and do as you have said. Promises to God should be remembered and kept in the same way. For example, we should not want to hurt God with our sins. We should promise or resolve to try never to sin.

When we talk to a friend, greeting, caring, thanking, asking, and promising are usually part of our conversation. It is the same with God. When we pray to Him, adoring, loving, thanking, asking, and resolving make up our conversation. The Mass is the greatest of all prayers, because it includes all of these things.

Activity: Tree of New Life

Find a large tree branch with several smaller branches on it. Spray paint it either brown or white. Place it in a pot or bucket. Use several rocks to support it. Cut out the leaf pattern from the Appendix. Use it to make paper leaves, one for each student. On the leaves have each student write something that he or she would like to pray for during Lent. The students can color their leaves. Make a hole at the top of each leaf and insert a piece of yarn or string. The leaves can then be hung on the tree. The tree will bloom with love.

Note to teachers: You may want to have extra copies made of the leaves so that a student can add a prayer request to the tree at any time.

Part D

Application

Materials needed: One 3″ x 5″ slip of paper and an envelope for each student.

Student Book, page 259

MAKING SACRIFICES

Prayer is one of the things that we can do during Lent to show our love for Jesus. Another thing we can do is sacrifice.

To sacrifice means to offer something to God as a sign of love. We make sacrifices when we give up something we like, or to do something good even though it might be difficult for us to do.

If your mom brings home your favorite treat from the store, and you eat only some of it and save some for later, that is a sacrifice. If you go outside and help your dad bag leaves instead of playing with a friend, that is a sacrifice.

When we make sacrifices we are following Jesus. By sacrificing Himself on the cross, Jesus shows us how to make sacrifices and offer them to God the Father. By following Jesus, grace is strengthened in us.

Living the Lesson

1. What is a sacrifice? (*To give up something we like or to do something good, even though it might be difficult for us to do, as a sign of our love for God.*)
2. Name something that you like to do.
3. Name something good that is difficult for you to do.
4. When we make sacrifices, whom are we following? (*Jesus.*)
5. Do we like to do things that are difficult? (*Not always.*)
6. What was Jesus' most important sacrifice? (*He died on the cross.*)
7. By dying on the cross, what did Jesus show us? (*How to make sacrifices and offer them to God the Father.*)
8. What is strengthened in us when we sacrifice? (*God's life, grace.*)

Activity

Tell the students to decide on something they would like to sacrifice for Lent. Remind them that a sacrifice means giving up something they like or doing good, even though it might be difficult for them, as a sign of their love for God. Tell the students not to tell anyone what their sacrifices are. Their sacrifices are between themselves and Jesus. Have the students write their sacrifices down on the slips of paper. Pass out an envelope to each student. Have the students put the piece of paper in the envelope and seal the envelope. On the front of the envelope have each student write, "My Sacrifice for Jesus". Have the students write their names on their envelopes and give the sealed envelopes to you for safekeeping. Tell them that you will give the envelopes back to them before Easter vacation, so that they will be reminded of their sacrifices and their stronger friendship with Jesus.

Part E

Application

Say to the class: "So far we have talked about prayer and sacrifices. Prayer is having a conversation with God. In prayer we:

Adore—tell God how great He is;
Love—tell God that we love Him;
Thank—thank God for everything;
Ask—ask God for something fair;
Resolve—promise not to sin.

"A sacrifice is giving up something we like or doing something good, even though it might be difficult for us to do, as a sign of our love for God. All of us can find something to sacrifice."

Student Book, pages 259 and 262

DOING KIND DEEDS

Another thing we can do during Lent, and other times as well, is a kind deed. A kind deed is a way of showing that we are images of God. There are many kind deeds that we can do to show that we are images of God. We can do things at home for our family. We can do kind deeds at school for our teacher and classmates. We can do kind deeds for other people we meet. We can also do kind deeds for ourselves. We all are capable of doing some kind deed each and every day.

By doing kind deeds we act like Jesus, and grace is strengthened in us.

Prayer, sacrifice, and kind deeds are things we can do during Lent to prepare for the celebration of Easter. Another thing we can do is celebrate the sacrament of Reconciliation. When we celebrate the sacrament of Reconciliation we should be sorry for our sins and ask forgiveness. Read the story about the young man who was sorry for his sins and asked for forgiveness.

THE PARABLE OF THE LOST SON

There once was a man who owned a great deal of land. He had servants who helped him take care of his property. He had two sons, whom he loved very much. The sons were given everything they needed to live comfortably—a nice home, clothes to wear, food to eat, and lots of love.

All the father asked of his two sons was their help in a small way with the daily chores. He wanted them to know how he ran the farm, so that when the time came for them to run the farm they would know what to do.

The older son helped his father. But the younger son became bored with the chores and thought he would rather have something more adventurous to do. He wanted to be on his own so that he could have fun and do as he pleased.

So the younger son went to his father and asked for his share of the money from the property. His father was disappointed that his son wanted to leave, but he gave him the money. A few days later, after the younger son had collected his belongings, he set off on a journey to a distant country, looking for fun and adventure.

Along the way the young man made many new friends. He spent his money entertaining his new friends. He found fun and adventure, but soon his money was all gone.

The young man's new friends all left him when his money was gone. Then a severe famine spread all through the country, and there was little food to be eaten. The young man was alone and hungry. He had no food, no shelter, no money, and no one to love him.

He finally found someone who would give him a job—feeding the pigs. The young man was so hungry that he wanted to eat the food that the pigs ate. All of a sudden he remembered his father and his home. How nice it had been to be well cared for. At home he had had everything that he needed. Here he had nothing. He longed to be back home again!

As he sat thinking about being back home he said, "Even my father's servants have food to eat, and I am here starving. I know what I will do. I will go back to my father and say to him, "Father, I have sinned against heaven and against you. I no longer deserve to be called your son." In other words, the young man was willing to work for his father as a servant. He started on his long journey home.

One day, as the father was taking his daily walk down the road, hoping to see his younger son, he saw a person walking toward him. He knew it was his son. The father ran to his son, threw his arms around him, and gave him a hug and kiss. The father was very happy to have his younger son home at last.

The young man, feeling welcomed home, said, "Father, I have sinned against heaven and against you; I no longer deserve to be called your son." He told his father he was sorry for his sins and asked for forgiveness.

The father was happy to see his son and forgave him. He called to the servants, "Bring out new clothes and put them on him. Put a ring on his finger and shoes on his feet. Find the fattened calf and kill it. We are having a feast to celebrate. My younger son, whom I thought was dead, is alive. He was lost, and now he is found. Let the celebration begin!"

During this time the older son had been doing work in one of the fields. As he came closer to the house, he heard a great noise. He asked one of the servants what was happening. The older son was angry when the servant explained that his father was giving a party because his younger brother had returned home. The older son did not go into the house to join the celebration, because he was so upset.

Soon the father came out of the house, touched his older son on the shoulder, and said to him, "Son, you are always here, and everything I own is yours. Let us all be happy, for your brother was lost and now is found." The celebration continued.

—Adapted from Luke 15:11–32

Living the Lesson

1. How many sons did the father have? (*Two.*)
2. What had the father given both sons? (*A home, clothes, food, and love.*)
3. What did the father ask in return? (*He asked his sons to help out in a small way with daily chores.*)
4. Did the younger son enjoy helping his father? (*No.*)
5. What did the younger son want to do instead? (*He wanted to be on his own, have fun, and do as he pleased.*)
6. What did the younger son ask for from his father? (*His share of the money from the property.*)
7. What did the younger son do with the money? (*He left for a distant country to spend his money on things that made him happy.*)
8. There was a great famine, and the younger son had no money. What did he do next? (*He got a job feeding pigs.*)
9. Did he enjoy his new job? (*No.*)
10. What did he spend his time thinking of? (*All of the things that he had had when he was at home.*)
11. What did the younger son decide to do? (*He decided to go back home, say he was sorry, and ask for forgiveness.*)
12. What did the father do when he saw his younger son coming up the road? (*He ran to his son, put his arms around him, gave him a hug and kiss, and forgave him.*)
13. What did the father plan for his younger son's return home? (*A celebration.*)
14. How did the older son feel when he discovered that a party was being held to celebrate his younger brother's return? (*He was angry, upset, and jealous.*)

Jesus, like the father in the story, loves us, forgives us, and welcomes us back in celebration even when we have sinned. However, we should be sorry for our sins and ask for forgiveness.

Reconciliation means "to bring back together". Jesus knows that we are unhappy when we sin. We need a way to be forgiven so we can feel good again. He gives us one of His greatest gifts, the sacrament of Reconciliation.

We do not like to tell people when we do something wrong and are sorry, because we are scared of what will happen to us.

However, we do not need to be scared or nervous when we talk to the priest in the sacrament of Reconciliation. The priest is there to remind us that God loves us, and he acts in the Person of Jesus, forgiving us for the times we did not act as images of God.

In case you are feeling nervous, here is a quick review you can follow for receiving the sacrament of Reconciliation.

Note to teachers: If your parish has the custom of using a passage from Scripture during the sacrament of Reconciliation, instruct the children on the appropriate places to say the words from Scripture.

STEPS FOR RECEIVING THE SACRAMENT OF RECONCILIATION

1. Make a good examination of conscience. Be ready to tell the priest your sins.
2. Go into the confessional and kneel down, or go into the reconciliation room and sit or kneel down. Greet the priest.
3. Make the Sign of the Cross and say, "Father, I have sinned. My last confession was . . . (tell the priest how long ago it was)."
4. Tell the priest your sins. When you are done, say, "I am sorry for all my sins."
5. The priest will talk with you and will help you find ways to be more loving to God and others.
6. The priest will give you a penance.
7. The priest will ask you to say an Act of Contrition.
8. The priest will give you absolution.
9. The priest will tell you to "Go in peace." Thank the priest and leave.
10. Do your penance right away.

We have to remember that the sacrament of Reconciliation is a great and powerful gift. We should take advantage of it frequently, not just during certain holiday seasons. Jesus wants to hear from us more than only a few times a year.

Activity

If possible, arrange an opportunity for the class to celebrate the sacrament of Reconciliation.

25

The Saints

1. Lesson Focus

Out of love, God made the world and everything in it. He created human beings in His image. He created us to love Him and others. He created us to serve Him and others. We should love Him with all our hearts, and we should love our neighbors as ourselves. That is what the saints did, and that is why they are saints.

Saints are holy men and women who live with God in heaven. They followed Jesus' teaching and example while they were living on earth. The saints were people with hearts filled with love for God. They showed courage, gentleness, and patience even when things were difficult. They always tried to act as images of God to the very end of their lives here on earth.

In this lesson, we will try to answer the following questions:

1. What is a saint?
2. Who can be a saint?
3. How is a person named a saint?
4. How can we become saints?

Note to CCD teachers. Use Part A in class. Part B can be sent home as family projects or used in class as time permits.

2. Concepts of Faith

Student Book, page 269

Things to Remember

Who are the saints?
Saints are holy men and women who live with God in heaven.

222

3. Lesson Presentation
Part A

Student Book, page 267

WHAT IS A SAINT?

The saints are holy men and women who live with God in heaven. They followed Jesus' teaching and example while they were living on earth. The saints loved God very much, and they tried to act as images of God while they were living on earth. They had hearts filled with love, courage, gentleness, and patience.

Some of these holy people became saints by doing very hard things. They offered these things as sacrifices to God to show their love for Him. Some of the saints gave up their lives rather than give up their belief in God. Other people became saints by doing small things very well. They offered these small things as sacrifices to God to show their love for Him.

Activity

Name some of the saints that you have heard about. Discuss briefly what you know about them.

Student Book, pages 267–268

Who can be a saint?
God calls all persons to become saints. He does not exclude anyone.

How is a person named a saint?
So far, we have talked about how important it is to try to act as images of God. If we do try, we are on our way to becoming saints.

Specific steps are followed when a person is named a saint. Here are the steps:

1. A person is known to have lived a very holy life.

2. That person dies.

3. People pray to the holy person for help in their lives.

4. When their prayers are answered, the people report what happened to an official of the Church.

5. This official investigates the life of the person and makes a recommendation to the Pope as to whether or not the person should be declared a saint in heaven.

6. If the Pope decides that this person should be declared a saint in heaven, the Pope makes an announcement to the world at a special ceremony called a canonization.

7. In the Mass that is celebrated as part of the canonization ceremony, the Pope mentions the name of the saint in the Eucharistic Prayer.

Of course, there are many people in heaven. Some have been named saints. But others too have lived as images of God, have died, and are in heaven. Some of our relatives who have died are probably in heaven. These people are saints, too, but they have not been *declared* (named) saints by the Church. In heaven, then, we have the declared saints and also others who have not been declared. We celebrate all the undeclared saints on the Feast of All Saints, November 1.

Activity

Write about one person living today who you think will be named a saint someday. Remember to list reasons why you think this person will be a saint.

HOW CAN WE BECOME SAINTS?

We do not have do great things to become saints. But acting like a saint can be difficult. We should try to act as images of God. We should try to do everyday things with love. We can look for times when we can do something or give up something for Jesus. We can do these things with love, and we can offer them as sacrifices to God. If we do these things, we are on our way to becoming saints. Being a saint takes a lot of love, courage, gentleness, and patience.

Activity

Make a list of three things you can do to become a more saintly person.

(1) _____

(2) _____

(3) _____

Note to teachers. Use the following list of feast days as you see fit. It would be advantageous for the students to study and learn about a few of the saints listed here.

January

1	Mary, Mother of God (*Holy Day of Obligation*)
2	Ss. Basil the Great and Gregory Nazianzen
4	St. Elizabeth Ann Seton (*in the United States*)
5	St. John Neumann (*in the United States*)
21	St. Agnes
24	St. Francis de Sales
25	Conversion of St. Paul
26	Ss. Timothy and Titus
28	St. Thomas Aquinas
31	St. John Bosco

February

2	Presentation of the Lord
5	St. Agatha
6	St. Paul Miki and companions
10	St. Scholastica
14	Ss. Cyril and Methodius
22	Chair of Peter

March

7	Ss. Perpetua and Felicity
17	St. Patrick
19	St. Joseph
25	The Annunciation

April

7	St. John Baptist de la Salle
13	St. Martin
21	St. Anselm
25	St. Mark
29	St. Catherine of Siena

May

1	St. Joseph the Worker
2	St. Athanasius
3	Ss. Philip and James
14	St. Matthias
26	St. Philip Neri
31	The Visitation

June

1	St. Justin
3	St. Charles Lwanga and companions
5	St. Boniface
11	St. Barnabas
13	St. Anthony of Padua
24	Birth of St. John the Baptist
29	Ss. Peter and Paul

July

3	St. Thomas
11	St. Benedict
15	St. Bonaventure
22	St. Mary Magdalene
25	St. James
26	Ss. Joachim and Ann, parents of Mary
29	St. Martha
31	St. Ignatius of Loyola

August

4	St. John Vianney
6	Transfiguration
8	St. Dominic
10	St. Lawrence
11	St. Clare
15	Assumption (*Holy Day of Obligation*)
22	The Queenship of Mary
24	St. Bartholomew
27	St. Monica
28	St. Augustine

September

3	St. Gregory the Great
8	Birth of Mary
9	St. Peter Claver
13	St. John Chrysostom
14	Triumph of the Cross
15	Our Lady of Sorrows
16	Ss. Cornelius and Cyprian
21	St. Matthew
27	St. Vincent de Paul
29	Archangels Michael, Gabriel, and Raphael
30	St. Jerome

October

1	St. Thérèse of the Child Jesus
2	Guardian Angels
4	St. Francis of Assisi
7	Our Lady of the Rosary
15	St. Teresa of Avila
17	St. Ignatius of Antioch
18	St. Luke
28	Ss. Simon and Jude

November

1	All Saints' Day (*Holy Day of Obligation*)
4	St. Charles Borromeo
9	Dedication of St. John Lateran
10	St. Leo the Great
11	St. Martin of Tours
12	St. Josaphat
13	St. Francis Xavier Cabrini
17	St. Elizabeth of Hungary
21	Presentation of Mary
22	St. Cecilia
30	St. Andrew

December

3	St. Francis Xavier
6	St. Nicholas
7	St. Ambrose
8	Immaculate Conception (*Holy Day of Obligation*)
12	Our Lady of Guadalupe
13	St. Lucy
14	St. John of the Cross
25	Christmas (*Holy Day of Obligation*)
26	St. Stephen
27	St. John the Apostle
28	Feast of the Holy Innocents
29	St. Thomas Becket
31	St. Sylvester

Part B

Have each of the students choose a saint to read about and research. Have them find the information indicated in the suggested report outline (below) and then put together a report booklet with pictures. (*Option*: Have the students give a short presentation to the class on the saints they have researched.)

Paragraph 1: background information.
1. Saint's full name.
2. Saint's birth date.
3. Saint's place of birth.
4. Names of the saint's parents.
5. Saint's nationality.
6. Kind of family the saint grew up in.

Paragraph 2: special relationship to God.
7. Education, occupation, interests, hobbies, etc.
8. Did the saint have to suffer for Christ?
9. When and how and where did the saint die?

Paragraph 3: reasons for sainthood.
10. What did the person do to become a saint?
11. Is the saint known as a patron saint?
12. What is the saint's feast day?
13. What Pope was responsible for canonizing the person a saint?

Conclusion: What do you find most admirable about this saint?

APPENDIX

Pattern of Cross
Lesson 2
page 15

SUN	MON	TUE	WED	THU	FRI	SAT

Calendar and Hearts Lesson 3, page 27

Hearts Lesson 3, page 27

CARD B

One person is standing alone on the playground. The rest of the group is playing baseball. Finally, the players notice the lonely person. The pitcher asks the person to play.

CARD D

One of you catches a baby bird in a net. All of you like the bird, but you notice that it will not eat. All of you decide to set it free. You remind each other not to touch it. A mother bird will not take care of her baby if it has been touched by people.

CARD A

Everyone in your group is fishing. Every time a fish is caught, it is thrown *carelessly* onto the shore and forgotten about.

CARD C

Everyone is at school. The whole class should be in their seats, doing their work, but they are not. Instead, they are fooling around.

Role Playing Cards Lesson 4, pages 33–34

CARD 1

Your mother told you to clean up your room. Instead, you go outside and play with your friends. What would Jesus do and what should you do as His image?

CARD 2

Your sister is building a castle out of building blocks. You accidentally knock it down. She cries. What would Jesus do and what should you do as His image?

CARD 3

You are choosing teams for kickball. One of the players cries because he doesn't play as well as the others. What would Jesus do and what should you do as His image?

CARD 4

Someone you know skips prayer in the morning and watches cartoons instead. What would Jesus do and what should you do as His image?

CARD 5

Someone doesn't have her homework done. She asks you if she can copy your paper. What would Jesus do and how should you act as His image?

Image of God Cards Lesson 9, page 65

KIND KAREN	LYING LUCY	PATIENT PATTY
helpful, thoughtful	dishonest, does not tell the truth	calm, waits for others, doesn't get angry
EFFICIENT ERICA	**HURTFUL HARRIET**	**DISRESPECTFUL DIANE**
does not waste time, gets the job done	dislikes everybody and everything	no honor, insults, calls names
OBEDIENT OLIVE	**STEALING SALLY**	**JEALOUS JUDY**
listens to parents and teachers	takes other people's things	does not want to share
TRUSTING TERI	**LAZY LAURA**	**MEAN MARGARET**
has faith in God and others	does nothing, never busy	unkind, crabby
BRAVE BECKY	**DEPENDABLE DAN**	**BOASTFUL BILLY**
self-controlled, not afraid	on time, there when you need him	brags
COURTEOUS KURT	**FORGETFUL FRED**	**GOOF-OFF GUS**
helpful, thoughtful	ignores time and promises	fools around when he should be working
PRAYERFUL PETE	**RUDE RYAN**	**ENVIOUS ED**
prays often	interrupts	wants what everyone else has
CHURCH-GOING CHARLIE	**HARMFUL HOWARD**	**QUIET QUINCY**
goes to Mass often	hurts people	does not speak when unkind things are said
CRABBY CASEY	**HONEST OTTO**	**GENEROUS JACK**
bad temper, mad	tells the truth	giving
UNKIND ULYSSES	**REVERENT ROY**	**ARROGANT ARNOLD**
cruel, unfriendly	believes in Christ, acts as an image of God	brags, mouthy

Imaginary Person Cards Lesson 9, page 70

Pitcher: I try to pitch the ball as close to the batter as I can in order to scare the batter.	**Umpire:** I call plays fairly.
Batter #1: After batting, I throw the bat, not caring whether or not it hits other players.	**Batter #2:** I make fun of other batters who cannot hit as well as I can.
Catcher: I drop the ball on purpose to help my friend take a base.	**First Baseman:** I stand out of the baseline to give runners the space they need.
Second Baseman: I carefully tag runners out without hurting them.	**Shortstop:** I stand in the baseline unfairly blocking runners.
Third Baseman: I compliment my teammates on a good play.	**Right Fielder:** I try my best to catch balls and throw them to the proper person on base.
Left Fielder: I miss the balls that my friends hit and catch the others.	**Center Fielder:** I catch the ball and "burn" it into another player's mitt.
Program Passer: I say to the people, "Here! Take your program and sit down!"	**Food Vender:** I say to the people, "Thanks for buying the hot dog. Is there anything else I could get you?"
Security Guard: I say to someone, "Hurry up and find your seat, slowpoke. You're holding everyone up."	**Ticket Checker:** I say to the people, "You can find your seats two steps down and to the right, folks. Let me help you."
Crowd Member: I stand up and holler, "Boooooooooo! Hisssssssssss!"	

Baseball Activity Cards Lesson 11, page 84

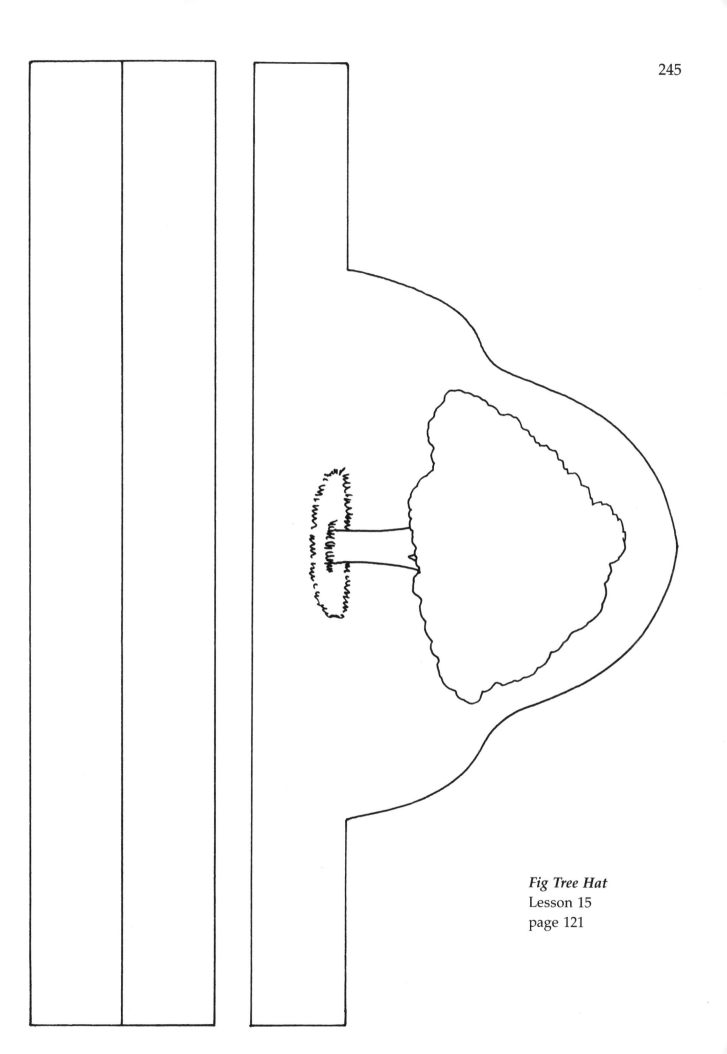

Fig Tree Hat
Lesson 15
page 121

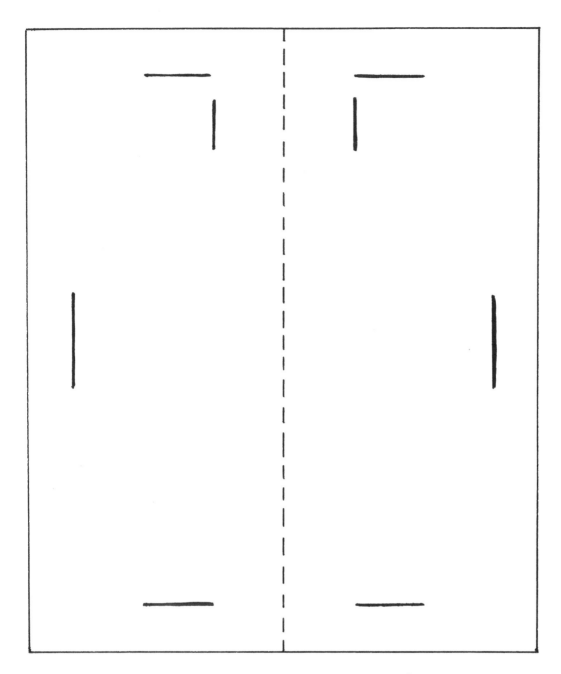

roof

chimney

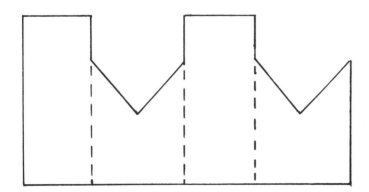

School House Pattern
Lesson 18
pages 146–47

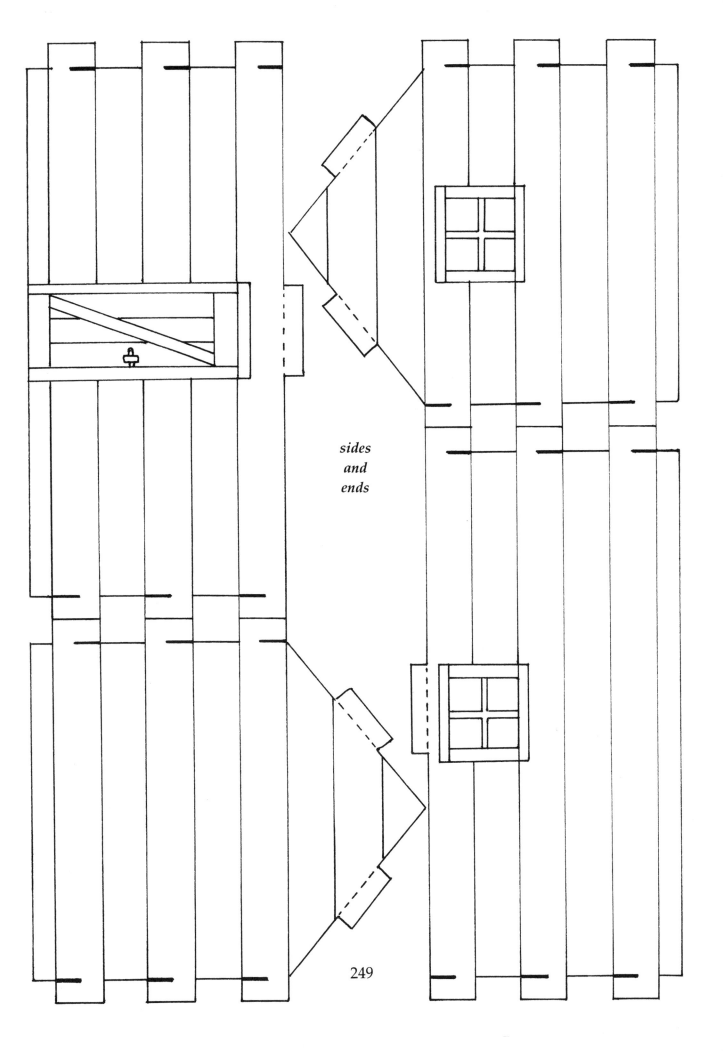

sides and ends

249

Shepherd
Lesson 19
page 154

251

Your teenage sister takes forever in the bathroom in the mornings before school. What can other family members say or do so that others can take their turns?

Mom is trying to cook supper, and your two-year-old brother keeps getting in the way. What can other family members do to help make Mom's job a little easier?

Both parents work, and the house is a mess. What can other family members do to help clean up?

Grandma is sick and in the hospital. What can other family members do to make her hospital stay as pleasant as it can be?

Dad works long hours and is tired and crabby when he gets home. What can other family members do for him before he gets home *and* after he gets home to help him relax?

Mom is busy cooking, and the table isn't set. What can other family members do to prepare the table and the food for that meal?

One of the kids in the family doesn't understand math, and the parents haven't got time to help. What can other family members do to help this child finish the math homework?

The family hasn't done anything together for a long time. What are some things that a family can do together?

Mom hasn't got any free time. She is always working or cleaning. What can other family members do to give Mom some free time?

Everyone in the family watches too much television. What can the children in the family suggest to do instead of watching television?

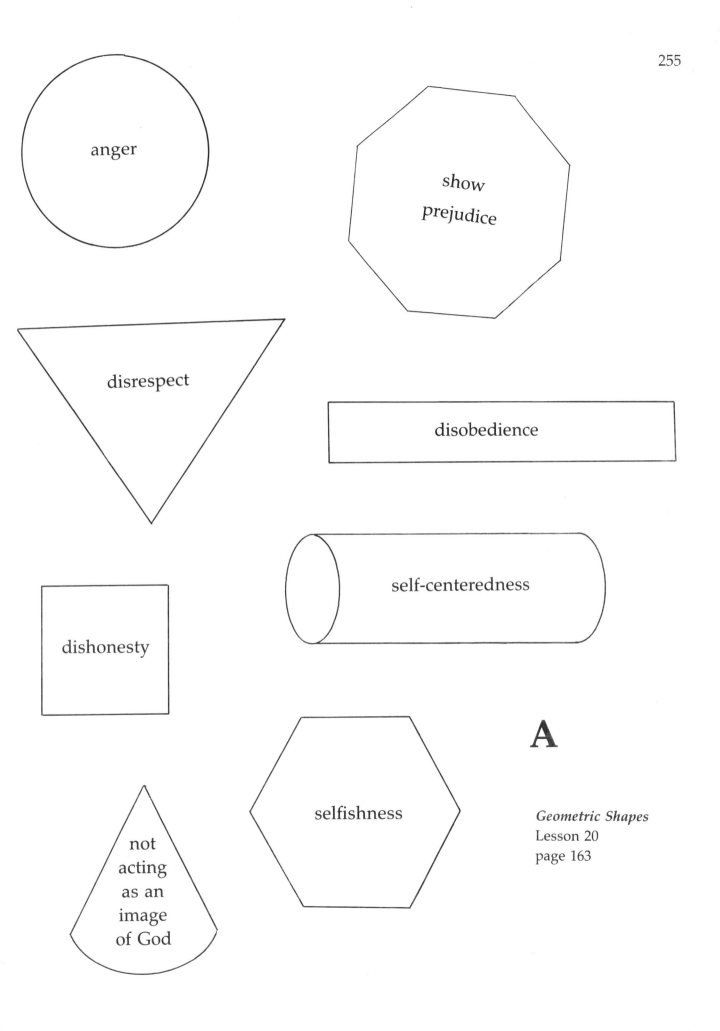

anger

show
prejudice

disrespect

disobedience

self-centeredness

dishonesty

A

not
acting
as an
image
of God

selfishness

Geometric Shapes
Lesson 20
page 163

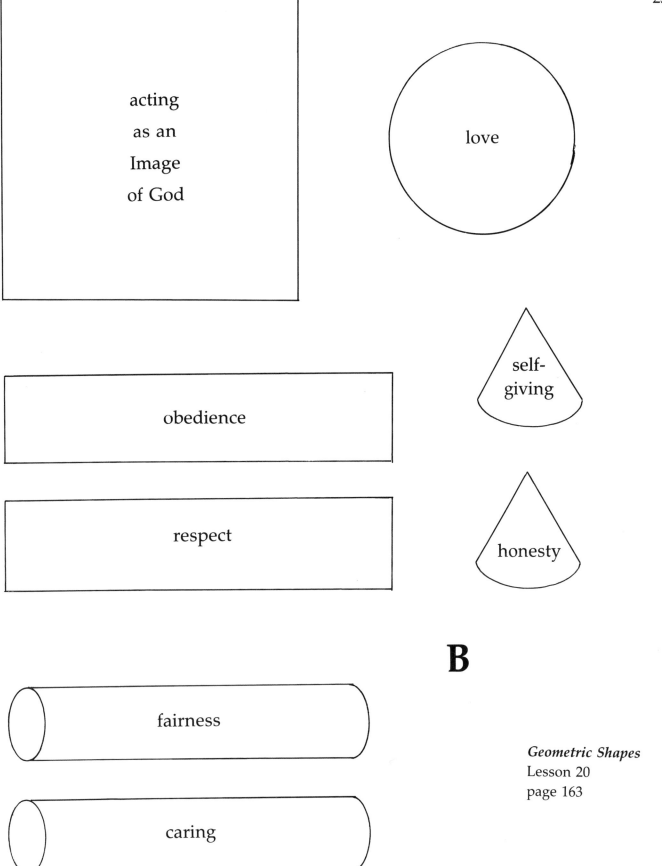

acting
as an
Image
of God

love

obedience

respect

self-giving

honesty

B

fairness

caring

Geometric Shapes
Lesson 20
page 163

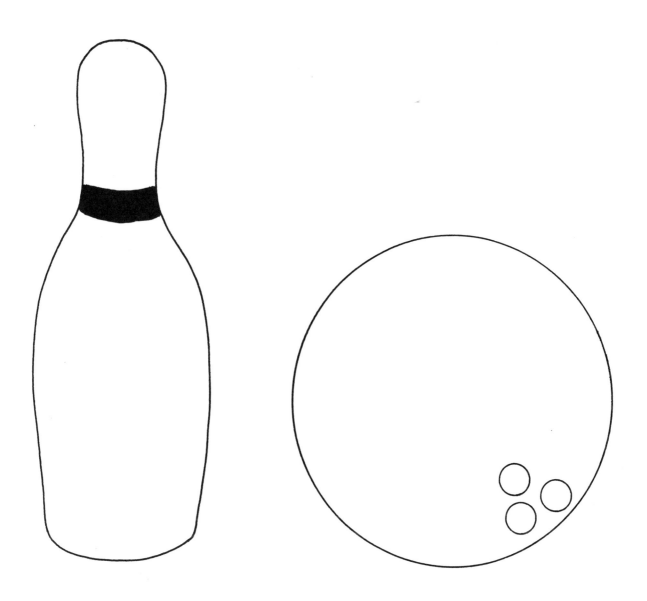

Bowling Ball and Pin   Lesson 22, pages 190–91

QUESTIONS

What did Jesus command the Apostles to do?

Who does the work of the Church today?

Where do we begin to help others?

How do we serve others within our own families?

When Jesus was on earth, how did He help the sick and needy?

What do the bishops and the members of the diocese do to benefit others by meeting their physical and material needs?

What do parishes do to meet the physical and material needs of others?

How does the Pope know when there are problems that need his help in the parishes around the world?

Although Adam and Eve did not return God's love, what did God continue to do?

What did Jesus do to repair our relationship with God?

Jesus' death on the cross was the greatest of all loves. Why?

What is grace?

What does grace do for us?

In which sacrament do a man and woman promise to love and care for each other for the rest of their lives?

Jesus feeds us with His Body and Blood and makes us one with Him in which sacrament?

In which sacrament does the priest bless the sick, the elderly, and the dying?

In which sacrament does God give us His life for the first time?

In which sacrament does the Holy Spirit give us the strength to love God in a more grown-up way?

We tell our sins to the priest and receive Jesus' forgiveness in which sacrament?

A man is ordained a priest in which sacrament?

How does Jesus do His work today?

What is a sacrament?

How many sacraments are there?

What happens each time we receive a sacrament?

Bowling Ball and Pin
Lesson 22
pages 190–91

ANSWERS

To teach all people the things He had taught them through the parables, to help all people celebrate the sacraments and receive God's life, and to show all people how to use their talents to benefit others.

The Pope, bishops, priests, and all members of the Church.

Within our own families.

By having the courage to use our own talents and abilities to help whenever possible.

By performing miracles.

The bishop and the talented people who work for him help others who need guidance, food, clothing, and shelter.

Priests and deacons show parishioners how to use their talents to benefit others. Parishioners clean and prepare the church, assist before and during Mass, donate food, clothing, shelter, time, and money to care for the health and happiness of others.

He has meetings in Rome with the bishops, sends letters to other bishops around the world, leads helpful organizations, and travels around the world.

God continued to love and care for them, but the love between Adam and Eve and God was weakened.

Died on the cross.

He did the Father's will and gave us a chance to share in God's life, grace.

God's life.

Grace enlightens our minds, strengthens our wills, and helps us to use self-discipline in the things we think, do, and say. It enables us to live forever in heaven with God.

Matrimony.

The Holy Eucharist.

The sacrament of the Anointing of the Sick.

Baptism.

Confirmation.

Reconciliation.

Holy Orders.

Through the teachings of the Church, the sacraments, and other works of love done by the Church.

A physical sign, given to us by Jesus, through which Jesus meets us and gives us His grace.

Seven.

God's life in us grows stronger.

Bowling Ball and Pin Lesson 22, pages 190–91

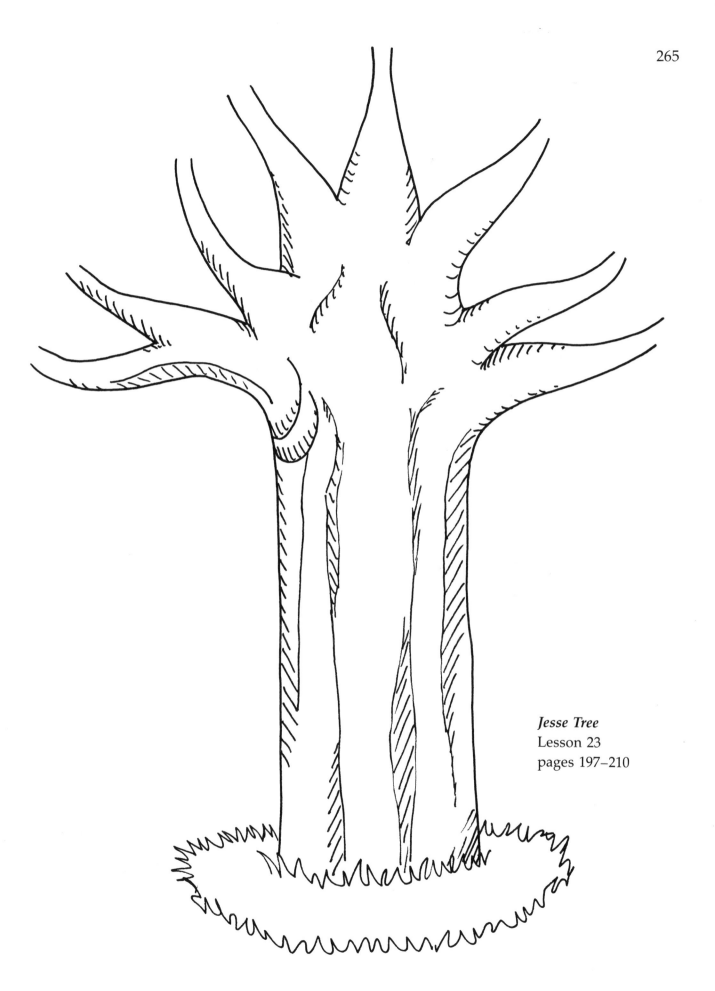

Jesse Tree
Lesson 23
pages 197–210

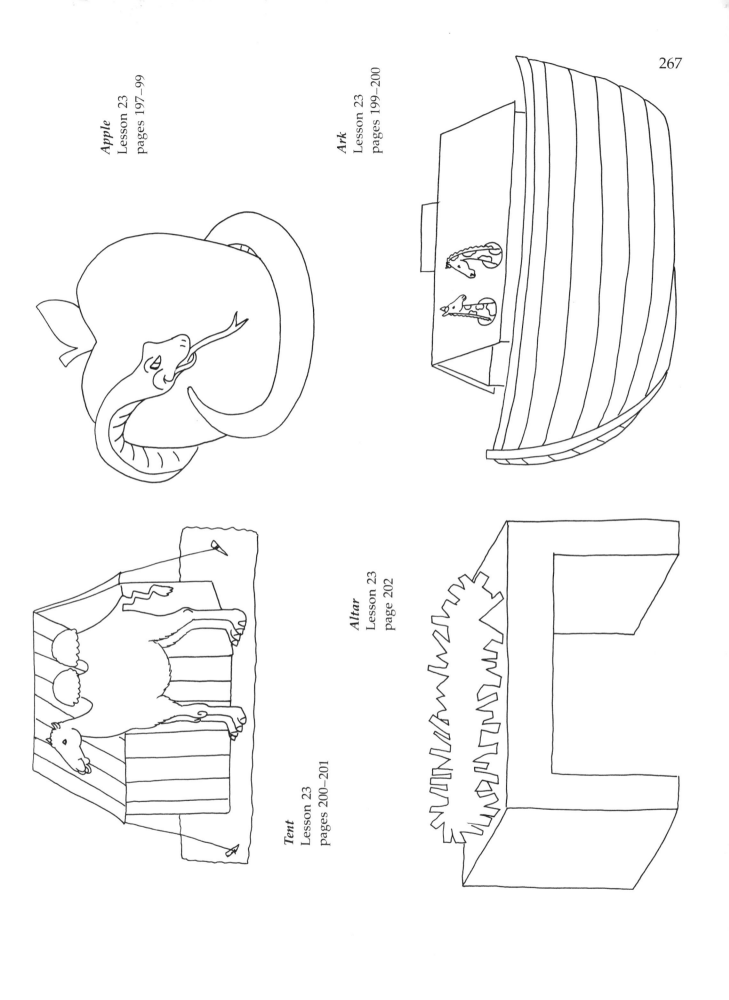

Apple
Lesson 23
pages 197–99

Ark
Lesson 23
pages 199–200

Tent
Lesson 23
pages 200–201

Altar
Lesson 23
page 202

269

Manger Lesson 23, pages 208–10

Robe Lesson 23, page 203

I

II

III

IV

V

VI

VII

VIII

IX

X

Tablets
Lesson 23
pages 205–206

Ladder Lesson 23, page 203

Crown Lesson 23, pages 207–8

Leaf Pattern Lesson 24, page 217